FINDING FIT

What Running Through an Arduous Childhood
and a Remote Marathon on Every Continent...
Can Help You Find.

CAREN WARE

No part of this publication may be reproduced, stored in a retrieval system, or transmitted in any form or by any means—electronic, photocopying, recording, or otherwise—without prior written permission, except in the case of brief excerpts in critical reviews and articles. For permission requests, contact the author at carenfasttrack@aol.com.

All rights reserved.

Copyright © 2023 Caren Ware

ISBN: 9798858876977 (Paperback)
ISBN: 9798871243879 (Hardcover)

The author disclaims responsibility for adverse effects or consequences from the misapplication or injudicious use of the information contained in this book. Mention of resources and associations does not imply an endorsement.

Editing and Publishing Assistance by Kelli Watson, Scriptor Publishing Group

This book is dedicated to all the struggles we face and FINDING healthy ways to RUN through them.

To Every BODY and everybody out there.
Move forward, onward, and upward.

Written to inspire YOU to FIND your FIT.

May my journey help you summit yours.

"Run to add days to your LIFE, and you will find running adds LIFE to your days."
-Caren Ware

Contents

Preface: Searching for Meaning 1

1. Racing Against the Setting Sun 3
2. Finding the Will to Survive 6
3. A Summit Experience 16
4. Surviving Childhood 27
5. A Master at Masking 34
6. It Took a Jog-a-Thon 40
7. Don't Die on Me 45
8. The Sound of a Shrug 53
9. When It Gets This Intense 62
10. Fear is a Liar 68
11. The Trigger 77
12. Summer Camp Came to the Rescue 83
13. Foundations Crack and Boats Sink 93
14. Let's Go to Alaska 103
15. It Stung 109
16. We Pushed the Gate Open to the Arctic Circle
    Prudhoe Bay, Alaska. 124
17. There's a First for Everything
    Continent 1: North America – Los Angeles Marathon 129

18. The Belmont Boys 138

19. A Miracle was Brewing 151

20. Leaving Legacy 159

21. Stuck in Paradise 167

22. I Ran a Good Time. He Had a Good Time.
    Continent 2: Europe—The Paris Marathon 183

23. What Pets, Sports, and Having Children Can Teach You 189

24. Only Silhouettes 200

25. Using Miles to Heal
    (The Midnight Sun Marathon, Alaska) 202

26. Touching the Void 206

27. Can the Earth be Orange?
    Continent 3: Australia—The Outback Marathon 220

28. The One that Didn't Count
    Continent 4: Asia: The Tokyo Marathon 230

29. Evolving Inward
    Continent 5: South America —
    The Galapagos Island Marathon 242

30. FINDING Myself… in the Middle of Nowhere 262

31. All Who Wander …Wander 272

32. Myself Went with Me
    Continent 6: Antarctica — The Antarctica Marathon 283

33. SERGEY No. 9 303

34. Getting to Africa 317

35. It Almost Killed Me
    Continent 7: Africa — The Kilimanjaro Marathon 324

36. Eaten Alive..331
37. It's -20°F in Africa?!
    Summiting Mount Kilimanjaro................................338
38. Enriched is Rich..354
39. "Hey, Sis. Dad Died." And the Butterfly.....................358
40. Summitting the Insurmountable
    Continent 4 Repeat: Asia — The Everest Marathon 367
41. Trekking to the Everest Marathon...............................376
42. Running the Everest Marathon....................................410
43. Patagonia: Bridges, the 7 Continents Medal,
    and a Windswept Marathon....................................426
44. Heart Shaped Rocks 435
45. A Healthy Life List: What's Yours?..............................441
46. Conclusion. My Challenge to You 443
About the Author..445

Preface

Searching for Meaning

I like *running*—the word and all that it means. It's a word that has action. Using your body to go somewhere faster. *Running* also means it is working, functioning as it should. This is opposed to *broken*. *Running* helped fix some of the broken parts of my life. That is why I am so passionate about it. In a very grateful way, physical running was the mentor, guide, excuse, and reason for other parts of my life to start running better.

In this book *FINDING FIT*, you will traverse through a childhood that somehow left me sad and serious. I had a dad bent on being bent. Yet, read how my mom was able to teach me things money could not buy. Discover how I found stability in *running* and the *outdoors*. How I raised my own two children and inner-city youth to all become college graduates. Enjoy stories that come from living an active life. But feel deeply with me when l stumble and life tumbles. It crashed often and even burned to the ground. Love was lost, love was gained, sometimes so misunderstood. I took the punches and got up and kept going…somehow. Determined.

Live with me in the pursuit of some lofty goals, like standing on a podium as a World Class Track & Field athlete. Adventure with me in the incredible experience of running a marathon on every continent, including Antarctica. I am a scrappy, under loved kid who developed a passion for the outdoors, people of all cultures, and the chance to race. Let my journey inspire yours and let us all be a story of experiences, relationships, overcoming, tenacity, and growth. This is what makes life interesting!

In the book, *Trapped in the Mirror* by Elan Golombjz, Ph.D. she advocates travel and states, "Travel is outstanding, because it teaches about how people can live." She explains how we do not really know ourselves as much as we do when we get to see life led in different ways. "Although initially fearful, I go without an accompanying group to feel myself 'there' as much as possible. I learn something of the language and make local friends."

This is exactly what I did. I ran the 7 continent marathons by traveling solo to discover what would make my life healthy and to help others live their healthiest lives.

FINDING FIT is the act of discovering. A conclusion reached as the result of inquiry, investigation, and trial. It also alludes to a sense of surprise. Like the joy in discovering hidden Easter Eggs. Even the hard stuff in life is worth discovering, because *finding* it means it is no longer *lost*, buried in a lack of understanding that muddies life. *Lost* means unable to find one's way, not knowing one's whereabouts. You will *find* me lost in many ways in this book. But you will also discover that I *find* a path that goes somewhere. It comes from within. We can rescue our own lives.

FINDING FIT is the meaning of sculpting new narratives that provide a sense of coherence around everything sad and wonderful in our lives. *finding* means *looking* and *searching* and finally reclaiming what once was lost in us. *Finding* we *fit* by *finding* how to be *fit* is a formula for an energized and rewarding direction. Purposing our lives to be *up* and *running* is the healthiest way to live. Not *down* but *up*. Not *lost* but *found*. Not *broken* but *running*. *Working* properly and in *shape*—putting all those puzzle pieces together to know you *fit* perfectly. This is when we are at our healthiest best and the journey is quite worth it. *FINDING FIT* is that kind of journey.

1

Racing Against the Setting Sun

Expensive computer boxes, wires, easy ups, generators, little cutters, start horns. Hordes of timing pieces are strewn across the driveway. I have a rake and am frantically piling up leaves to bag. A freak storm is closing in and there is going to be snow at this 6,000-foot level. Abandoned in the tasks, I also grapple with mountains of personal life issues I have too little time to resolve. The deadlines of these race contracts are intense. I can't call any of the contracts off. "Oh, I'm sorry, but we are not ready for your race. Could you please postpone your marathon until next week?" My head is racing faster than my body.

The sun has already splashed its hues of red, yellow, and orange and the tinge has just turned grey. It is getting dark. I bail on the pine needles and frantically start tossing equipment in vehicles. The temperature is dropping dramatically. Clouds have moved in. I get all the equipment in, but all the tools and racks are disappearing in the darkness.

The phone rings. This is more important to me than any "thing." I take the call. Such an inviting voice. It always captures me. Something about it. It has a mildness mixed with an east coast, Long Islander accent. I must have been huffing into the phone. Silence on the other end.

Finally, the voice speaks, and it has some tone of condemnation which I react to. I look for an answer that will please even before any question is asked, "What are you doing?"

I am at 6,000 feet. I try to catch my breath to answer in a calmer way to pretend that my pat answer is how I really feel. In the short pause, the world turns black, as if on cue. I am in the dark. I drop on a stump and blurt, "I AM RACING AGAINST…." I look around. I can't see a thing. It is pitch black. In exasperation I finish the sentence, "…THE SETTING SUN."

I slump. I'm not used to not being able to finish what I set out to accomplish. I have a strong will, and it makes me try the impossible. But I can't beat the setting sun. I can't turn back time. I can't stop it from ticking so fast. I can't believe I cannot do the impossible, and I am stunned. I am….? Failure overwhelms me. It's not a bad place. I can't be God. I need to know that. Nor can I please someone who thinks they are God. I don't know that yet.

I hear distancing in the voice. A disdain. A tone that punishes crimes that do not exist. I have no idea it is being used as an effective weapon to force me to grovel. I feel a panic of pending loss as the voice trails off in indifference. I am about to be cut off. Permanently. And I have given up too much in adoring this voice. I have harmed my own life and all those I should have loved properly.

A few sentences of idle chatter and the conversation is over. I hang up. I am utterly and positively alone. I can't see. I cannot see straight. I sacrificed my foundations for this voice in my life. I feel the darkness around me like no other time in my life. It is so clearly dark. I know that this is not true, but I feel at this moment there is no God near enough to save me from a life wreck. Left in the dark which is so blinding. Is there even a way to find…meaning from here?

My family is struggling. After 25 years in a marriage making ends meet, I am in trenches. I can't keep up anymore. Am I divorcing? What race am I trying to win? I had tried to make the impossible happen. Friendships, marriage, and good relationships are hard to keep healthy on the road and on the go. And something in me was trying to be bigger than I am, driving me to be more capable than possible. I finally can't do it anymore. I set a pace I can no longer master. Somehow, I tried too hard. Rigid things snap.

It is so very dark. It is cold. I can't hold back the tears. Pain engulfs me and saps even the spark in my soul. I feel my arms reach around my body and try to shield myself from this very black of blacks. This is where I must begin to bring light back into my life. This is where I must examine all my RACING through life. I thought I could actually outrun it. But you can't beat the setting sun.

This is my story.

2

Finding the Will to Survive

Dusty and I in the Eastern Sierras

The trail was steep. It was on the eastern side of the Sierra Nevada Mountain range. From various trailheads arduous paths twist sharply up canyons to lazy lakes nestled in basins above the tree line. Our trail traversed in switchbacks and was unrelenting in its upward climb. My husband and I, still newlyweds, were backpacking with our new puppy. Dusty was an adolescent yellow Labrador.

We were training him to carry his own pack. He was already an exceptional dog. Two light, red pouches swayed on his sides, brushing rocks and tree trunks. He exuberantly zoomed around catching new scents in that sense of pure freedom…off a leash and outdoors. I related completely. Our packs were no nuisance to us if they got us outdoors. The labor was freeing. The dog seemed to agree. My spirits ran amuck just watching the puppy do what I felt. I loved this. And I loved the man I was hiking with because he loved this also.

Dusty paid little attention to the bouncing load, save an occasional neck straining sniff backward. The scent of his dry food was in the packs. Our destination was one of those high terrain lakes that rarely get human footprints but are stocked by helicopter with delicate trout. It was early in the season. Too early for fishing. Too early to really be hiking. We would be punching through snow. But this was on purpose. We knew we would have the expanse and peaks and our echoes to ourselves. We felt smugly prepared for the cold. We had spent our adventure months in Alaska. This was our choice of the best weekend getaway.

We knew the mountains may not want to give up winter quite yet. The weather reports forbode of a probable snowstorm. We hiked toward it with a taunt. We could not think of a better, more relaxing place to be than snowed in, inside our tent for a few days. A weekend away from the demands of work and the buzz of a metropolitan area like Southern California? This would be epic and worth the strain of carrying our own goods up a mountain.

The higher we hiked, the more solidly frozen the lakes were. We finally left patches of snow behind and were crunching over the winter's snowpack. When we arrived at our chosen lake, it was completely frozen over. The landscape was shades of white with occasional grey rock slabs poking through. Dusty was as thrilled as we hoped he would be. Lighter, more nimble, and on all fours, he zipped with unmistakable joy through the undulating snow fields.

Those of you that have had pets before children, or still have pets and no children, know that pleasure which is derived from our animals having fun. It is as if we use them for an excuse to do so also. This is important for us to FIND FUN as human beings. It is a fulfilling connection to share. Animal or human. Animal with human. We loved this dog and what he added to our lives. We even bought booties for him.

Once the four fuzzy soles were strapped on, Dusty stood still as if we just sentenced him to prison. He looked annoyingly at us and waited for us to take them off. Finally, he tugged with his teeth and flipped all over the snow trying to shake each one free. He had to get used to them. We could tell his feet were getting too cold. As with getting braces, or having to wear glasses for the first time, one finally gives up the fight and allows acceptance and adjustment to set in. Dusty took off leaping once again. The opportunity to play in the snow outweighed the unwanted shoes. I wish I felt like leaping as our pup did. Instead, I had a slight headache.

Two things can happen in the mountains at this elevation. Dehydration and altitude sickness. Usually, one kicks the other off, and you can be dealing with both. A throbbing headache is a symptom for either. Drink plenty of fluids. Watch that you have an intake of potassium and replace lost salts from sweating are the directives this high up. You hear everyone cheering about their electrolytes. It is important. Lack of the right balance can cause cramping, nausea, and headaches. Luckily, my headache diminished once we boiled snow and cooled it to replenish our drinking water. I, so far, had been blessed with little reaction to altitude.

We had to pitch our tent on a granite slab, and gratefully brought our thick Thermarest pads so we were not sleeping right on the solid rock. The view out the unzipped front flaps of the tent was spectacular. It spanned over treetops and the canyon below. Waterfalls were cascading and disappearing under the snow drifted by our plateau like a fine wine or melody. The faint feel of the little town of Bishop and Hwy 395 was somewhere beyond our gaze. White clouds were popping over the wall of a mountain behind us. A breeze kicked up and pushed them. We knew the storm was coming.

Once our freeze-dried dinner in a mylar pouch was brewed, we called the pup and all three of us crawled into the tent. Dusty curled up at our feet and was instantly asleep. That was quite a day for a young dog. As we watched stars pop out from the view out our window, the fuzzy ball in the tent twitched and yelped with his dreams. We imagined he was recounting the glee of running in the snow. The stars started to disappear as clouds shrouded.

The quiet of this place was so peaceful. But there is also an extra quiet, and that comes when it is snowing. It started to snow in the middle of the night. And continued the entire next day. Dusty obliged to be with us in our new home. We came here to rest. To relax. And to relate as we loved best to do. It brought back Alaska for us. And we were so content to sit in our sleeping bags, read the books we brought, adorned in our wool beanies.

The puppy was soaking up the warmth and we all were enjoying our igloo party. To break up the day, we took turns bumping the snow off the tent and sweeping the flurries off our rock slab. Home chores were melting snow for drinking water and taking turns boiling mush to eat. There was no wind now, just the steady snow fall. Our happy souls were bright on this white canvas. It quieted our inner being as we had sought.

We knew we had a champion dog. It did help that he came from a top line breeder. But that does not make a champion. Character does. Dusty was noble, loyal, and instant in taking our cues. We hardly were training him. He just knew. He watched, responded, sensed without a command how to be man's best friend. And that he was.

To my husband, Dusty was a best buddy. This dog was so in tune with his owner. It is one of those rare and precious miracles when you get to have that kind of bond with a pet. I am a fond lover of Labradors as a breed, and what they are generally like in composure. There is a reason they are used as seeing eye dogs, companion dogs, rescue dogs, and are great bird and water dogs. But Dusty was exceptional.

For me, Dusty was my faithful running companion already. For my husband, he was his buddy. He rode shotgun, and my husband took him to work every day. This dog was a gift that bonded our young marriage in a deeper way. The dog allowed us naturally and organically to react to life, and somehow gave us the excuse to look for play and experiences.

Dusty was an instant and excellent swimmer. His thick fur seemed impermeable to cold. And the dog loved to swim. If there was water, he was in it. Many times, in trouble. He fell in a backyard pool as a puppy, and we could see by all the scratch marks on the sides of the concrete lip that he had been trying for some time to FIND a way out. There was none. We discovered the small, exhausted puppy hanging desperately to a ladder rung. Taken to a California beach, he also learned that waves could flip him over.

After hours of dutifully being in the tent, Dusty would start to wiggle and pace. Little whines were his way of saying he had enough of this thing called rest. He would start to yelp with a plea to be let outside to play. And with a zip of the tent front flaps, his powerful and youthful muscles were let loose to glean and flex as the happy beast frolicked in the fresh, new powder. He dug and pawed and came up with a nose of sticky snow. When he wanted to come back in, we commanded him to wiggle. Flinging wet spray in all directions, it was as if he knew he needed to wipe his feet before coming back in. We liked this animal so much we didn't even care that the tent had the musty order of wet dog fur.

The second day, the snow stopped falling and it was time to pack up and leave. As we rolled our bags and strategically placed all our gear back into our packs, we let Dusty out for one last recess before his pack was strapped on.

"I don't hear Dusty running around anymore." My husband had his head cocked, trying to listen.

"Neither do I."

We both pulled on our outer layers and scrambled into our boots. We scanned from our perch. Dusty's paw prints were everywhere and in every direction. They patterned a maze of exploration. The circles led further and further away as we traced the indents of his paws in the sea of white. That is when we both spotted it, almost simultaneously. Jim grabbed my wrist with a tight squeeze. I was already looking. A dark spot, a small portion in the middle of the lake, was cracked and showing blue water. In it, splashing dramatically in small circles was Dusty.

We had heard the lake cracking and popping in the night as the temperatures were rising after the storm. You could now see thin ice on the edges of the shoreline. But somehow, our beloved pet was light enough to make it to the middle of the lake before he punched through. There was no way we could go out on the ice and get him.

We both started yelling. Our voices were ricocheting like cannon fire off the mountain backdrop, a chorus of high pitch screams and a gruff man's panic. "Dusty, Dusty boy. Oh, no. DUSTY!"

My husband was lurching with all his might in waist deep snow trying to reach the unreachable. He strained to get to at least the edge of the lake. Each powerful surge I knew was an effort to try and stop love from being lost. I followed him, though my head knew our rescue ability was feeble. Dusty was trying to get out. He clawed at the ice, but slid right back in.

He saw us moving toward him, and I am sure the young dog could hear our yells. He started trying to jump out in our direction. Each attempt was met with more ice cracking off and the dog landing back in the chilly water. Who knows how long he had been in the lake already?

Dusty started to bark. He rarely did, only to voice a warning or a greeting. But this bark had a sound in it we had never heard before. Desperation. It was weak and it rippled to us. "Hey, mom and dad. I am in trouble." He let out a few, very audible whimpers, as if saddened to have failed us. He could not get out. His attempts to leap out were lessening. And, as we watched, he slid under the surface, but weakly popped back up. It was just a matter of time. We stood on the edge of this huge ice block with the edges of the lake now showing blue and could do nothing to physically save our dog.

My husband kneeled and dropped his head in his hands for a long moment. He slowly looked up and started coaxing. "Dusty. Boy. Come. Dusty, come." He made his plea, and it was the only way he could reach the dog cracked through the ice. A sound of *please, dear animal, you mean the world to me. Find the will to survive. Find it boy.*

"Dusty, come," he commanded.

Dusty did ignite, with higher pitched whimpers, and more frantic leaps. He just slid back in, slid back in, slid back in. Jim kept coaxing, like a coach bent on finding that turn in the dial that makes a champion race past the competition to the finish. My husband was willing our dog to find the will to survive. I heard him say under his breath. "You can do it, boy. You've got to. Do it for me, buddy."

He commanded forcefully. "Dusty. COME!"

And with that Dusty tried with an effort beyond measure. He got a toenail of a hold on the ice, and those youthful muscles bulged with will power. Tiny inches were being gained. The two humans on the shoreline were frozen in a fixation for the outcome. Finally, Dusty's toe gripping had leveraged enough weight of his body onto the ice. He was dragging his hindlegs out of the water. The soggy fur just laid there, unmoving for the longest time. Finally, on very wobbling legs, like a newborn colt, Dusty started walking toward us. We held our breath and prayed his body weight would not punch through any more of the ice. Our loyal Labrador made it to the shore. He punched through the last thin ice, but his feet touched the ground. In wet leaps he was in my husband's arms.

He took off toward the tent with the strength of a soldier carrying his stricken comrade. He retraced his entrenched boot marks so powerfully I couldn't even keep up. He had the limp dog inside the tent before I was able to get to the rock slab. We pulled out a sleeping bag and rubbed our pet's fur and let the animal curl up in a deep sleep while we both sat there, stunned. Neither of us said a word for the longest time. Finally, the pondering conversation drifted between us.

What if we had lost something we loved that day? What if the dog had not found that super charge of will to try and live? What if? What if? And more what ifs? And then we turned to only images. No, we did not want to fathom such a loss. What if that was a child? We brushed upon a hurt so deep it makes you back away from it. I could only imagine what it would feel like to lose a child or a loved one. I vowed to be sensitive and honor that place no one would ever want to deal with. It's a place I am sure God knows our human pain. God sent a Savior to bridge the pain of death.

We agreed that day, if we lived long enough and vibrant enough, there could be mishaps, emergencies, and loss could happen at any time. Needing to find the will to live is required of any of us. On that craggy ledge, we had to take a deep look at our own will to survive. Could we conjure up the superhuman desire to rise out of a fallen situation? It is a question we should all ask ourselves. Any one of us could have the misfortune to have to answer it. You never expect to fall through the ice, but life can put you in unfathomable places which might require you to find your own will and way out. I would end up there.

To return to living after a tragedy, or a bad circumstance. A situation, or a crash, or calamity. Or an unthinkable pandemic. All take a warrior will. Surviving my childhood asked for that same kind of championing. So, I campaign. Predetermine. Decide now. That when knocked down, you will claw your way back up, and out, with fortitude toward life and better living. We all have to.

Our pup went on to be a stellar dog. He accepted each of our two children as they were born. He patiently tolerated ear pulling and collar tugging. He kept a watchful eye on their play. He knew with some internal instinct that his special place in the family was the teacher of character. Our kids learned to love our dog as much as we did. And so, so many times, when life made me look loss straight in the face, I remember him finding the WILL TO SURVIVE.

—m—

Dusty lived to a golden age. His muzzle grayed and his limbs started twisting inward. He was getting so frail. As is a common mishap in the breed of Labradors, Dusty's hips started giving out. He was such a faithful dog. He did not want to soil anything inside. We would find him half on a rock or on a hillside, unable to drag himself back to the porch door.

My husband said he would be the one that took the ole boy to the vet. When he did not return for a long time, I called the animal hospital.

The receptionist excused herself. "Um, ahh." Deep sigh. "Can you hold on for a minute? I just witnessed the most heart wrenching exchange between a man and a dog, right now. We put animals down all the time. But this one. Whew," she cried. "I am sorry." Sniffle.

"You see," she retold the scene to what she thought was a stranger. "This man in working Cardiffs and a hunter's cap came in carrying his beloved yellow Labrador. He laid the dog on the table and proceeded to tell him what a champion dog he had been to him and his family. He slowly unhooked the collar and told the dog he would keep it. The dog lifted his head and licked his hand. I have never witnessed such a strong exchange between an animal and a human. That was so…unbelievably touching."

The receptionist cried more, then continued. "Some touch of life and loss that showed love. It was… beautiful. Is that an odd thing to say?" The receptionist rambled all this to her unknown caller.

"I'm sorry," she said, sniffling, "to be sharing this to a complete stranger." I could hear her wiping away her tears. "It was just so… touching. Umm… can I help you?"

It takes something fibrous to FIND the will to live when we feel like we are barely hanging on for dear life. The deepest loss I can think of is losing someone you love or something irreplaceably beholden and all our traction seems out of reach. We were just losing our dog. There were to be bigger losses. Sinkable losses. Life tsunamis that left me wading through refuse. Losses that battle wearied. I wanted to sink and just stay under. Life can be like a roll of dice sometimes, and we FIND ourselves in some horrible bottom of a pit almost too difficult to get out of.

We can learn to have the darndest of determined wills to get back on our feet. Tough things can make us DISCOVER tenacity. Making FIT happen helped me. As opposed to just hoping or waiting for something to happen. Going after goals that took fortitude and making my life active was a healthy solution when life tried to slide into slumps. I hope this book motivates a toe hold to crawl on to more solid places from life's tough spots. A better future. A chosen choice in taking hold of your own action. Let's all FIND the will to more than survive.

3

A Summit Experience

"Being Challenged in life is inevitable, being defeated is optional."
– Roger Crawford

My pure love of the outdoors is rooted in smells, sounds, and a deep feeling that nature and space is made for wellbeing. My earliest remembrances include blue birds—Stellar Jays—making chaw, chaw barks above my head. The fresh scent of pine. Wind swaying the tall, shiny trees playing a soothing creak, creak song. The sun reaching through and grabbing a tiny soul standing in its warm beams. Looking up. Sensitive to it all. I was spellbound by this magical place. We were in Big Bear, California on a first vacation with my young parents. My mother says I was too little to possibly remember that.

And though I would experience a tense childhood—a reality that would have me conclude that the world was an unsafe place for me—though I was pitted with unmet needs, I knew from that early sun-beamed moment that there was a Creator and an amazing creation to be a part of by just being OUTSIDE. Soaking in the wafted hues of sunrises and sunsets are reminders that there is color in life. Rippling streams, high mountains, and vast oceans were free to all and a playground to test stamina, find reflection, and dive internally to discover more about who I was. It is a gift from God.

A God-given reminder of something we can't see but should discover. And it is free to all.

I loved any and every opportunity to be…OUTSIDE. Out in it. It was a great place for that kid in me, already bent for survival, to find play. Peace. Toughened by the drive of my father, whom, in a twisted way was giving his kids a purposed drill camp upbringing, I was rugged. Gritty. Able and willing to tackle any natural terrain and challenges most shied away from. I already knew I was fighting whatever his agenda was. I knew if I could take the life punches of his bullying, I could also turn that grit into something that climbed real mountains. I was trained to strive, go, and not quit almost before I could walk.

My dad arrived home one day from a trip with some fellow police officers. He had been to the top of Mt. Whitney, the highest peak in the contiguous United States. At 14,505 feet in elevation, this towering high point tucks atop the Sierra Nevada range outside of a small town on Hwy 395 called Lone Pine. The Sierra Nevada Mountain range is a kind of spine between California and Nevada. If one peers through the telescope pipe welded to the pole in a park in Lone Pine, it zeros in on two pinnacle sister pillars and then the mounded higher doom which is the summit of Mt Whitney.

My dad had his sleeves rolled up and an orange-colored hunter's cap on as he burst through the door. His browned, sunbaked skin caught my attention, though I still jumped to stand at attention in respect and fear. An unusual brush of being refreshed came in with him as he triumphantly smirked while tramping in with a fully loaded backpack, slung off his one shoulder. This enthusiasm was rare. I was spellbound.

I showered questions at him as he stood in the entrance, sliding the pack off his shoulder and propping it against the wall. Questions he never even bothered to answer. He rarely did. He went upstairs to shower. I listened for the water to go on. Then I gingerly unhooked the flap of the pack and rustled through its contents. Conditioned that the shower time was a safe zone to snoop, I knew in my body exactly how long that stretch lasted. I had about ten minutes.

In the top of the pack, I found a camp stove, small lantern, and a poncho. All so interesting. I struggled, but I lifted and shouldered the pack to feel its weight. I stepped my little feet in his new, but dusty hiking boots. The shower clunked off. The hot water pipe always made that pop sound and was my cue that time was up. I quickly placed the pack exactly as it had leaned. My dad had that crime scene detective in him that kept account of all his scenes. I set the boots in the same configuration they were kicked off and drifted out the door to the sounds of neighborhood kids playing a game of "kick the can."

"My dad just summited a mountain!" I yelled.

None of the kids reacted to my announcement. We were all in that new era of just entering junior high. No one wanted to say or do anything that would make one stick out or be different. No one except my sister.

She galloped by on her imaginary horse, on her way to pull weeds for a neighbor so she could buy that horse someday. She would go on to purchase two horses and pay for feed and board before she even graduated from high school. She didn't stop there but continued to own and operate a ranch that now has barns full of horses, and with a purpose in teaching youth confidence and experience through tending the farm and learning to ride. I viewed my sister as "very cool". She did not bend into someone else's definition but chose her own dared-to-be-different mold.

It wasn't easy. The kids, as a mass, went after her, teasing and taunting, and mercilessly choosing to use her as the scapegoat was despicable. I admittedly feared being hurled with the same attack and tried not to stick out as being so different. Yet, I felt it. I was different in some shoulder-slumping way.

As most youth, I was trying to FIND, or maybe more like fight for, my own signature mark. It found root in active outdoors. Sports. Not just organized competition…but adventure and exploration. Backpacking. Climbing. Cycling. Running. My arousal to combining nature with camaraderie was more worthy of this pursuit than conforming to my peers. When in the woods or on a climb or in the midst of running at a track meet what they thought no longer mattered. What I felt when I was doing these activities felt better than conforming. My shoulders would roll back to their proper alignment atop my body and my sense of happiness would flourish.

"My dad climbed a mountain!" I blurted again and ran toward my favorite paths that traversed the hills. I kind of galloped my own trot that day, as my lungs burned and my whirling feet ran the twists and switchbacks of my worn path that led to our secret fort, a makeshift pile of used lumber that leaned against a tree. I sat on the hillside and listened to the birds. My mind wandered up mountain ranges with tall peaks. I knew I wanted to climb mountains.

I badgered my father. I wanted him to know, without a doubt, I was up to the challenge of climbing a mountain. When his pictures came in from the trip, I shuffled through them, over, and over again. The tents and the tarps stood out as bright tiny spots on the landscape. A terrain of looming grey boulders, dark blue lakes, an even bluer sky, above the cragged, treeless peaks. Everybody seemed 'buddied' in the pictures. Shadowed and unshaken faces with gleaming eyes. Smirks. Grins. And arms over each other's shoulders. Even my dad was smiling, authentically enjoying it. Those were the pictures I peered at most. And the ones where they all stood shoulder to shoulder, victoriously atop a vast, far-reaching drop to the world below. The summit picture.

The summit moment captured on a piece of paper captured me. Weather was warning in the distant ominous clouds, but the "team" of hikers had beaten something big. Donned in sunglasses, I could confirm that above the tree line, the light was reckoning. It drew me. And so did the knowledge that camaraderie could be found in a shared outdoor activity. I longed for the health of it.

My dad finally conceded to taking my sister and I to Mt. Whitney when I was twelve. I really don't remember much of the trip, which tells me that my dad's ways of interacting could decimate even the most anticipated desires and dreams. I can only know that he probably made it such a regimented check off list in which we, the unworthy, worthless bother of offspring, did something to make him not feel just right or our actions angered him. Even if we hadn't done anything so-called "wrong," we were in the path of his hurt to hurt. He must have found his false item to slam in how we didn't measure up to something or did something hellishly wrong and "selfish."

It was a from birth-on experience to be bulleted with harm-filled words shot in a way that stripped our sense of security and esteem. The hurt to hurt was a confusing swirl others rarely detected in that towering figure I had as a father. I learned to take a lot and tried to shut out a lot. I armored on the outside and told myself the lie that it didn't bother me, but it deeply did.

I felt I was alone on this earth in this battle, save my siblings, who were left to find their own ways to cope. Surviving such an invisible, motivated monster placed us on our own islands, even though we grew up together. I would experience a repeat, more detached, and more sinister trip years later, with my brother, as my dad trekked us rim to rim across the Grand Canyon. Sleeping in his own tent, my brother and I awoke to a note that said, "Pack up your stuff and start hiking until you find me."

My brother fought the game and started to turn around and go back to the south rim. I pleaded with him. "But mom and grandma are already driving to the North Rim. We will be lost in this vastness forever," I cried. We had to go after him. Up the 7000-foot climb of the North Rim, and an endless day of switchbacks a thirteen- and eleven-year-old found him leaning at the North Rim Lodge trailhead sign, showered and sipping coffee. It was dusk. "Oh, you finally made it," he said.

But on the trip to Mt. Whitney, as my sister, dad, and I were hiking to the top, my sister got extremely sick. She had a history of migraine headaches that numbed her arms and left her slurring her words. Altitude sickness stimulates this. The headaches can be excruciating and produce vomiting. She was experiencing all these. My dad never nursed any ailments. In fact, he attacked the emotional core of the one who showed such weakness. So, my sister groaned and suffered, and I think she either made it to the top or my dad left her alone in the tent at our pre-summit camp. We weren't stopping until the goal was accomplished.

I complied. I grabbed my day pack and chased after him. I was the skinny, dogged, and determined kid with the tenacity to stand on that peak with him. He liked that. I liked it for other reasons.

What I do remember of that first trip over 14,000 feet is that it was hard. I could hardly breathe. I felt like a one-hundred-year-old lady at twelve years old. Above 11,000 feet, at every switch back, every few minutes, I plopped down on a rock and tried to regain oxygen and the muscle strength to keep going. Once I got above 12,000 feet, I started counting 10 steps, 10 deliberate steps before I allowed myself to stop. It was that hard. Hands on my thighs. Pushing. Determined. Push up. Push on. Plop. Get up. Push on. Time turned into eternity. My dad, with his lanky stride and height was switchbacks ahead. He soon disappeared.

As the day wore into early afternoon, I became concerned. The trail was barely apparent. Past hikers had picked countless different ways to get up the huge shale slope. Over time, there was no clear trail. Then the wind hit. The wind didn't just pick up, it pitched up. An invisible demon appeared out of nowhere and toppled me backward with a 60-mph shove. I righted myself. And another blast took a swack. And another. Then, a steady, mad blowing gall engulfed me. My dad was nowhere in sight. I picked out an off-color, lighter string among the rocks that looked like a worn path and headed toward it. But it led me to a ledge.

I was at that spot you can see through the pipe in Lone Pine. The exposed ledges between the two sister pinnacles before you get to the summit mound. The wind funneled through these crags and the blasts could easily knock me off my feet and down the sheer precipice. It was at least a 1000-foot drop. I was overwhelmed. Stuffed-down fear started to gurgle up and erupt out of my inner being. Intimidated. My fears of death, heights, and open spaces were rumbling and stirred up an emotional wind more aggressive than the demon winds of the mountain. They both felt bent on destroying me. My answer was to panic.

I took a few steps back, turned my back to the cliff, and buried my head into the crag rock face. How was I going to walk this narrow ribbon of a trail past the drop offs? I couldn't walk on water, and this is what this felt like the trail was asking me to do. I hugged the granite wall. "You can't panic," I told myself. Something inside me screamed back, "I already am!" My breathing became staccato and rapid. Though the day was starting to rapidly cool, I felt sweat beading on my brow. I let one eyeball venture back to the overhang.

I caught a glimpse of that valley almost 12,000 feet below. There were specks of dotted color and an almost black colored lake in this light and angle. That must be Consultation Lake and the summit camp. My sister was somewhere between there and here. I looked out, and way across the valley was another mountain range dabbed with snow caps. That must be the White Mountains. My heart that had been pounding in my chest found its place back where it belonged. I could do this.

"I WILL do this!" I declared. My eyes involuntarily snapped shut, but I tried to take in that I was truly above the timberline. I forced them open and stared at a scene I had never experienced before. I started to like what I saw. Expanse. Openness. Rock and sky. Yes, way off in the distance and miles and miles away I could see other mountains at the eye level of where I was. I was high above even the clouds. I was near the summit.

I dug a windbreaker out of my pack. I ate a handful of peanut M&Ms. and being in the present moment where I was at my young age, was life changing. Life enhancing. Life calming. Life fulfilling. I was proud to be here. I had never been UP so far looking DOWN. In fact, I had never flown in an airplane. This must be what it is like. And yet, I got here on my own willpower with my own determination. This was big.

I decided to be cautious, but I was going forward. I was going to summit Mt. Whitney at twelve years old. I stayed low to the ground, almost on all fours, and got past each rushing wind opening. From here, I knew UP was the trail. And UP was the way I was going to go. I think this is the best kind of proud.

I picked through the boulders in an upward route. Around each mound there seemed to be more rocks and more rocks, until time and enduring perseverance produced blue sky overhead. I passed stacked rock shelters made by human hands to make wind shelters. Wind must be a constant threat this up this high. I hadn't seen a soul all day. These erected walls seemed like something from an Inca ruin. It had been a long, lone day with my own soul. I felt a shrine in the stack rocks. A rite of passage. I was summitting.

A forest service hut was erected on the summit and the door was ajar. I found my father relaxing inside. He had finished his lunch. Upon my arrival, he stepped out of the structure, ready to start down. An afterthought spread across his face. He dug out his camera and handed it to me. He motioned me to take a picture of him. He struck that movie star, practiced pose with his perfect physique, smart reflections playing off the sunglasses. Snap. He snatched the camera out of my hands and in his inventory fashion, carefully put it back in its case and into the pocket of the pack. Nodding his head was his manner of checking the task off his list. And telling me to fall in line. It was time to go down. He had waited for me long enough.

He headed down with his lanky stride. I hurriedly looked around. I rushed over to the geo marker signifying the height of the mountain and stomped my foot, gladiator style, upon it. There. I climbed Mt. Whitney. Though he was already on his way down, with that stomp, I stomped something in my cells. Not just the zeal to be accomplishing a mountain, but the mountain experience and what it felt like and taught me. I knew this was a great place and space for all of us. I knew that the world had life and lessons out there. And that adventuring to and through nature, being active, picking peaks to conquer would be life enhancing.

I knew that GOD was bigger than all of this. And I knew that getting outside was worth sharing, telling, and encouraging others to do. This was a teachable moment, and I felt the confidence and character-building ability the outdoors was offering me. I sucked this serene, real breath of life in deeply. And I let out a very healthy exhale filled with self-admiration.

My dad did stop in Lone Pine for a celebratory burger before we returned. And he did say he was proud of us. We did get to spend that valued time he took off from his demanding job to be with us. In the café, there was a small rack of patches that boasted, "I climbed Mt. Whitney. Elevation 14, 508 feet." I bought one and hand stitched it onto a windbreaker. I wore it almost daily to junior high. Who does that?! I didn't care. I knew I could summit. No amount of unfashionable chiding from an entire school of preteens could take that from me. It was a badge I honored.

I do thank my dad, sincerely…for giving me that mountain top experience. I am so thankful for the first chance to claim victory to a high peak's geo marker. It marked me for life. Thank you, Dad, for grit and tenacity. I learned through years of my own ruined choices that my dad operated from a core of his own immense hurt, but it was masterfully locked up forever in his perfection. As a kid, I knew I had champion status to go after and everything to prove in what I did not know was a game I could never win. I was striving to be his trophy child.

I wanted my dad to be proud and approving of me more than the value of my own self. I learned to be ultra in tune to the silent terms and twisted conditional childhood roles he had each of his children and wife play. I somehow knew my role was to excel, though it never had a label. I got skilled at a silent language of keeping him happy by winning. I became proficient at accomplishing. My grades were A plus. My pursuits, overly lofty. Unfortunately, growing up, I excelled more to survive him than to be able to glean champion confidence. It felt very mixed up. There is honorable drive that is healthy, and there is drive trying to prove self-worthiness that is unhealthy. I heard people describe me as the most capable, under esteemed person they had ever met.

Though I was visibly skinny, stiff, and an awkward athlete, I held a mojo to never give up. The outdoors gave me a place appropriate for that kind of dogma. I was hurting for something to summit. To validate me. I didn't know to acknowledge that I was just plain hurting.

4

Surviving Childhood

We have the ability to bloom on rocky soil.

Why was I such a serious kid? It was hard for me to tell. Maybe, because it was constant. A constant unknown of what the flair ups would be. Remember tetherball? My childhood was like getting hit and spun, faster and harder, until you were wound so tight, he won. Then he would back off and let you relax your way to unsuspecting… and bang, go at it again. It was always unpredictable. The knots in my stomach never left. I almost began to fear the quiet and seemingly normal times because I knew it was an eye of a storm. And I knew my mom was in for the worst of the rounds. The tetherball in my life was the hold my dad had on me.

What ignited him? Something he would blame on you, something you never even did. He needed to punch with momentum at your crushable self-esteem for some hidden, warped reason. It was very disorienting. He had only his sibling, mom, wife, and kids tethered to the game. Coworkers, a handful of acquaintances, and extended family were not tossed around like we were. So, my angst was judged just being an uptight child. My mom's weariness and ragged appearance was judged as her being unstable emotionally. He was a cool, successful cat to everyone else.

It was a teeter totter ride. He seemed to look for ways to slam me into the ground, with his mightier shove and I would, almost defiantly, shove my way back up. My childhood became times of 'normal' living pushed back down by intensity that were not fights, but a one-sided kill switch to bring one of us kids, or my mom, crushingly down. A sense of healthy self gets lost in such a game. The way he inflicted damage must have started in childhood and still reached out and landed on his own brother and mother whenever possible. We lived with him in the walls of a place that should have been called 'home' but was more of a baffling war ground with stealth artillery that left fear, anxiety, indecisiveness, and low esteem as wounds.

My mom battled back in unhealthy ways. She took her three kids out for a lavish meal on the first day of each week when he issued her the food money allowance. We then ate a can of veg-all and a box of macaroni and cheese (or what I called the less-than-a-dollar meals) each night thereafter. I will forever dislike frozen fish sticks. She rang up accounts for clothes and food and had us pretend to play by the mailbox on Saturdays to grab the bills and hide them so my dad would not find out.

We learned how to turn the speedometer back on the lavish Cadillac that was quarantined to the garage and not to be driven more than 10 miles a day. My mom piled all the neighborhood kids into that lemon, and we would steal beach days during the summer. The neighborhood kids understood there was some sneak to our tattered mom. They liked the trips even better because they had that covertness about them. My mom brought sandwiches that sometimes only had butter on them. She made adventures out of nothing, like when she tied bait to strings, so we thought we were real fishermen hanging them over the railings of the pier. To our delight, sometimes a starfish would hang onto the baited bread.

Big Bear Lake, CA Age 4, 1966. I learned I liked being outdoors.

The adventure had to be returned home before the curfew, and bad traffic days elevated our fear. Summer fun in the sun happened in our childhood, but it came at a cost. We had to scramble and vacuum every grain of sand out of the carpet of the car before my dad returned from work. Then act as if our tans came from being lazy around the back yard. We begged the neighborhood kids to flee and pretend to not know us, or to also act like they had just had a great day in the surf…without us. This set the neighborhood kids up to play on our situation. We were the kids that lived in a different house of rules that made us weird to other kids, and something they would not know to have empathy for.

They went out of their way to tease us, tagging us as targets. We never had friends sleep over. When my dad arrived home, everyone knew they must be gone, and they did so by fleeing out the side door and crawling over the back fence. They knew the rules were as different around my mom and dad as we did. It became a game for some of the kids to crawl back over the backyard fence and make funny faces at us through the window, knowing we were imprisoned in a routine that involved lack of socializing when my dad was home.

In his routine, he spent a good portion watching his programs with the rule if the television was on, we could not talk. Not much conversation ever happened around the dinner table. He had a strong and set routine, very efficient for preparing for high level presentations and advancement exams. He obtained his master's degrees and doctorate while we were still small children. He practiced his hobby of performing stage magic… relentlessly. We learned our parts.

He put on company parties. And holiday parties. And we, including my mom, were the indentured servants to scrub, polish, and prep these lavish get togethers. And then, at the invitation hour his children were sent to our rooms to hide out the party. We couldn't even be seen going to the bathroom. Maybe that is where my bed wetting started. I wasn't sure. Was it because I also could not disturb my dad, the giant sleeping at night? I would hold my pee painfully if I had to rather than risk it. There was wrath to pay if I woke him by getting up and going to the bathroom. The kid's bedroom in the house was on the same top story adjacent to the master bedroom. So, I tried to hold it, fell asleep, and failed.

Of course, news like that leaked to the neighborhood and ended up at the elementary school. I decided being shy was the best defense. I said and offered very little about myself, and I acted like I did not care when I heard the taunts. But honestly, I was getting devoured and felt defenseless. It was not the heathiest environment for self-esteem to have an elementary school of personalities use someone's struggles to further wound them, but it seems to be the nature when there is a mass gathering of youth. A kid society likes to find someone and something to pick on. I felt the words. They hurt worse than sticks and stones.

—⚋—

One day, my second-grade teacher called on me to get in front of the class to recite a poem. I nodded my head in a slow "No." She insisted, thinking that this would push me past my shyness. What she didn't know was I was afraid to go to the restroom in fear of getting teased, so I didn't go all day long while at school. On this day, I had to go. Badly. I was sitting on my foot to hold it in. The teacher came to my desk and her standing there told me I had no choice.

I moved to the front of the class and looked at all the faces as ones that could hurt me in a way that I might not survive. They had no idea how injured my insides already were. And as I tried to get my lines out, the warm pee just came and ran down my legs and into an obvious puddle. This is hard for any child to go through. But for me, it felt like death. Now the kids would have material to really go after me. The teacher, in a commotion of not knowing what to do, sent me to the office. I walked, head down from the front of the chalkboard to the back door past a hysterical classroom of kids laughing in one huge chorus.

The office issued me a "to borrow" set of underwear and a used dress and put my soiled clothes in a baggie. If they had these items on hand, I wondered how many other poor souls had soiled things in this demoralizing way while at school. I felt like I was the only and forever one, except for my sister. I moved at a snail's pace down the hall. I wasn't about to go back into that class. Time ticked mercilessly slow. I was waiting for the end of school and that final bell to ring.

Ring…. Ring. I bolted for the gate and slammed right into my sister. She had been waiting. She had already heard. That is how fast the "attack you" virus travels through a school population. She grabbed my hand. "Come on. We must get out of here… and fast."

We took off on a run. We could hear the roar of kids pouring out of the confines of the school. And above the normal noise, some yells and taunting.

"Hurry." She commanded.

She was outrunning me. I geared in to stay up. She veered around a corner and was pulling me up and over a fence. We landed, hidden, on a weedy concrete storm drain. She climbed me up and out of it and onto a footpath she might have worn down herself. It led secretly between the manicured housing track and to the hills where the horse ranches were. I was dangling my baggie of soiled clothes and trying to keep up.

Once clearly away from the torment, I looked around her world in awe. "This is so-and-so," she said, petting a horse that came to the fence solely to be petted by her. "I'm not sure if that is his name, but that is what I call him." A very skinny, shabby horse wandered over. "I think this one needs me." It cautiously nosed her. I reached to pet them also. They shied away from me, but not from her. They knew her.

"Oh, do be careful. This is a hot wire to keep them from chewing the fence." She looked at me seriously. I would have put my arm on it. I had grass in my hand to get them to come to me. I didn't know. "It hurts," she warned. I was protected by her in a big sister way.

My sister said she had permission to pick the avocados on this property in exchange for cleaning stalls. She took my baggie of peed upon clothes from me and started washing them out at a hose spigot.

"We can dry them here. Help me pick some avocados." She had set up a little cardboard box on a street corner that had stop signs. Deliberate letters scribbled on a piece of cardboard read, "Odocados. 10 cents. For buying my horse."

"I am going to get a horse someday, "she said. And I knew she would.

What an industrious kid my sister was. She sold avocados and polliwogs in baby food jars. She cleaned stalls and pulled weeds in people's yards. But kids, like ravenous wolves, went after her more than me. She was tall. Too tall. And that gave them the excuse to tear her apart. She was scrappy, though, and she refused to cower. She developed her own style and stuck to her guns with her love for horses. She trotted right by all their teasing, and she lived for the bell to ring so she could get away and wander through the properties that boarded horses. She was a year and half older and got out of school 15 minutes before me. I rarely saw her after school. We walked home alone in our own pain.

That was how our upbringing was, navigating childhood by learning about the hurts only after they fried us. Somehow, other kids had a sense that we were already suffering. We, as humans, can peck at hurts as the chickens do, especially a pen of children. It was a tumultuous journey that was leaving scars.

My sister and I never told my parents I peed my pants at school. To this day, I am grateful that she protected me from suffering some of the things that she had to learn the hard way.

As for the rest of that school year? I just became sadder and even more shy. And I'm not sure I ever got better at playing tetherball.

5

A Master at Masking

I'm the middle child.

My mom, trying to be very involved with us, and operating on a shoestring budget, made my sister and I matching flower patterned overalls. It was clear that she needed us to accept them. We went out the door and toward school knowing we were committing social suicide. But we had to. To reject my mom's act of love would also kill something that was barely staying alive in our own mom.

A Master at Masking

As soon as we got outside, my sister announced, "I'm not going," and took off toward the ranches. I went to school. I was a studious student.

I could get away with one day at school dressed like that, but when my mom produced a second set of matching overalls, my sister and I looked at each other in total horror. My sister knew she couldn't get away with ditching school every day either, so she came up with a plan. She came downstairs with a brown bag. When my mom asked what was in the bag, my sister told her that it was something for a school project.

"Let's go," she said, grabbing my hand in a protective way.

My mom snapped a picture of our "cute" overalls and the matching sisters, arm-in- arm as we raced from the porch. We did not feel the closeness my mom was trying to capture in that snapshot. We just pretended, masking our deception with fast forced smiles. We knew my mom needed that.

My sister had a plan, and I hoped it was a good one. She pulled me into the bushes. "Here, put this on," she said.

To our delight, a new style was emerging in the late sixties. Girls were wearing jeans and a t-shirt, and long, straight hair. She had grabbed jeans and a t-shirt for each of us. We left the material my mom had painstakingly hand sewn in the bag, stashing it back under the bush and we headed to school. We kept those hidden clothes in the bushes for a long time and did this routine many mornings. One day, I guess my mom drove home from the store a different way, and at an earlier time. On the sidewalk, she must have witnessed her daughters walking home, wearing jeans and t-shirts. She slowed to see us crawling into the bushes and coming out in the matching pairs of psychedelic overalls. She was waiting for us on the front steps to our house when we rounded the corner.

"Why didn't you tell me that wearing my outfits I made was a hardship? I love you girls. I wouldn't ever want to hurt you." She looked so pained, almost pierced. And that was the problem. We didn't want to hurt her any more than she already was having to experience. And in doing so, probably hurt her worse.

That was a spiral scenario in our home. I still feel it to this day. I still do it. And am affected by it. Confused by it. When do you tell the truth? When do you hide the truth? If ever. Think of the people that hid the Jews from the German Nazis. They were courageous in their way to survive and keep people alive. That is where I found myself. Making those hard kinds of choices at too young of an age. Survival choices. I learned to maneuver, outsmart, and keep the hurt from smarting to the point of no return. I knew these kinds of hidden wounds were doing damage and could kill the soul. But so could lying. It didn't matter which choice I made. Damage was done. It felt damned. My skill box was filling with tactics that would not make sense to a love showered environment. Tactics that could foster future bad choices.

I became a master at masking. I was watching people put my mom in a fall-apart category, saying behind her back that she was too emotional, too needy, or too under impressive. Very few could find that refined and pretty woman she was when she began the relationship with my dad. Now she was overweight and weighed down with volcanizing emotion. She complained, bitterly. She tried to explain her prison, but few liked to listen. And fewer saw her as the victim.

My dad was a master at masking in a different way. Most people easily agreed with the conclusion my dad manipulated so hard to make them believe was the truth. He stood there, fully groomed, affluent, educated and decorated. He was strategic in the impressions he left. And for my mom also. It was twistedly forced so that she didn't amount to anything while my dad rose to higher callings and steadily better positions.

The Bible says that God looks not at the outward appearance, as man does, but the inward appearance of the heart. We should try to do so also.

My mom was destroyed into something that no longer got to be her, except for that true center of the heart each of us can have that is truly beautiful and shouldn't ever be taken away. My mom had God at her core. My dad couldn't get to that. It annoyed him. But wouldn't a God annoy when you had become your own god?

Mission accomplished on my dad's part. My mom looked, acted, and was a wreck. Watching that as a child, I knew and felt my dad was accomplishing missions on his own children. I was the chosen trophy child. I just didn't know I was playing out a role. I was raised to produce straight As, win awards, and be called the smart one. But I was also pinned in so as to never rise enough to lift above and surpass him. That was punishable. He made sure I knew the rules.

I took piano lessons. I had no natural ear or gift for music, but I won awards. I practiced incessantly because I knew he expected the accolades. I was able to bang out a mechanical tune with no grace or natural feel to it. But it won awards because it was so complicated and astounding for a kid my age to be playing that level of a piece. To this day, I couldn't tell you what I played. I just did it for the recitals and the awards to be lined atop the piano. It felt like the void that it was. People would defend him saying, "Your dad is just giving you opportunities." I knew better. It had nothing to do with me and what value music or grades or sports had to my life.

School came easy to me. I was a bright student, and the school put me through an IQ test. I found the questions odd and nonsensical. Apparently, I scored high and the discussions of me skipping a grade began. My dad's IQ was phenomenal. I already knew that without a test. But so was my mom's. Her artistic gift of expressing in writing and photography were signs of her intellectual equality which my dad never recognized. She was also mothering three kids who were so different, and different in the way we learned. She creatively parented each of us with our own bents. Smartly.

My mom knew to sit side-by-side with my over-active brother when in kindergarten to allow the teacher to attend to the rest of the classroom. He was just naturally wired to poke, move, knock things over, and be interested in cause and effect. He was real, natural, fun, fun-loving and about people in an "upset the apple cart" kind of way. I loved my siblings, and so did my mom. For my sister, it was modeling and horses and my mom did whatever she could to nudge us along in life experiences that cost little.

My siblings and I fought. A lot. It was a warped means to release tension. My sister was left-handed. Not that it made a difference until you had to sit next to her to eat. Then her elbow annoyingly tapped your ribs with every bite. So, we fought over who had to sit next to her. And we fought over who had to sit next to my brother in the back seat of the station wagon. Sitting next to my brother, we were sure to get poked or have our hair pulled and our nerves tousled. If we shrilled in complaint, we got in trouble. That fact kept our little brother fully entertained. He would make faces and pretend to poke by putting his finger just a smidgen away from touching, but not actually touching. I am not sure which was more irritating, actual poking or the pretend poke.

One time we were all in the back seat on a long drive to the Sequoia Redwood National Park. My mom said it was my turn to sit in the middle next to him. My mom always made it my turn on long trips. I had the higher tolerance level. But on a seven-hour drive on this hot summer day, he made sure he pushed me to that last straw. It was usually hard to break my camel's back, but this trip, my brother would not let up. It was the only way to stay entertained on an otherwise silent drive. My dad was listening to his news.

In that back seat I had been mouthing mad faces to convey for him to stop. I had to do so in between my dad's eyes that randomly appeared in the rearview mirror. He always kept a watch on us. He instituted this silent rule as it made his programs paramount, making him King of the Convoy. We secretly fought each other beyond the gaze of his eyes.

My little brother kept it up for hours, and I finally slapped him. It was a rare response from me, but we had developed into a twine of taking the tension out on each other. Ridiculous damaging flare ups were happening more frequently. I did a dramatic pretend swing across his face, without really trying to punch him. I respected his way of living through silence, I just didn't like the tension it put me through. I meant it to be a final caution to make him stop.

My action did something neither of us fathomed. My pinky finger caught the edge of his brand-new glasses and flung them right out the crack in the back seat window. We both jumped backward and watched the tiny frames bounce a few times on the freeway. We watched in horror as the next car's tire smashed right over the fragile plastic and glass. We flipped back around and sat upright, rigid, and dazed. My sister looked at us, astonished. Written corner to corner on her face was the look a sibling gives you when they know you are about to get demolished yourself; killed by real punishment.

My dad's eyes met ours in the rear-view mirror.

"What's going on?" his officer voice demanded. My sister blurted out what had just happened. The family station wagon moved over lanes and came to a complete halt on the side of the freeway. I paid for my intolerance. My brother paid for it, also. We all did. I think I started selling 'ovacados' and pollywogs and pulled weeds after that. I paid for the glasses and kept up trying to earn money as an entrepreneur in the hope to live past all this. I started a money jar for college to pay my own way to somewhere other than here. Somehow. Someday. I was going to go somewhere.

6

It Took a Jog-a-Thon

I remember the exact day running became important to me. A bursting sea of rapacious and rambunctious school kids were being ushered by teachers from the classrooms into the elementary school's auditorium. The buzz was about a school fund raiser they called a jog-a-thon. The assembly explained how each child could earn the school money by accumulating pledge amounts per lap each child could run. The lady in charge of the Parent Teacher Association held up the largest candy bar I had ever seen—a supersized Sugar Daddy– and I instantly yearned to be its recipient. Not because I even liked Sugar Daddy candy or candy in general. It was because it was so gigantic. And it was the top prize. I decided I was going to WIN that biggest prize.

This assembly triggered a drive I already had. If I could sell pollywogs in baby food jars, could I not go door to door and muster up donations? I knew I could run. The equation for winning the ginormous candy was endurance (running) and perseverance (getting the most sponsors). This gave my walk home from school a new purpose. I picked a new path every day and knocked on doors. Pushing back my shyness, I got better at presenting my project at each house I doggedly approached. I ran out of time before I ran out of neighborhoods.

It Took a Jog-a-Thon

I wandered miles and miles filling up the pages and being okay with the doors that closed on my hopes. I knew if I knocked on enough of them, I might have a chance at winning that supersized Sugar Daddy.

On jog-a-thon day, I had more pages with signatures on them than any other child. And on that day, ambition kept me running long past the recess bell. The rules said the big candy bar went to the kid who ran the most laps. So, I kept on running. To the entire school's delight, I was still running around the cones on the field when the kids piled back out to the playground at the lunch bell. They all started running with me, cheering, and begging me to make it through the entire lunch period.

They were enamored because I was doing something extraordinary. They were giggling and taunting, but in a good way for once. They were wishing me well and sincerely wanting me to accomplish some champion distance. I was so glued to not stopping that my skinny legs kept churning in a running motion. Though they had become numb with lactic acid, I kept going. When the bell rang, I staggered to a stop and felt hands slapping my back in fun approval. With that one feat came a respect the kids had never offered. Not only did I win a silly candy bar I never could finish eating, but I also earned something much more valuable. I earned a title, a stamp of approval. I became the runner chick.

Around that time, the President introduced the Presidential Physical Fitness Awards for elementary schools to encourage health and activity. It was a coveted patch earned by being able to produce a certain amount of sit ups, pushups, pull ups, and timed running tasks. All eyes veered toward me. How fast and how far could Caren go?

Again, I took the challenge as something interesting. I practiced for it. Scrappy counted for something…finally. I liked being active and now it had awards to incentivize me. I earned a patch each year and sewed them onto the same jacket with the "I climbed Mt Whitney" patch. It was dorky, but I didn't care. There's something about having a uniform that makes you realize you can belong and can be connected as a teammate to your own self, if that is all you have.

In 1972, something spellbinding also happened. The Olympic Games were televised. I was smitten. I learned what track and field events were. I believe I watched every single broadcast. I saw athletes doing their ultimate best in swimming, cycling, horse jumping, diving, and multi-events like the decathlon. But mainly I fixated on track and field with all its jumping, throwing, sprinting, and endurance races. They won my admiration.

The rest of the summer, our backyard and back hills became Olympic games. We set up makeshift obstacle courses and pulled strings to set lane lines in the pool. We played at being champions. We dreamed. We picked events we liked best and pretended we were the winners. It was a summer of bests. Ten years old is a great age to dream. A healthy foundation of who I enjoyed being was developing and formulated in those formative years. The 1972 Olympic games stamped possibilities into my fiber.

When I entered junior high, I knew to include sports. It was a place I could safely be myself, though I was hardly talented at any activity that involved a ball. At that time, these were the only sports available to girls: volleyball, basketball, and softball. But our junior high announced the school would be conducting a one-mile run. The top boy and girl would go on to regional meets that led to county and state cross country championships.

I discovered that running required something core, and that core was an effective place in developing a better me. I wanted to run in high school, but the coaches felt not enough interest would arise to warrant a girls' team. I would not go away and pestered their office for the opportunity. The athletic department finally conceded that I could run with the boys' team, only because they were worn out by my asking. They thought that would get rid of the problem by adding a clause so unreachable I would not faithfully serve the terms. I was a freshman. They said if I ran three years in a row, by my senior year they would consider a girls' team. I know they never thought I would last. And they probably never thought they would be inheriting a long legged, skinny, over-motivated girl who they nicknamed "chicken legs." I was theirs for keeps. I ran every season.

I ran every practice. I loaded on the bus and went to every meet. Those first two years, I came in far behind physical bodies built differently than mine. I respect that and the God that designed each of our physical differences. I wasn't there to be a boy or to beat them. I just wanted the opportunity to run and jump. And I felt, what better place to train for dreams and aspirations than against a field that was better than me. I developed explosiveness coming out of the blocks. I learned to attack hurdles aggressively. And I listened and watched what made some better runners than others. I enjoyed the busload of guys. They were fun. And the interactions were pricelessly natural. I was on a team.

One of the most valuable by-products of doing a sport is camaraderie, and one of the beautiful things that was happening to me was conversation and connection. I was learning to enjoy other teens in an organic way. I was getting to learn what being myself was freely like. This was far removed from the charade inside the walls of my home. Healthy friendships grew in the moments before practice, traveling to meets, warming down, and waiting to be picked up, or walking off the track. Soon, the girls of my high school were noticing. I had a natural in with a busload of guys they were hoping to at least get a date from.

Track and field taught me how to have friends and be a friend. By my senior year (1980), I am not kidding, a full-fledged team of girls signed up. They also wanted to enjoy this same easy-flowing magic that gets to happen in sport. All the teammates, guys and girls, learned to be together. It helped gift me something extremely healthy in those two ways that doing FIT can. Besides allowing me to get in incredible FIT shape by being on a track team, I learned to FIT in with a community of kids. I liked my senior year.

To this day, I still marvel that a candy bar was what initiated the entrepreneur in me. It wasn't the candy bar so much as wanting to develop the skill to get over the bar which was set at a new height. No wonder I love the mechanics needed to succeed in the high jump in track and field. Or the mechanics for entrepreneurship.

A simple quest to win that Sugar Daddy fanned a lifetime of being a fan of running, and being an entrepreneur, and the endless pursuit that running could award my life with interesting enhancement. That jog-a-thon taught me that hard work and the ability to have stamina could move the needle toward success. It did not matter if I won. It was trying to win which fueled the driving force and produced the will to do what it takes. This one act set in high motion the path to pursue. It added interest to my life, like high octane fuel does in a race car. Learning to go after a goal, learning to try, was really the supersized prize. It was a lesson that would stick with me the rest of my life. Going after the goals, seeing if I could win top tier made me realize that striving alone is a prize in itself.

7

Don't Die on Me

Even flowers try to bloom on rocky ground.

I am not sure what made my mom finally fold into a shell of a person, but I gather emotional scars are flimsy like a stack of cards and have a topple height.

She was a nice person. Too nice. It was as if she was overcompensating for all the meanness the world had already given her. She never developed boundaries for who deserved appropriate portions of getting her love. She tolerated the intolerable and loved even those who hurt her. She was wide open with no protective shield to abuse and was constantly taken advantage of or devalued. She had no limits to her giving, and it destroyed her.

Yet, she had something. Something deep. Something strong. She had character. Caliber. She had depth as seen in the likes of Mother Theresa. She was a talented writer and photographer. She saw into the eyes of people and beams of light and angles on landscape. She was a mom who loved being a mom and wanted nothing grander than for her kids to have experiences she did not get.

But during my seventh and eighth grade years, my mom ghosted away. Her outer body was there, but her inner spirit was gone. Her words were shallow, and she stopped speaking unless you insisted she answer. But usually, it became an only a one-word reply. I knew she was slipping away, and I tried all kinds of interactive antics to keep a thread of her connected. She mopped floors and pressed my dad's shirts… emotionless. She no longer got dressed to go anywhere except to buy groceries. We no longer took the secret trips to the beach. She rarely brushed her hair. I was trying to find her, but all that met me was an unresponsive shell with no person inside. I was scared.

I would rush home from school to see if she had changed back. No. There was only that blank stare. There was no rise. No beautiful person that took us to church. Nothing. And nothing seemed to matter to her anymore. Even us. I have no idea if there was one breaking incident that threw this switch or just the accumulation of being so consistently chipped apart. But she disappeared, and it was terrifying. Between my shoulder blades developed a knot that would not go away. It shallowed even taking my own breaths.

I was panicked. We needed her. What would happen to us if we were left with my dad? What would we do if my mom died? I didn't recognize it, but I was trying to keep her from committing suicide. Our house was two streets above the junior high. I would run home in between every class, racing through the house, tapping my mom on the shoulders, making sure she was at least breathing, and race back to make it to the next class before the tardy bell rang. Remember, I was the straight A student. I was having to be both—a kid who skipped out on school, and a kid who was in the desk ready for every test and every question. Talk about suicide. My own inner self was casting into lead.

I would come home for lunch. No one ever knew I was running off campus. I did this for most my eighth-grade year. I was deep into sports because that gave me an excuse to have some time away from home and feel some realm of normalcy. I knew my siblings would be home in the afternoon, and I had a window of time to do afterschool sports. I can look back and see that sports rescued me. They were the place that relationships, communication, interaction, learning, and yearning could happen normally and naturally. Yet, I would cut out right after practice and get home. I did the dishes, straightened the house, and propped my mom up for my dad's return from work. My dad said and did nothing about this change in my mom.

Just months before she had been working feverishly on a book for a woman who had lost her husband, an LAPD officer in the line of duty. It was interesting and put a buzz in our home. Publishers came. Editors took the manuscript. There was talk of a movie. The woman and her children hummed around our house waiting to be interviewed as my mom typed constantly, day and night, to put the story on paper. Back in the 70s you still had to manually type transcripts. A pile two inches deep was already done. Every day she proudly let us come and see how much higher the stack of pages was rising.

She turned our bathroom into a black and white dark room and was producing pictures from negatives. That was even more interesting. Many of the photos were from combat in Vietnam. There was one that stole my attention. A man she was writing the book about was handing out toothbrushes and toothpaste to families standing in a long line in front of a rows of outhouses. My mom added the caption, "The military brought in sanitation. The Vietnamese refugees used each one as an entire family home, spreading the toothpaste over the k-ration biscuits and sleeping inside the plastic structure with the safety of a locked door regardless of the odor." I looked at the war weary, stricken, skinny faces filled with fear. I hurt for all they were going through and was glad my mom was giving them a voice in the book.

But as the project neared completion, it disappeared out of our house. There were many loud, yet muffled arguments. My mom's outcry pierced through the walls in a battle between my parents. We were tucked in our rooms early and just had to listen to the wails of a women's voice and the staccato jabs of the man's voice in our home. One night, my mom's voice turned to screams for help. My fists were cringed so tight the nails dug in. My teeth clenched so tight I feared I would shatter them. I couldn't stay in my room any longer. I fiercely slid down the staircase, missing most of the steps. I opened my mouth and entered the den in our home… screaming. My mom was curled in a ball, in a fetal position. She was rolling around and pleading.

"Stop it, stop it. Oh, please stop it. Somebody help. Please. Please help me. Stop him." Her whimpers sounded for real.

My dad turned on me with yellow in his eyes. "I am not hurting her. She is just crazy. I don't know what to do with her. She is lying to me."

I joined in the screaming, "YOU, Stop it. Stop it. YOU."

I wanted to hit him so badly. He walked away. He never landed, or rarely landed, a blow on my mom. He didn't need to. His weapon was words. Twisted words. Twisted actions. In some warped way, he was robbing her of the joy of accomplishment. Joy of life. Getting to be nothing other than an endured woman to his demented manner was her fate. I was so mad, but unable to be mad. It tore in a way that did not heal. We should all leave. My head wanted to explode.

By this time my brother and sister were standing at the top of the stairs.

"Go ahead. You can all go to hell," my dad spit." I never wanted any of you anyway. I never did. She did. I don't need you. I don't need this. I don't need any of this."

He heavily pushed my brother and sister aside and went to his bedroom, the master. The bolt on the door slid shut. What family has a bolt on their master bedroom door? Ours did. My mom's book never got finished. Or at least, my mom never got to finish it. They came one day and picked up the almost done piles and talked of the new writer and publisher. That was the day my mom started sleeping on the couch in the den. And she slipped away.

The teacher of my accelerated class for gifted students knew I was dealing with some form of turmoil. She asked me to do projects after school. I couldn't. She probed for information. I provided none. She offered to let me weed her yard. I could do that on the weekends because my brother and sister would be in the house so my mom couldn't pass away. I applied the money I made to go on a State Capitol field trip our class was planning and made sure my brother was home.

I never talked about my home. My fears. My mother's situation. How could I? How do you? I didn't even know what was happening to me and why. I had no clue why we were spinning and dangling in this house that felt more like surviving a prison camp than a home. It made me feel uncomfortable being in anyone else's home. My dad said it was my mom's fault. We all tried to be better. Every day felt desperate and without a shield. I knew I needed my mother to survive and had to find a way for her to come back to life.

One day, I came running through the house, and she was gasping in an odd manner. She said she needed to go to the doctors. I liked the sound of that. I hoped a doctor would rescue and intervene. My dad was ignoring her. Maybe the doctors could help us. But she asked me to do something that I feared was more than I thought I could do.

"Here, you have to drive." And I knew she meant it. She was barely breathing, pasty pale with blue lips. She already looked dead, like a Halloween character. I was thirteen years old.

"I don't know how to drive mom."

She got in the driver's seat and slumped back. I jumped around into the passenger seat. We had no portable cell phones at this time. Or GPS. She headed, not in the direction of a hospital, but toward the doctor's office. She pushed the gas pedal. I leaned over and was trying to keep my steering within the lines. The car jerked nervously back and forth as I overcompensated. I tried my hardest to focus, and the car took on the pattern of a drunk driver. It was one of the more frightening times in my life.

"If…" she tried to talk. She couldn't. She just weakly pointed if we were coming to a turn. It took more time than I thought eternity could take to finally get to the parking lot of the doctor's office. Like a cruel dream where time ticked but went nowhere. We did not even pull into a parking space. The rusty family station wagon that had been purchased for us kids to be hauled around, rolled to a stop. My dad had discovered we were sneaking the Cadillac for trips to the beaches so either my mom or dad had bought this used vehicle. I looked at my mom, and her chest was no longer going up and down. She had stopped breathing. FUCKKKKK! I knew that word was reserved for something this bad.

I pounded wildly on the back door of the doctor's building screaming that my mom had stopped breathing. Two nurses came out, looking wary at my wildness. I dragged them over to the body sliding closer to the floor in the front seat. The nurses jumped to action. One nurse worked at unlocking the seat belt, the other took off on the run for oxygen and a doctor. I just stood there and watched my mom's face start to turn blue, matching her lips and her arms. There was nothing I could do.

The nurse was now pumping her chest and counting. The other nurse returned, shaking her head that she could not find the doctor, but she had a portable oxygen tank. Both seemed so caught off guard. I am sure it is not every day someone comes pounding on the back door and announces they have a mom who is not breathing. The one nurse could not get the gauge turned on for the oxygen tank. I tried to help them by loudly shouting, though I was normally such a quiet kid. "Hurry! Please hurry!"

They called an ambulance, but I knew the team of trained specialists would not arrive in time. It was up to these nurses, and they looked perplexed. One actually started reading the step-by-step instructions on the outside of the tank to try and master how to operate it. My mom's eyes were wide open and unblinking this entire time as if she was already gone. Going.

But that is when I caught a very slight heave in her chest. Like a last effort. That toe grip on the ice Dusty had found. An airy swish sound followed, and her chest started rising and falling. My mom had only one lung and half of another. She had lost a portion of one as a teenager battling pneumonia five times in one year. But that was not the reason right now. Later, we were told her lungs had collapsed for no known medical reason that they could determine. She was held in the hospital for a week of testing. They found nothing.

The heave, she later shared, was a laugh. She realized she was dying and found it funny that these nurses could not start a bottle of oxygen. She finally had a reaction to something for the first time in months and thankfully, it was to laugh. That ability to laugh activated her diaphragm muscles and triggered an inflation of her deflated lungs, naturally. I believe she would have died that day had the reflex to laugh not boiled up somewhere from her pancaked emotions.

And I believe beyond measure that laughter and joyful things in our life are what keeps us alive and so beautifully human. We should put a lot of value on this. FIND so many reasons to laugh. Fill our lives with fun and things worthy of humor. Not at the expense of anyone, but the valuable kind of laughter from the recipe of joy, delight, and the depths of our souls. Silly and playful moments that make us giggle and enjoy. I know, for a fact, it can save lives. It saved hers.

The three of us siblings had a makeshift fort my brother had constructed from a large refrigerator cardboard box. We felt it to be more of a cozy place than our huge home on the hill with the view, the pool, and the manicured yard. My dad threatened to throw it away, so we dragged it behind the trash cans and hid it at the side of the house. It became our command center. The three of us squeezed into it the afternoon my mom almost died. Neighbors, meaning well, came over and left a meal. They offered pity we did not know how to accept. We left it all on the table and crawled back into our fort, waiting for my dad to come in from his shift.

One of the nurses had driven me home, sweet with small talk I barely engaged in. I sat stoic as a statue shocked by what had just happened. The silence spread like a disease to my siblings. We all were worried into silence. What would happen to us now?

I wanted to cry, but I did not know how anymore. I felt old. I desired more than anything for my mom to get air back into her entire life. I wanted her to have reason to laugh…and laugh often. But at our present moment, life seemed so lacking in humor. We left the huge house empty and let the food brought by our neighbors grow as cold as we felt.

8

The Sound of a Shrug

A great thing happened after my eighth-grade graduation. Our church decided it wanted to do a choir tour and come up with a play that we could perform in national park campgrounds. My mom wrote the play. It was real, touching, engaging, and captivating. And the music choices told a story of how life could be redeemed, be turned around, and be filled with grace just by getting to know the God who made those amazing national parks.

It was a high school activity, but because my mom wrote the play, I got to tag along. We had a week-long excursion filled with people, laughter, and camping out. I, of course, was still considered an eighth grader, so I developed crushes on every cute high school guy. My mom got praised for writing something that resonated with people. It reached out and touched on needs that really were changing lives, even ours.

My sister came home with a boyfriend. I was happy with my crushes. We sighed in relief to know that hanging out with people, doing something creative, and being outdoors could have a fullness worth living for—not just sports, but enjoyable time outside. And how much more enjoyable it was to be outside with a group of others. It gifted my sister, mom, and I a touch of life beyond the walls of our home. It showed me the type of freedom I should head toward.

It is sad to add that the rest of the summer felt heavy. Being back in that house felt stiffer. It felt like being exposed to an invisible gas leak that made you feel nauseated all the time. The oppression was now obvious. We had experienced a taste of carefree love, play, and enjoyment. I signed up for every camp and every reason to stay away from home after that. I was away as much as possible. I had an endless appetite for the nourishment I lacked called natural healthy living. I knew I had afterschool sports to hide in, and now this organic means to enjoy the planet in a creative way called camping gave me even greater doses.

My mom didn't have this luxury. It was torturous. Every opportunity that propelled me toward my own life, left me feeling so responsible for abandoning her in her sinking ship.

My mom came to my track meets. All of them. She had to. She had to drive me. But she also wanted to. She liked being outside in the stands, with the kids, and being a part of our lives. I never saw my dad at any of those meets.

My dad at the only meet he came to.

He did attend one master's National competition far into my adulthood. It was hosted near a university town he had moved to when he entered into a new relationship and a third career. By then he was a highly rated department head and college professor. I was 45 years old. I was surprised he said he was going to show up. It just so happened to be one of the few track meets where I really struggled.

I thought his presence was possibly making me feel weak and winded. I still had a hard time reading my own needs coming from my own body, even as a mature adult. It ended up I was low in iron. The line had dropped to the level of anemia. Fatigue, pale skin, pallor, and shortness of breath are signs of low iron and lack of vitamin B. Iron levels can fall low enough to cause not enough production of red blood cells. Red blood cells are the carriers of oxygen to your organs and most definitely needed in high level competition. It took eight weeks of good supplements to bring my levels back, and here I was thinking that I needed to train harder. This national meet was not to be a podium winning performance weekend for me, and my dad lost interest in the stands.

"Caren, I have got to go. Something came up." He brushed past me as I was conferring with the sports medical tent as to why I would be so winded when I was in the kind of top shape I was.

My dad whispered in my ear, "I thought you said you were good."

It didn't have the air of a cutdown. Just his factual voice. It almost had the sound of a shrug. I now was old enough to refuse to let the voice take seed. I had spent all these adult years taking a tweezer to his voice, like plucking cactus thorns out of my skin. They were weeds in my garden that wanted to choke out joy and confidence. I made a mental note to let him be just who he was, though I was baffled by it. And I tried my darndest to not let his disinterest knife in.

Wailing about unmet needs is petty, but I feel this kind of childhood needs a voice. My dad knew that destroying us subtly would leave us sounding and looking like we did not know how to handle ourselves. And underneath that a narcissist, sociopath, or abuser can take cover and stay undetected. That's why the word "covert" floats around. I think the damage it causes needs a voice because it so easily gets brushed under or excused away. Drawn out in the open, it can't continue as unaddressed. Actions, even words that harm, need to be called out as the abuse they really are, and for the impactful damage they really do cause. In recognition, there is healing that can then take root.

Those affected or entrapped by neglect, abuse, or indifference need to know they can have a voice about misbehavior and harmful conduct. That they can get on with living a healthier life. My mom did not know she had the right to be treated better. I feel compassion for anyone trying to live through someone else's chaos and forced harm. It is difficult to explain the voluminous, subtle, but real damage it all causes. It gets to hide behind comments like, "It is not that bad," or "Don't be too sensitive." It made me feel so ruined for no reason. It seemed better left swept under the carpet. So that is what I did. I got very good with that broom and the denial of the damage. I brushed it away.

Things swept under don't go away. Soon I had a bulge I was tripping over. It broke bones and caused life crashes for me, literally and figuratively. It seemed hard to paint a relatable picture for anyone to grasp who had never had to live with "it" or through "it." Whatever "IT" was. A kind of unwelcomed, ghostly vapor that was sapping sound happiness. This is where I plead for empathy. Empathy to be had for anyone that has had to live through something others do not. Empathy for living through damage.

FINDING the way to sweep it out the door and not under the carpet would have been a win. But, instead, I decided to race after a life that was full of all the "fulfilling" things and ignore the root of my tension and the seeds of my pain. I tried to run away from it. That part of running didn't go very well.

My dad was good at his cover up. There are people who operate narcissistically. It is a disorder. Yet it works for them. I didn't know this. My dad was a master at looking good, and he enjoyed his craftiness. His own family always came out of the coverup looking like the losers. No storehouse of scenarios, even with added exaggeration, would sound criminal enough, nor convincing enough, that someone just taunting you all your life could be so emptying. All my trying to paint the true picture of the tension came out sounding like I was not very good at dealing with life. Worse, I was perceived as just insecure and uptight. So, I stopped trying to tell anyone, and I tried to ignore the knots that never went away in my stomach.

I learned to do something asked of me, but but it robbed me of myself. I learned to pretend something wasn't wrong, or it didn't matter, or actions were justified. Or, worse, I accepted what I was being told – that I deserved to be made to feel bad. I learned to lie, exaggerate, or deny. Not to ever be dishonest. I almost overcompensated in honesty. But to protect against harm.

I am also astounded. But I learned to do my own self-punishing, self-down talk. I dove harder into myself where my dad left off. How does that become the case? That the abused learns to hate themselves for being abused, and so they jump in and treat themselves just as badly, or worse, than anyone else? These were bad habits with huge consequences.

It's been hard to share some of the childhood hurt. It has taken me years to be able to put it into words, though I love language and writing. Years of walking away from these emotions, hurts, and issues. But I must walk down the right paths and give myself my own empathy in doing so. That's how to FIND the best me. Just as important as seeking to be FIT, I was needing to FIND that I FIT. I was an empty, yet very accomplished child, that didn't know how to put all these pieces together to make the best adult me.

I asked a gal who lived a few doors down to describe what she saw of our home. She said, "Your dad was stinking intense." She found me on social media and texted. "I could not be more proud of you and your drive to do well. Your own kids look so happy, which in my opinion is the most important thing in the world. But let's remember, and say now, what we never could as children. I cannot believe how your dad treated your family. Yet, the strength you have has come out of that. The strength you have as a woman for yourself and your own kids is something to be proud of. Your mother. She was an amazing human being and had a huge effect on my own childhood." All these years later, this was good to hear.

How good were we at painting the picture that everything was perfectly fine? The neighborhood kids saw through the perfection. My dad even sprayed our lawns green if any sunspots or fade appeared. Living in this picture-perfect neighborhood, my dad made sure his children were painted also. As a child, you would think I was hoping someone would see past all this and find me. Instead, if a reference was made to it possibly being wrong, I cringed and scolded myself and determined a better way to hide it. I was a perfect pretender, a master at masking. It became a way of life. And I was not about to entertain a discussion on the subject as a child.

I had a girl come up to me in high school. She poked my arm. Jab, jab.

"What are you doing?" I wailed.

"Seeing if you would break in a million pieces," she chided in a destructive way. "You are so rigid, I thought if I touched you, you would shatter." She laughed and took her circle of friends waggling away.

She had touched what I spent most of my energy hoping to hide. It did shatter. I watched the keenly dressed group, swirling their curled hair, linked in a snickering community, disappear around the corner. The style had changed to curled hair and puka beads and frilled skirts. These were the same girls who had followed me through the halls and off campus, loudly letting the world know that I had started my period while wearing white pants. We all have embarrassing moments. They are humbling and good for us to learn to navigate. But there was more to this for me, and I wonder how many others. Hurt upon hurt really hurts. These girls were going after a person they knew was already getting knocked down, and they sensed they could score a kill. And by doing so, elevate themselves. This made me sad. Sad at an entire childhood of this. Sad that people do this.

I made a vow. I was going to either cave in or courage up. I was headed for young adulthood, and I was determined to get a college scholarship. It hurts me that people will go out of their way to peck a person who is already injured. Even in chickens, pecking bothers me.

"CHICKEN!" My head screamed back after those girls who had teased me but had rounded the corner.

What if we reached down and picked up the downtrodden instead of snickering at the problem, or the injured, or hurting? What if we cared instead? NOW, that is BRAVE, I decided. It is chicken to cruelly attack the cracks or weaknesses in another. I vowed to try and not do that. I vowed to care, see others' struggles, and respond to them as people deserving of equal treatment. I would try to be sensitive and recognize real needs, real people, and demonstrate love. That would take not being a frail bird. I vowed to create the impact of an eagle, making life soar for myself, and others. It was a good vow I hope to keep. It was who my mom was.

I have met so many people who, despite all odds, are wonderful. It's because they chose to be. They chose character despite their circumstances. I decided that I wanted to be one of those types of people—a kind person. With boundaries. Not one to be walked all over, but someone with genuine actions and acts of kindness. Love that changed lives.

Bringing up childhood things shouldn't be blaming someone else for what we really need to take responsibility for, which is ourselves. I fervently know that we are at our best when we are totally responsible for the attitudes and the actions we take. No matter what age. No matter our situations and circumstances. We cannot blame how we feel and what we do on another person. We are responsible for ourselves. No doubt. But pretending that pain and abuse was not harming me was a factor that got my life in trouble. I lost me.

I was glad that childhood would soon be over and some rite of passage of becoming a certain age would declare me an adult. I hoped it would offer me wings. I was sixteen and beautiful, just like any other sixteen-year-old on this earth is. I just didn't know it. All I knew was that the kids at school and the conditions happening in my home were leaving me in a pile of pieces. I did not FIT in very well. And I had no idea how the puzzle of me FIT together…anywhere. I think this is when people can and do… and often… give up.

After running into my 40s, and 6 years of training, learning, & striving, I accomplished the goal of winning a world competition in the 400m hurdles and Heptathlon. I became a 12-time Masters National Champion and 2-time World Masters Champion.

9

When It Gets This Intense

The relationship with my mom was hard on me. I loved her because she had such a true, unwavering love for me. But the voids and lack of her life made mine also destructive. I obsessively over-helped others, did not have a clue what I really liked or felt, and was always thinking that all outcomes depended on me. And, for the most part, they did. It was the role I was put into. I am not sure if I learned to be good at it, or I was chosen to be the accommodator and repairer because I just naturally had that bent. Whichever it was, I was molded to smooth situations over. I rarely, if ever, thought of what would be best for me. I was always, and still am, unsure.

All this would get me in trouble as an adult as I tried to experiment to find myself. I honestly had no clue what I liked. So many things I hadn't had a chance to try or decide for myself. I was robbed of childhood play, that sense of safe discovery. Yet, I always had a wonder of nature. I also found clarity in sports and education. It was the emotional side of life I was bewildered by. And the relational. I was weary and trying to not be crushed by the fear of being underexperienced.

I watched how hard my mom's life was in search of love in a world that wasn't going to give it to her. I, at least, had sports and a solid youth group from a church. Both gave me a healthy outlet and doses of regular friendships. I also used it as an escape hatch. My mom didn't get access to any extra doses of enhancing life lift-me-ups. It destroyed me to leave her behind as I grew old enough to leave. I would survive. She would not. I knew that.

Learning to be the "perfect child," the "trophy child," is a set up to fail. No one ever told me that it wasn't my job to make the world work. It had taken me far too long to accept there is an Overseer. It's His job, God's job, not mine. I had to find that out the hard way. Through years of trying too hard. By thinking I had to make the world function, I set a never-ending pace I raced.

Being with my mom or away from my mom was a lose-lose. It never felt like either place was right. I wanted to be that fiercely independent person I was, but keeping the home together made me carry a load that felt like weights were shackled to my momentum. Secrets disconnected me. I had so much to hide I became a super capable loner. I lived in real dread, a consciousness that something bad could happen at home at any unpredictable moment. I also would rather drag along a burden alone than have to explain it to anyone. As I was excelling through high school and headed to college on a scholarship, my mom was getting grinded. It did not make sense.

There is a strength in being educated. Now, I can Google and read about what was really happening. Narcissists have an inner agenda to make others crazy. My dad was making my mom go mad. He was needling her, blaming, insulting, ripping the skin off her self-esteem. He felt powerful and mighty by putting his heel in and twisting with all his might at her self-worth. Her ability to appear calm and be put together was gone. It was an effective prisoner guard technique on his part. She was hysterical. She was fear-filled, anxious, needy, and a desperate mess. And people stopped wanting to be around her. She had no access to knowledge to inform her of what was happening.

She cried too much in social settings. She was over-clingy. And her physical appearance was starting to hide the beautiful lady she once was.

He needed her to look like that so he could excuse himself and leave. He would make her grovel for food and clothing. Even for peace and rest. He found some warped pleasure in making her lie, catching her in the act he forced, and then disciplining her in front of others as a liar. He called us kids "selfish no-goods" more often than he called us by our names. And the sad, and very haunting truth, was that he was the liar. He was the pretender. And yet, he looked so put together. And we looked haggard. This is not a whine, nor a complaint. This was a harsh reality that we were so trained to let no one know, probably because we did not know ourselves why we felt so held underwater and so much like damaged goods.

Things escalated as us children headed off in different directions during our teens. My sister headed right into an immature first marriage because they were young. I headed off to college. My brother was impulsive and more free-spirited, and he just went away and partied whenever possible. It took nearly a lifetime to put a tag on the thing that was rotting us from the inside out. I had no idea there was a disorder to it. I thought we were just not living up to a stronger personality. The outcome of children who have had to live under narcissism is not a good one because they do not get to enjoy many aspects a home should have. And it goes through most family histories unconfronted, discussed, or addressed point blank. How do you?

I walked into the house one evening right as my dad was finishing off a session of "push my mom to a frenzy." She usually ended up in a fetal position, rocking back and forth with her hands over her ears begging, "Please stop. Please stop. You know I can't take this." Neither could we. My sister crawled out the window and drove away. My brother spent the night at a friend's. Then my dad would ask me if I could do anything to help his hysterical wife. My own mom.

But this day, he did not expect me home. He was inflicting damage just because he was in that kind of a mood. As I walked in, my mom was at the kitchen sink and my dad was towering over her in that stance he took on when he needed to be king. He was rattling off how she didn't clean the house right, that his shirts were always wrinkled, that the dinner vegetables were cold. But he was adding in how wormy, and miserable, and poor of a specimen of a human being she was. Where did these kinds of words erupt from inside my dad? I can only think they came from his own crazy upbringing. How sad a home he must have had to grow up in. I could hear my mom's weakened pleas, "Please, please." Sob. "Please, stop," she begged. He never did.

Finally, in an act of desperation, she grabbed the knife in the sink and started stabbing her own hand. "Stop it. Stop it," she screamed. With every scream, she stabbed her own hand. I rushed in between them.

My dad looked at me and rather emotionlessly said, "Maybe I took this too far." He understood exactly what he was doing. I grabbed the phone to call 911. He put his hand on mine and hung up the phone. In his professional voice he said, "I will take care of this." He wrapped my mom's hand in a towel and directed her to the car. He took her to an urgent care, not our primary hospital and paid cash for the stitches. This was not something that he was going to allow to be put in a record. And, eerily, it was never talked about, even by my mom. She told people she cut herself doing the dishes. I think she was willing to take the wounds in silence because my dad was super attentive and nice to her, for a while, after every incident.

So, did my mom get hysterical to get my dad to show some semblance of tenderness, caring, acts of love, or concern? Either way, it was whacked out, and the way my parents were relating was so wrong. Writing this all these years later still leaves me in knots.

My childhood had times of true craziness. To harm yourself instead of dealing with the one who is trying to hurt you is mind-boggling. But my mom stabbing herself is the truthful picture of what happens in this kind of caustic relationship between a narcissist and a broken codependent. The softer one finally starts taking the hurt like they deserve it. They come to believe they are unworthy or did something to be neglected and abused. They lose sight of their needs ever being met. And they think the problem is in changing and bettering their behavior to keep that person happy. It's blinding.

I could hardly wait to find a way to live life so differently. And leave.

The summer between my high school graduation and college, I turned eighteen. My dad loved puns. He loved teasing, but it was the kind that made you uneasy. His jokes were at your expense. My mom had wrapped a few gifts and bought a cake. To my horror, she also invited a group of my closest friends to have some form of graduation celebration. They were excited to finally get to come all the way to my house—the house on the hill with the evenly landscaped yard. They laughed and played games. We served chips and dip. My mom was so happy to have them all enjoying our lavish home.

My dad was not. He felt like my mom pulled something over on him. At 9:30 p.m. he declared a curfew on the party. My friends were interested in taking the party to the nearest Bob's Big Boy (A big deal hangout at the time), but I bowed out. I was afraid to leave my mom home alone with the consequences of doing this for me. My dad literally herded them up like cattle and shooed them out the door. They thought he was kidding and left laughing as he shut the door.

My dad was staring at my mom and me. To end the evening, as we could hear the cars drive away, he made his announcement. I already knew it was coming. He looked at me, and the corners of his mouth widened out into a smirk.

"So, you are eighteen." It wasn't a question. "You know what that means? You are your own adult. I am no longer responsible for having the cost of paying for you." He was really smiling now. He took a coin from his pocket that he had ceremoniously placed there. Who carries a dime in their pocket? He opened the door and threw the dime out and looked at me. His arm motioned the act of leaving. Here came the ceremony pun, "Don't ever say I didn't give you a dime." The dime flipped through the air and bounced across the walkway, disappearing in the spray-painted green grass. He seemed to be enjoying himself.

This did not feel funny. I felt impoverished and in rags on the inside and out. I was heading off to college at the top of my class and as a track athlete, but with the emotions of a confused, marred, and mixed-up child. Still, I was glad for this gesture. I could finally be out of here and on my way to better choices, stronger relationships, freer living. I was so relieved to be turning eighteen. I accepted that tossed coin. And tossed me out with it.

10

Fear is a Liar

During my first year of college, I wanted to diminish the swirling storm of fears that followed me. Instead of ignoring them, I decided to dagger each one with dogged determination and replace anxiety with skilled confidence. Though I could dog paddle to stay above the surface in water, I could not swim. My mom's soothing patience taught me to trust closing the door to the restroom, and to take an elevator instead of climbing all the stairs to avoid that claustrophobic feeling in small, enclosed spaces, yet I still couldn't put my face under water. By the time I hit college, I still did not want to have anything take my breath away. I hated being under water and not able to breathe.

I think a particular incident happened early in my childhood that somehow set some of these phobic fears in motion. It was when I got dried in the dryer. The reasons I ended in among the towels and the fabric softener is a mystery. The story told is that I crawled in and shut the door. But the story I lived does not feel the same.

My foggy memory wants to imagine someone standing outside the hinged dryer door. I had carefully left it open to let light come in. I was hiding, I think. Then click, the door closed. Without warning, I went tumbling into unconsciousness. Our barking dog, and my mom hearing the dryer turn on, rescued me. This "incident" sent a clear message. Some things were not safe. Some things could hurt or even kill you. I learned that day that the world could be an unsafe place. For me, at least. I became terrified of enclosed, tightly squeezed in places. And to just balance that out, I decided to be petrified of heights.

But in college, I was no longer a toddler, and something was still triggering that instant and intense fight or flight response in me. The minute my face went underwater, it triggered the same panic I had as a child in confined places. It evoked a dreadful feeling of not being able to breathe. If I could learn to calmly accept being in confined places, could I also become at peace with other fears? I was determined to find out. I vowed to learn to put my head underwater. And challenge becoming competent on ledges.

There was a pool on campus, so I signed up for a Water Safety Instructor class and a Lifesaving course. In addition, there was a Quonset hut on campus that bore a sign: The Recreation and Camp Administration Department. It had canoes and rubber rafts out front and a notice for an upcoming rock-climbing course. I put my name on the list. Neither of these courses ended up being easy. These classes, easily accomplished by so many, were disquieting to me. Yet, I was desirous of the outcome. My ability to learn skills in my dreaded environment would somehow help me overcome my targeted fears. I inwardly knew there was victory in trying. I put my willpower fists into the power punch position and sought grit. My fate was set. The courses were on my roster.

The first day of WSI, the coach told us to swim four laps as a warm-up. I could not make it one length of the pool. She fished me out with a shepherd's hook and said I had signed up for the wrong class.

"Why are you in this class? You can't even swim," she barked like a gruff coach.

"Isn't this a class that teaches you how to teach other people to swim?" I tried to give my case some foundation. "If I learn what it takes to teach swimming, won't I learn to swim also?" I added, like a beggar needing a morsel.

She started walking down the deck. She had already given up on me.

"It's your wasted time," she yelled over her shoulder. "If you can't pass all the four strokes of swimming, each in four laps at the end of class, or dive to the bottom of the deep end and rescue a ten-pound brick, you won't pass this class."

Her words got further away as she walked. And so did my goal. But I had enrolled in college to take hold of my own life and build my own character. I was determined to learn to swim past my fear. I was determined to learn to swim.

"I will," I declared to myself, now left alone on the deck. "I will to will," I retold myself. I practiced every weekday morning that first semester, and I took notes during the class. I mimicked and watched during the in-pool drills. I triumphantly learned to swim at eighteen years old with precision in my strokes. At the end of the semester, we had a makeshift swim meet. I won two of the four strokes in the female category. I was rightfully proud of myself.

Of course, I still had to pass that final element—the brick rescue. Though I could now fluidly swing my head for a calibrated breath on each stroke and swim, I still hadn't tackled my fullest fear. That was holding my breath underwater long enough without fully panicking. I hated being under water. Something in it really bothered me. It felt like it could kill me. It felt like I was being dried in the dryer or suffocating under sheets too tightly wound around my face receiving punches. It felt like my childhood.

I failed self-inflicted brick tests over and over. Initially, I would not even make it past diving under. I was up to the surface in almost no strokes and jumping up on the side of the pool deck in stricken breaths with the brick disappearing and settling to the bottom. I would have to ask someone else swimming laps to retrieve it. They did so effortlessly, which made me want to give up even more. I was just too afraid. But every morning I kept trying. I got deeper and deeper before I clawed back up, never touching the bottom, but at least relaxing more in that lack-of-oxygen liquid which felt like a coffin to me.

So, on the day of the test, I knew I must take a deep breath and let myself relax and drop under that water until my feet felt solid ground. I was sure I was going to die, but I would die trying. I was so resolved I was surreally relaxed for the first time. And bonk…there was the bottom of the pool. I quickly felt around for the brick. I clutched it, pushed off, and shot for the surface. I pumped it above my head, which was miraculously above the water line. I couldn't hold onto it and tread water, so the brick slipped from my hands. No one took notice I had dropped it because I had brought it above the surface. I had passed.

Incredibly, I would be required to use this learned skill in my future. It would save my life and someone else's.

In contrast to swimming, I instantly liked the rock-climbing class and its earthy instructor and equally swarthy classmates. I liked learning the terminology, the climbing lingo and connecting the sport with each other in a kind of outdoorsy club. "Belay on?" "On belay!" "Climbing." "Climb on." "Repelling, rock, rope." These words sounded so raw and basic. They were beautiful. I liked learning the knots, how to use devices to jam into cracks or clip on pitons for protection. There was an art to being safely anchored, and I now knew it.

Having the proper protection (a rack full of devices to fit different cracks or crevassed scenarios) and knowing how to anchor them was crucial. And, done properly, climbing was very safe. It was another strong team sport, and within it, I found huge life parallels. Somehow, learning to rock climb taught me that I could anchor my own life. Confidence and self-sufficiency went from something others had to something taking root in me. I was hooked on the sport and used it as a tool to nurture a healthy self.

Yet, on my very first actual climb in Joshua Tree National Park, I froze. Halfway between the bottom and the final top ledge, I shimmied away from the relatively smooth wall face to a crack. When my left hand found a solid knob to grab ahold of deep in that fissure, my fear refused to release it. I looked down, not up. Terror overtook me. I would not let go. I could not move on. I was stuck.

I jammed my body as tightly as I could squeeze into this crack, somehow, no longer thinking, but letting fear make silly decisions. This struck me as very peculiar. I was trying to protect myself from the heights by shoving myself into a confined space. So, which was it? Fear surely wasn't allowing me to successfully complete this route. My inner voice said, "Caren, take a look around." I made myself glance outward, and I saw that there was a world out there past my fear.

Strewn across this desert area were an array of cragged boulders, as if God had played marbles here. The Joshua Trees dotted the desert valley like monumental soldiers standing against all odds. These heroically hardy desert succulents are revered for growing in this fiercely adverse and arid area. Their rough-barked bases store water while their limbs reach out and upward to the heavens with pricker-tufted opened arms like they are praying to God. I was one of those. I did not know how to win my battle with this rock route. I was wilting into fatigue, and fear was looking like the winner.

A rope appeared and started wiggling as the instructor adeptly rappelled down to me. He had that collected calm in his voice and started coaxing me to trust the tips of my toes on what he called footholds. I looked down at the millimeter knobs he was pointing to. He said, "Watch. When you are afraid and pull yourself into the crack and wall, the weight of your body pushes your feet out from under you. You start slipping. But if you stand erect, and keep the wall at arm's length, your weight is over your feet, and you stick." I was not convinced.

"Plus, there's a belayer. If you fall, he has you." I looked down at the very patient body who had me on hold and how taut the rope was kept. I had never had a belayer in life and had forgotten he was there. I had a hard time trusting a person would catch me if I fell. That is the beauty of climbing as a sport. This is the beauty of good relationships.

There is a verse in the Old Testament that reminds that "Two are better than one, for if either of them falls, one can help the other up." (Ecclesiastes 4:9-10) This sounds like something we should be doing—taking hold of each other, helping each other up, and learning to reach out for help. I was seeing the life picture, and I was so grateful for this sport and what it had to teach me. I moved out on that face. I stood over my feet on those little stubby knobs, and I moved onward and upward.

"Fear not" is mentioned in the Bible over 365 times. God must have known mankind was prone to fear. All kinds and forms of it—tangible fears and getting over phobias. Real fears and fake fears. Fears that leave us gripping to something called stuck. There are so many fears. They tend to accomplish very little, save paralyzing us from peace, balance, and experiencing life in a more abundant way. "Fear not" is easier said than done. Facing our fears takes something, something like the strength of a Joshua Tree plant to stand tall in a parched circumstance. We can triumph over them. I liked Joshua Tree and moved onto Yosemite, the Grand Tetons, scaling Mt. Kilimanjaro, and even running in slippery places like Antarctica, and the base of Mt. Everest.

I went on that year to run a very successful season in track and field, full of personal best marks for a skinny college freshman. It was filled with the same rewards of teammates, travel, camaraderie, and the learning that high school track had been, but with a broader array of maturity and a required sense of discipline.

The only job I had time to fit in with my sports-filled scholarship and my extra classes was to wash dishes for the campus cafeteria. Instead of eating dinner with my colleagues, I took advantage of the time and stuck my exam notes on the wall in front of the conveyor belt as I sloshed suds to clean the plates, cups, silverware, and trays. That is where and how I studied my way through college. People would ask, how do you get such grades when we never see you studying. I learned to double duty tasks.

These college years were solid years that chiseled my growth. I was taking on a form and becoming a whom. I was learning to replace fear with personhood. That did not eradicate hardship, but it gave me my own source of experiences to tool myself for what lay ahead.

Fear can be a good thing. It keeps us from getting too close to harm's way. We need that kind of fear. But fear that robs us and holds us back is a wrongful fear. If it is a debilitating thing that keeps us from enjoying victory in experiencing doable things, clobber that fear. Give it an adult dose of conquer. I no longer wanted fear holding me back.

There is a song Zach Williams wrote called "Fear is A Liar." His lyrics resound, sonorously echoing off the walls of those rocks in my life. They bounce off the fears that have been foe to my journey, and maybe yours also.

When he told you you're not good enough
When he told you you're not right
When he told you you're not strong enough
To put up a good fight.
When he told you you're not worthy
When he told you you're not loved
When he told you you're not beautiful
That you'll never be enough.
Fear he is a liar
He will take your breath
Stop you in your steps
Fear he is a liar
He will rob your rest
Steal your happiness
Cast your fear in the fire
Cause fear he is a liar

When he told you were troubled
You'll forever be alone
When he told you you should run away
You'll never find a home
When he told you you were dirty
And you should be ashamed.
When he told you you could be the one
That grace could never change. Fear is a liar!

Is fear convincing you of things that are not true? Replace fear with boldness. Replace that fear with bravery. Tell yourself the beautiful truth about yourself. You are a success just because you are…you. You can make your own life summits past failures and setbacks. Don't let fear keep you from living the best you.

It is a journey, albeit a courageous one, pitted with unknowns, storms, and obstacles. Hunker down into it anyway. Face your fears. And call out the ones that are lies.

Splash. I put my face under water. Tap. I reached the top of the climb.

11

The Trigger

I accepted to attend a solid, but small, private Christian college so I could live on campus and run track as their token female runner. I had some scholarships and had a student loan to cover tuition and most of the housing. But my meal plan only went from Monday morning to Friday afternoon. I lived on peanut butter and jelly sandwiches, the avocados my sister could still get from the ranches, and popcorn on most weekends. I was perfectly content to do so.

I decided it would be a good idea to utilize the campus counseling services to work through carrying any childhood baggage into my future, my future marriage, and my future family. It took a few mismatches to weed through funky, awkward therapists, but I finally found a solid woman in the counseling profession who didn't pull punches with me and that I couldn't outsmart. We worked on the issues. It took work. But with it, came a calmness and confidence that would prep me for my own better home.

I also very decisively tackled those two phobias that had accumulated in my childhood. I can attest, as my own example, that you can work through issues, situations, and circumstances. Even the toughest of ones. It's not easy, but you can "work through it" if you are patient and purposeful. It requires action, like reorganizing and cleaning a closet, but is two hundred percent harder. Yet, what a reward there is if you can learn to not repeat some of the same mishaps or mistakes done to you.

It took understanding and good self-talk, self-care, and self-love. And, as I would have to learn, a revisiting of a lot of issues. Remember I had ignored such a large lump of my own debris. I kept it swept under my skin. And it would welt up in times, though I thought I had fully dealt with it. Just a disclaimer. Make learning and tackling issues, ongoing. There is a lot to learn and grapple with. Be willing.

I loved being in college, though I was a starving college student. I loved young adulthood. The people I was meeting, the classes I was getting to take, living in a dorm, and running on the track team. I was the only one who showed up with a bedroll and backpack to college, though. I had no sheets, nor a bedspread, or matching pillows. My roommates thought that to be odd. I also had no provisions. Shampoo, make up, song recordings, or cool outfits. I had a backpack, a tent, and cross-country skis, a bike, and all my running shoes. But I did have a soft heart which my mom gave me, and a tenacious determination my dad said made me the kid most like him. And, luckily, I had an appetite for formal education.

But the girls in my housing situations had to teach me some simple things I ought to have known. Like, it is okay to enjoy a hot shower, and that I had poor choices of hair shampoo.

"What? No makeup. Unheard of. We will have to fix that," they would chide.

"And where are your dresses? You only brought one?". How did I tell them I only had one, and one pair of dress shoes?

My first semester in college I got a call from my dad. He didn't come out and say what he needed me to do, but I knew he wanted me home to fix my mom. "I thought you would at least be thoughtful enough to come home on a weekend a month and help by doing the yardwork. It is the least you could do." I could hear, "Please no. No, please. Stop it," in the background.

"Dad, what did you do to mom?" Fury erupted in me.

I didn't have a car. Well, I had one. But we named it Curby because it spent more time by the curb than running. It was an army camouflaged Baja bug that was given to me for $1 so they could write it off as a sold vehicle. It should have been written off as mechanically unsound. It had been used to jump sand dunes in the desert and even the main frame was cracked.

But my roommates loved Curby because we could fit it on the sidewalks. We would dart it across campus to class and park before someone official noticed we were driving on the campus sidewalks. And it, at least, falsely made me feel like I had transportation. I didn't know if Curby would make it home. It had been blowing blue smoke.

Fortunately, it did make it. When I arrived, I parked Curby a block below our house. My dad said he refused for it to ever be parked in front of the house. He never offered to help me buy any decent transportation, but he grizzled that my crappy car would ruin the ambience of his landscape. The command. It should never be parked on our street. Even more tacky than the car, he said, was the fact that I was in overalls. It was kind of a thing in the 1980s.

But I had dropped everything of my weekend life at college and headed to fix my mom… still in my overalls. He was going to have to deal with at least that.

When I entered, the house was quiet. My dad was sipping a glass of wine.

"Where's mom?"

He pointed upstairs.

As I headed up the stairwell, I heard him explain. "I think I told her something like I was leaving her."

She was in a corner of the huge master bedroom, rocking with her arms wrapped around her knees.

"Mom," I said gently. She sprung for me and grabbed onto me like I had never had to endure before. Tight. So tight her nails were digging into the flesh of the back of my arms.

"Mom," I tried to pull away and she clung on sobbing. Too tight. I wanted to panic.

You know, that feeling from being claustrophobic and not wanting to be pinned down? It had most likely come from my dad, but it was made worse the time that my mom had an emotional meltdown on me. She wrapped me in the sheets I had wet the bed with and pushed me around, punching me and living out something I think happened often to her in her childhood. Her reaction had cemented to me that neither parent, nor my home was a safe place. And claustrophobia became the demon.

At this present moment, I had to talk myself out of that childhood memory and squelch my reaction that said to panic. We couldn't have two of us panicking here.

"Mom." She started to cry out all the years of pain. This was her high school sweetheart. This was the father of her three children. This was all she was left with. I was gone.

"Oh, mom. I'm so sorry."

I finally thought of a possible plan. Her grip was starting to leave marks on my triceps.

"Why don't I call Grandma, and maybe you could live with grandma and grandpa for a while?" This suggestion bubbled up too much past, causing her to get hysterical. Grandma was the bedrock source of her void of love and her empty cistern. I had just poured pain upon pain and the idea of it was beyond what my mom wanted to live through.

She let go of me and flung open my dad's closet. The master bedroom had two closets. We were forbidden to ever open my dad's side. So, of course, as kids, we dared each other to sneak in when my dad was surely gone. We found stacks of Playboy Magazines that my dad said had good articles in them. My dad was well accomplished and well educated, and he kept up on all current affairs. Smart of the magazine to include current articles. But even as a kid, I felt like the magazines could hurt my mom.

I thought that was what she was doing in his closet. She had slid the door shut on herself. All the fumbling noise was from her pulling his clothes down and the magazines in response to trying to keep him from leaving. I thought it best to leave her in there and let her try to deal with her own pain. I could hear her pulling things off the shelf and mumbling, "No more. No more. I can't take this."

That is when I remembered my dad's closet was off limits, not because of the magazines, but because that is where he kept his gun.

"Sh....zzzzz", squelched out of my esophagus.

I flung the closet door open as my mom had the gun to her head. I entered a tug-of-war with her. I think her true concern for me made her finally let go. The gun flinging out of her hand could easily have fired a shot into either of us. She had managed to get bullets in it, and the safety switch was off.

It was horrible.

I pulled her out and onto the floor, and I let her grab hold of me and hang on for dear life. I wanted her to. I wanted her to live and to have something to live for. I no longer cared that her nails were digging in.

"Cling on, mom. Cling on."

I sat with her all night and only returned to college on Monday morning when my father had to leave for work. Again, this incident was never talked about by any of us. They went into a period of working things out together and "getting along." I went back to college. But I knew it was a matter of strategic timing. I believe my dad had decided upon another woman.

My armor clamped on as I left. *Oh, mom, how hurt you must be.* My mom loved animals, plants, people, and everything. And strangely, she still loved him.

12

Summer Camp Came to the Rescue

One morning towards the end of my freshman year, I walked my patterned route past the recreation program's Quonset hut. I liked what that tin-domed storage garage represented. I liked the Rock Climbing 101, Outdoor Survival 202, and Wilderness Camping 303 classes I was taking, and every time I walked by, action was taking place there. Rafts were being washed, climbing ropes coiled, and there was a fun buzz from people coming back from a trip or getting ready to go out on an outing.

It was the same camaraderie I experienced before and after practice and at the meets in track and field. On this day, I had my head down deep in thought, and I stepped on a piece of paper. I could tell it had been there a while because there was a muddy imprint of a boot on it. The corner had a Yosemite Sierra Summer Camp logo and a picture of a smiling kid. That caught my interest enough to reach down and pick it up. I wiped it off, but the waffle image from the bottom of someone's shoe was like permanent ink left on it.

I could see that it was an application for a camp counselor position. I took it to the library, uncrumpled it as much as possible. And, though stained, I filled it out anyway. It had a PO Box in Bass Lake, California. I gathered it must be somewhere near Yosemite since Yosemite was part of the name of the camp. That sounded exciting enough. I went to the campus postal center, bought a stamp, and mailed it with huge hopes.

A week later I got a call. A soft, gravelly voice introduced himself as Jim Slevcove. He conveyed right away that all the positions for the summer had been filled. The interviews had been done a few months earlier, but he was calling because he was curious as to why there was a boot imprint on the application. He found it creative that I would do that so that my application would stand out. Finding that application created hope for an opportunity. Maybe, much like a foreigner hoping to win a lotto entrance or a work visa to the United States. I sent that paper in hoping some form of an angel would appear and lead me far away from having to go back home.

I shared the truth. I told him where I was attending school and that I had found it on the ground by the Camp & Recreation Hut. Biola University happened to be his alma mater also. I shared with him about the fun Quonset hut, the camp courses, and that my name was Caren with a C with the word Care in it. We laughed about the boot imprint, but when I hung up, my soul sank. I had applied to all the camp programs and had the same answer from all of them—they had all interviewed and filled the positions months earlier.

Summer Camp Came to the Rescue

My two paper sacks of belongings, my sleeping bag and backpack, and the newly acquired climbing rope with a rack of protective chocks and carabiners were neatly arranged near the dorm room door. They sat already prepared for dread. We were in finals week at college, and I had nowhere to go but home. There was no "giddy" in this for me.

Suddenly, the loudspeaker in the dorm crackled on and I jumped from my thoughts. It announced a call for Caren Ware. As I tripped over my pinecone box and stumbled out the door to the phone hanging on the wall down the hall, I wondered who it could be.

When I answered, I heard that same quiet voice asking, "Would you still be available for the summer? We had a counselor cancel. There is a pile of college students to pick from, but everyone agreed they wanted the girl that would send in an application with a boot print on it. Caren with a C, would you like to come work for Yosemite Sierra Summer camp? We only hire the world's best counselors."

"Would I?!! "YES!" I tried to make my answer not sound like a squeal.

He told me he had a series of questions he needed to know. It intrigued me when he went on to ask, "What number child are you?"

Confused, I answered, "The middle of three."

"Hmm. I have a daughter your age who will be working at camp with you. She is also the middle of three. You two will get along smartly."

He asked a host of other questions, and I could see he was searching for personality type. This wise man realized that there are all types of people, and he would need a balance of counselors to match his all types of campers. He believed it divinely special to have such a balance of different personalities. Jim Slevcove got to know me and was placing my personality in a position to flourish. He gave me something I did not think was imaginable—the gift of functioning and being who I naturally was born to be.

When we hung up, I screamed down the dorm hallway, "I am going to camp" and kissed the phone. I was elated. Summer Camp, here I come!

But wait. When? He never told me when. I called the camp the next morning and asked when they opened. I wrote the date down.

On the last day of my freshman year of college, I stuffed my backpack full of the contents in the bags and had the gentleman I was dating, who would become my future husband, drive me a full day's drive to Bass Lake. Because I wanted to use this as an adult coming-of-age-summer on my own, I let him drop me off at the gate of the camp. After giving him the commitment to see him in the fall, I slung the backpack over my shoulder and headed to what would be some of the greatest times spent in those precious college years. This was to become one of my world's greatest places being a world's greatest counselor.

Yosemite Sierra Summer Camp was nestled on forest service land in an alcove called Emerald Bay. It was in the foothills of the Sierra Nevada Mountains at Bass Lake, California. One winding half hour's drive was the south entrance gate of Yosemite National Park, and another winding hour's drive down the road, you arrived at the valley floor of Yosemite. A grove of impressive Sequoia trees was on the right at this entrance so you could get the best of both: giant redwoods and the granite walls in one impressive day's visit.

But there was a bit of a glitch. When I got up to the camp buildings, no one was there.

"Hello," I timidly yelled out. "Hello?" A little louder. I walked around voicing out hellos. No one was anywhere on the entire premise. I sat down on the porch as the hues of sunset were turning and then a maintenance pickup truck bounced in. The driver got out and wanted to know if he could help me. I explained I was here to be a camp counselor for the summer.

He snickered, "Oh my gosh. They are not arriving until next week. The date they gave you was when I come to open the camp and get the buildings ready."

Despite the mistake, I had no choice but to stay. I camped out there, on the porch of the Mess Hall, for the next week. I helped the guy get the pool, cabins, and buildings ready. He was delighted I rock climbed and could set up all the climbing gear. He taught me how to drive the ski boats. It was a chilling experience as we had to swim out each morning and get the boats that were moored to buoys in a bay. There was no dock. This frigid, daily experience helped prepare me to handle the swim portions of triathlons years later, and it made me competent with all the equipment. I was the camp expert by the time everyone else arrived.

It set a foundation that boosted my confidence, and again, affirmed to me that learning skills adds to the opportunity to experience more things in a better way. Don't be afraid to try. Always be willing to learn. Master skills you think you could never do. And watch life open up for you. I did.

I began to passion for firsts. I love to hear someone say this is their first time, or better yet, to offer them an experience for the first time. My life was so filled with firsts, and notably, this was my first experience in an environment centered on building each other up, rather than getting torn down. Camp became a good form of a family for me.

The camp held some magical years. I had the life privilege of being a camp counselor and a camp activities director all four summers I was in college. Living and working with the camp director and his wife and their three children, all around my age, had been a four-year, gifted opportunity. I bet they never knew how much healing was happening in me. But maybe they did. They were in the business of changing lives.

The Slevcove family modeled for me what a wholesome, freely forgiving, easy flowing, people-oriented family could be. Not perfect, but perfectly real. The heart purpose of the camp was to grant great experiences and build up self-esteem in youth while mentoring the college counselors in the same process. What a formula this world needs. We, as people, need. Wholesome time devoted to being and feeling happy, healthy, and accepted.

Jim wanted every single person who came near the camp to feel uniquely special. He felt all people needed was to know and believe they were born to enjoy a rich journey. That was the world's greatest news to me. It wasn't the location of the camp that made it so special, it was the heart and foundation of the Slevcoves. The fact that it was tucked away in a pine forest on a lake did help, though. And backpacking the upper Sierras, tackling the challenges of ascending Half Dome, or just staring up to the towering tops of Sequoia Redwoods swirled with grand emotion that life doesn't get much better than this.

Jim Slevcove said extraordinarily little. He was a very quiet, but strong man. He created influence through experience. He was a strategic businessman, very set in his ways of negotiating good deals. He loved to repurpose things and found ridiculous use for so many items for the camp. He did the same with people. He picked the slightly used people because he knew the dents and peeling paint on them added character and charm, and authenticity. He knew that we could become a fine piece of furniture. All we needed was a fresh coat of varnish called specialness.

Jim Slevcove and his family. His kids were the exact same ages as my siblings and me.

He loved the diversity of personalities. He planned his business around how we operate out of these four personality grids: Type A driver, analytical, expressive, and amiable. He knew, most are in the corners of more than one type and people are not to be boxed up or labeled but will flourish if given an opportunity to be their best selves in their natural ways. He knew how to FIND how people FIT into a community.

This was so polar to how my dad had used his kids as his stage props. This was an important change for me. To be asked to operate as myself. It helped me FIND me. Just getting to be myself for the first time in a long-term way allowed a lot of potentials to strengthen within me. It changed me.

Camp put play in my life which I had a hard time doing as a child.

Jim Slevcove was one of ten children born to Russian immigrants. His parents spoke no English and were trying to scrap out a meager living in Boyle Heights, the poorest section of Los Angeles. Jim spent his entire childhood on the tough streets of LA. He pointed out that the Russian kids had to be the toughest, but that he also learned good work ethics. He was on his way to being one of the worst hoodlums with a drop out reputation, though. His story was of getting saved by the least likely people—two old ladies.

Two missionary women decided to retire in that hardcore neighborhood and start a kid's club for the street kids. They had been serving in Mexico and spoke fluent Spanish. They were so surprised to find these tough Russian speaking kids. The ladies were unrelenting with true love. For him, it took root. He said no matter how bad he was or how poorly he treated them, they respected him with kindness. They also gathered their meager money together and sent him to a summer camp.

He had no idea that fresh air and fun existed. All he had ever known were the concrete streets of Los Angeles. Being in the mountains among pine trees was so life refreshing and eye opening, he wanted this experience to save lots of lives, not just his. Now guided with a goal to own a camp, he turned his street toughness into industriousness. Hard work got him to get a college degree, to own businesses, and to earn enough to lease the property and build buildings for this summer camp in Bass Lake, CA. Those women helped Jim FIND FIT in the outdoors, and he used that experience to help so many others, including me.

I sometimes think about what my life would have been had I not ended up at Yosemite Sierra Summer Camp. What if I had not had a place where the goal and purpose was to enhance great experiences? A place that treasured exactly and naturally who I was? Where I was told, over, and over again, that we were the world's greatest staff, and our kids were the world's greatest campers. Thank you, Jim Slevcove, for knowing there was a world who needed your camp experience.

Well into my late fifties, and just a week before the Covid-19 stay-at-home order hit in California, there was a memorial service for the passing of Jim Slevcove. The sanctuary was filled, and there was standing room only in the back when I arrived. All these people were the lives this man had planted seeds in and watered. We all knew it. We all were here, smiling together, because by Jim Slevcove believing in us, we were able to believe in ourselves. He lived his conviction that a Creator made us each so divinely different and perfect just the way each of us was. By making magical moments in a camp environment which had changed his own life, others would flourish and grow into their own beautiful gardens.

I believe that Jim Slevcove would have smiled at his own services with a chuckle at all the potentials sitting and standing in that auditorium. Everyone was greeting each other with so many good memories and stories. There was no grieving at this funeral. There was a respectful awe. This man's life mission was accomplished.

This is the kind of funeral I hope to have. This is the kind of life I hope I live. Mission accomplished. Passion fulfilled. Well done, good and faithful servant. Jim Slevcove. You didn't die. You passed on.

13

Foundations Crack and Boats Sink

It was going to be my mom's birthday, so after school I gave her a call. I tried to talk to her about organizing a half marathon in which Mary Decker was inquiring about participating, and in which I already had two of the fastest Kenyans signed up. I trailed off. I could tell she was not able to listen.

"Your dad has been really working on our marriage." I didn't trust that.

"He is going to meet me at the Ritz Carlton in Dana Point on Tuesday at four p.m. for my birthday. Isn't that sweet?"

Now, I really did not trust that.

"Why four p.m.? And on a Tuesday, mom?"

"Because he is gone at a convention and will meet me there when his flight lands."

"Oh. That sounds nice mom," I lied.

"Hey, we are going to go to the beach on Monday. It is Memorial Day. It may be crowded. But you are welcome to join us."

"I would like that," she said.

I really did not mean to invite her, but how could I let her be left alone all weekend on a holiday? My husband gave me a strained look, but also could not say no. He knew my mom needed to be around someone.

She met us at the beach with way too many items—a chair, an umbrella, a towel to look like she was there to enjoy the beach, yet she was so tattered. She acted happy and precious, looking at tide pools and focusing her professional camera lens on shots of waves crashing, the sunlight, crabs, and sea urchins. But she couldn't hide the hurt. She was overweight. Poorly out of shape. Her hair was cheaply colored. And she had a puffy look to her skin. She was beaten, the kind of beaten people ignore and avoid, insuring they do not have to get involved.

It is not easy to cross over and reach out and care for the tattered. It takes something most of us are not willing to risk. I drove home from the beach in silence. I felt if I said even a word, all these years of what my mom had endured would flood into unexplainable grief and tears. We had walked my mom to her car from our time on the beach. She was out of breath and seemed so weak.

In a poor attempt to sound normal, she departed with, "It was a nice day. And, tomorrow, your dad and I are going to have dinner at the Ritz Carlton," she again reminded me.

In the morning I told my husband I was going to call in sick from my teaching job.

"Whatever for?" he asked. "It is just a regular classroom day. You're not sick."

"I think I should drive all the way to my parents' house around noon and just sit there." I told him my dad was going to leave my mom. We both agreed on that, but I added, he is going to do it today.

"No, he is not, Caren. He is going to take your mom to dinner and, no…he wouldn't send her there and then go to the house and get his things and leave. Who would do that? Besides, what a waste of your sick leave day. We could use it to go a day early on this Mt. Whitney trip next weekend."

He talked me out of driving to my childhood home on the hill with the grass painted green and the manicured yard.

You know how you kick yourself for things you should have done? This is one of them. My gut was screaming at me. I just knew. And I knew it wouldn't be a simple leaving. It would be a maneuvered, calibrated act. He never did anything otherwise. Like a smooth predator lurking unbeknownst. He operated somehow as the slinking mountain lion type. Leaving would be a warped win he worked for. To take with him everything material but leave behind the broken spirit. Shattering another's soul was his masterpiece, like a painter paints a painting that seemed so perplexing to understand. It was a warped victory in this phase of his life plan. The man was on the top of his game.

My mom called me from a pay phone in the lavish lobby of the Ritz Carlton.

"Your dad never came. I guess he got stuck on the flight. I will go home. Oh, you should see how pretty I am. I bought a new dress. It has Hawaiian scenes on it and pretty flowers."

"I bet it is pretty, mom. I bet you are beautiful." I hung up the phone, yelling insults to myself for not cutting off the chess piece in its final move to checkmate. I grabbed the car keys.

"Where are you going?" I heard my husband ask as I headed out the front door.

"To beat her home!"

I didn't. When I pulled up to the front of the house, the lemon of a Cadillac was parked in the driveway. The front door was left open. I felt like I was stepping into a morgue, not sure what death would look like. I was sure I already knew what it felt like. I was still shocked. I heard myself gasp.

The entire house was empty. Completely empty. Empty of all furniture, and even the pictures on the walls. The drawers and cabinets were flung open and empty. Indents in the carpet and on the walls marked where the contents used to be. A hasty and premeditated robbery had taken place. I thought he would take his own things, but not everything. A few things were left. Oh, the used-up piano was still there. And odds and ends of no value. But the entire property, including contents in the garage, were gone. He felt he owned and deserved everything.

I could hear my mom upstairs in the master bedroom by the creaking of her rocking. More haunting to me was that she was not voicing any sound. There was no soft crying or saying, "Why did you leave? Oh, no. Don't leave me." There was just the rhythm of rolling back and forth. I bolted up the stairs. She was in the furthest corner of the empty room. His closet doors were open and everything, even the magazines, were gone.

My mom was faced in my direction. A hurt that I can't even put in words stared back at me. All I could see was a piercing that is so beyond what anyone on earth should ever have to shoulder. It was a hurt that I could not do anything to take it away. A hurt that is so wrong. A hurt so real. So raw. So deep. So final. And so full it encompasses everything. The only thing else left to grab for was a finger hold on a promise of eternity. And that very sincere cry out to the only One who can rescue you. "Oh, dear, God. Help us."

I let her hold me tight. For hours. I didn't care if she left nail marks. We just rocked and I stroked her hand and her curled hair and felt the hair spray. I just stared at the flower patterns in her dress and told her how lovely of a person she was. Over, and over again. Way into the darkness of the night, with the moon beaming in, we sat in that empty room in that huge empty house. We did not even have a lamp or lampstand left. The light went out in my mom. She begged me to tell no one. I think she hoped to win him back as all her good behavior antics had been for in the past. I knew this was final.

Ironically, I had a trip set to go up and summit Mt. Whitney. I enjoyed backpacking frequently in the Sierras and had a reputation of leading good trips. A solid childhood friend had come along with us, and I tossed and turned in the tent next to his on the ascent. I couldn't sleep. I could only beat myself up for not going to my parents' house when my instinct told me to. Somehow, I felt that calling my dad on his next move, catching him in the act, would have eased the shot-up lives he left behind. Gut instinct had told me to go and get to be that fencer's riposte, the lunge with a stabbing sword, like what gets to happen in movies. But it did not get to happen. Instead, I harbored my emotions, and as I promised my mom, I told no one.

My dad started the negotiations. If she agreed to settle out of court, he would give her the house and some of the family photo albums back. How do you give dignity back? He would not allow us children to be a part of the wagering. We were over eighteen. I am not sure how it all played out. My mom went to get gas and all the credit cards were cashed out and maxed out. She barely had a part-time job and was truly penniless.

She went in search of who would hire a person in their midlife without loads of experience. She had to put the house up for sale. She could not afford the remaining payments, and she certainly could not afford furnishings. She slept on the carpet with a blanket and pillow I brought her. She didn't want to rebuild. She did not have anything left to try with, but cry.

The house finally got picked up and was in escrow the following fall. That had to have been a heartbreaking summer for my mother. Do you remember an earthquake that happened in Southern California with the epicenter in Rosemead? The Whittier Earthquake occurred at 7:42 a.m. on October 1, 1987. It had a 5.9 magnitude and occurred on the Whittier Fault, which is part of a larger Puente Hills fault in Southern California. This was only a few miles from the house. It rolled and shook with a force out of our control. Just like the pain of the divorce.

The totality of Southern California felt it. My husband and I did, living more than an hour away. I sprang for the archway in the hall and held on. My husband marveled at my fight or flight tendencies, so super overcharged and over wired that I reacted to situations like a James Bond. He waited until all the rolling stopped to join me. We knew this was a big deal and immediately wondered where the epicenter was. It was at MY childhood home.

The foundation of the house, the one in escrow, cracked that day. The backyard sidewalks and the main foundation split as the ground shifted six inches. Eight people lost their lives in that Whittier Quake. Over one hundred million dollars in damage happened in 20 seconds. My mom was in an empty, three-story home riding out the shaking on a blanket with a pillow over her head. The close of escrow was delayed by months trying to get engineers to properly assess the damage. She couldn't make the monthly payments, and the house turned over to the bank, who continued the escrow and successfully closed it at a lesser value.

The proceeds that could have come from the sale vaporized and my mom began living in rented rooms and cheap apartments. She somehow, finally, purchased a home in Lake Arrowhead. She decorated it nicely and saw it as a place that would bring the family together for holidays. We did have lots of family get togethers in the fresh air and wooded location, but she could barely make the mortgage payments. Another problem was she worked in Los Angeles. The commute was unrealistic.

As a solution, she rented a boat in Marina Del Rey. It was a fishing boat that the owner thought he could pay for the monthly dock fees with a commercial catch of fish. When his inexperience was unable to even catch fish, he resorted to finding someone who would live in the cabin berth and pay rent so he could pay the dock fees. My mom said it was a new adventure. She was okay with it.

She liked the smell of the salt air and the swaying in the bay helped offer a rocking lullaby to her life. She was working as a media clerk for a company in Los Angeles. She would soon transfer and be the lead photographer and media person for the private Jonathon Club in downtown Los Angeles. This position required her ability to take high valued photos with top national and world leaders and celebrities.

One day I got a call from a nurse at St. John's Hospital in Santa Monica, California. "Your mom will be ready for pick up this afternoon. She is recovering nicely from her surgery and wants to leave today. She will not be allowed to drive. She says she has her car in the hospital parking lot. She gave us your number to call to have her picked up."

My mom had not told me that she was having surgery or that she was even in the hospital. The nurses explained she had been there for a week. I would have to make the long drive to Los Angeles in rush hour traffic to pick her up in time. Doing this on this unexpected day was enough of a reason to understand why my mom could not live in the mountains and work way in the city. The traffic was debilitatingly thick and slow. I thought as we drove, "no wonder she rents the boat." My husband so graciously drove me and dropped me off.

It had been raining all that week and I picked through the puddles to get to the front entrance of the hospital. When they looked for my mom's name on their admittance lists, they said she was not on any of them.

That was strange. I insisted the hospital had called.

Another nurse looked through the records. "Oh, here. Her name is not here. She is across the way at the John Wayne Cancer Institute."

As I jumped more pools of water gathered in the cracks of the sidewalk, I wondered why they would have done her hysterectomy at the Cancer Institute. They must be overfilled, I easily concluded. I, again checked into this new lobby with the clerks that had the lists of admittances. I made sure I commented to the nurses looking up what room I was heading to. "So, why are you doing hysterectomies over here?"

Both nurses looked at each other and back at me. "Your mom is here because she has cancer. We removed areas of organs it could spread to in hopes to stop it. She will begin radiation treatments next week. This is a week for her to rest."

I went into a blurred swirl, like the reflective lines in the splashed puddles outside. How long? What kind? What had she been shouldering alone? My mind went numb. The poor nurses explained as much as they could. There really wasn't much they could say except, "Your mom has cancer." I wheeled my very pale mother to her car with pots of flowers sent by her office that were now trying to topple over in her lap.

"Mom?" I asked. She just raised her shoulders in a shrug.

I had not been to her fishing boat yet. That is where she wanted me to drive her since she still called it an adventure of fresh salt air. I wondered how she would be able to step up a ladder to board. She was trying to decide how she was going to manage that also, but we would not need to figure that out. When I wheeled her to the slip, the boat was gone. She looked at me.

"Mom, are you sure that this is the slip number and the slip?"

"Absolutely. This is it." She was standing up out of the wheelchair peering into the dark water of the murky bay. I noticed four heavy marine ropes leading from each mooring. She sat down on the edge of the planks of the slip and gingerly slipped her legs to dangle over the water. She patted a spot for me to sit and join her. I obligingly sat down.

We swung our legs back and forth for a few silent minutes, as kids do on a swing. She took a deep sip of the salty air and watched a pelican float by before she turned to me with the largest smile. She started to laugh—a true, this is such a funny, good-part-of-life laugh like you just heard the best joke.

"Mom. What is so funny?"

"That's my boat down there." She pointed. "It must have sunk while I was gone." She looked at me with a face of resolve. "I can't take any of it with me anyway," she continued. "My business clothes are down there. My microwave. Maybe my curling iron and all my belongings. Good thing I have my work camera in my car." She was so entertained. "They are all at the bottom of the sea. Imagine that." And my mom meant it. She knew there was no treasure in things. There was only treasure in people.

She reached over and squeezed my hand, and I felt the current of real love gently squeezing mine. She had been through so much. She was a warrior of real making, and here she was able to find humor in material losses because they held no value to her. What mattered were the lives she was able to connect with, the eyes and hearts of people.

I started to laugh with her. I felt all she had done for me. Our feet were still dangling, and we could lean over and see our glimmering faces in the waters of that bay. A mom and her daughter were giggling. I etched those smiles in the recesses of my memories, and once again, watched my mom let laughter be the life lightener.

To this day, I cannot think about that moment on the dock in Marina Del Rey without a glimpse of what is truly rich and valuable. I am so grateful I got to have my life garden watered by my mom. Though the years after my dad divorced her were not wealthy, they were rich in something money could not buy. You know the saying, "stop and smell the roses"? My mom did. And people were the best roses to her. If they hadn't budded yet, even more reason to stop and notice, befriend them, and watch them grow.

One out of one of us die. Eventually, we all will. We sincerely cannot take any of this earth's material things with us. So… are the valuable nuggets of life something intrinsic? Something felt or shared? Not something owned. Not a thing. But an experience? I was learning that to be so.

That day on the dock was the start of a struggle for my mom's life. It was a war that stage four cancer said she would not win. But she had already won the bigger battle. She knew what was meaningful to her life. And what more could you ask for?

14

Let's Go to Alaska

Being decisive was a rare trait in me, so why was I not hesitant on this decision? I had made up my mind, instantly. No wavering. My second year as a fifth and sixth grade elementary school teacher was in its final weeks. One night over the evening meal, I placed my renewal teaching contract on the kitchen table. I had a plan brewing. I pushed the paperwork toward my husband and told him I was not renewing the teaching contract.

I had his attention.

"I want to explore your Alaska instead."

He kept munching. He didn't seem to think I was serious. But there had been an announcement that a giant store called Costco was opening in our town. I slid a flyer that had just come in the mailbox toward him. He hardly glanced at it, knowing that I was on a pipe dream. I was telling him we should buy supplies and pack up and go. He did not see how we could.

So, I went to the grand opening of Costco the next morning and came home with a summer's worth of provisions—an odd assortment of canned goods and such. I saw a boyish grin creep into his face when he realized I was serious about going. It never left. He was all in, and the project to explore Alaska filled our home with a unified buzz.

After getting my bachelor's degree, I considered whether to go after a teaching credential or get a master's degree in public service and pursue my passion—a career in recreation. I ended up taking the teaching job to avoid judgment and appease my dad. Making that choice meant I shied away from my own passion and that huge-hearted hope of doing what I loved… and running a camp slipped away. Instead, I did what others thought I should do, and it gnawed at me, like not following your passions should.

I quickly found I was not wired for the inside walls of a classroom. I knew that kids loved to play. If I felt cooped up, what did they feel like? I believed giving them active opportunities was a good teaching style. I took them outside… a lot. To learn math. To soak in English concepts. I had the kids role play history rather than merely listen to it. Outside. I thought experiencing science hands-on was more impressionable, so we went on as many field trips as I could finagle.

But coming up with 12 subjects a day for a combo class was a juggling act that drained me. Since I was trying too hard, I felt doomed to be doing this year after year. I did not like regulated classroom teaching. At least I had some affirmation later down the road that my teaching style was not a total wash. I still run into young adults over the years who had been my students. Many of them shared. "Mrs. Ware, you made class fun. I remember so many things from that year. You kept us moving and interested. More like a coach, rather than a teacher."

The principal had an opposing opinion about my technique. I was unconventional, and at a private school, I rattled their cage. I was in the principal's office more than the kids. She wanted to know why, when she passed through the hall, my kids were not sitting in their seats. I had no answer other than I preferred letting them move around. How could I tell her I preferred being outside?

I knew how to resolve my yearning for a world with no walls. My husband had been hugely influenced by a summer his grandfather inflicted upon him at sixteen. His "Daddy Bill" packed up a bag of beans, a sack of flour, fishing poles, a shot gun, and a pistol, and promised his grandson he was going to teach him how to be a real man. They headed to Alaska. It worked. My husband was a quiet Jedediah Smith, a seasoned frontiersman, and an avid outdoorsman.

I was so surprised to discover a wilderness man in someone having been raised in Southern California. Of course, I was smitten. He could live off the land. He could hunt, fish, start a fire with a flint. He was that kind of man. I fell in love with his easy-going manner in the mountains. I wanted to embrace that, not tuck it away in a tract home. Bonding over our mutual love for the outdoors was a reason we had married each other. Teaching elementary school subjects seemed less of a life than discovering Alaska and building who we were as a couple.

To prepare for the trip, my husband built a huge mess frame out of steel and welded it to the front of our mini diesel pickup truck. We looked like one of those police vehicles that were being used to bust down drug houses. This sparked inquiries as we raced around a metropolitan suburb getting more supplies and fortifying the truck with extra gas cans and off-road tires. The armored front was to shield it from rocks on the lengthy dirt road called the Alaskan Highway we would be driving on.

We bought a camper shell, and every evening the sound of plywood being cut drifted from the garage. Soon we had an elevated shelf in the camper shell. We put a cushion on it and made it our bed. My Costco provisions slid nicely underneath the platform. In went fishing poles, a shotgun, the pistol, our backpacks, and our ambition. We were packed.

Waving good-bye to the young family who rented our home for the summer, we drove toward the Yukon Territories. A stashed copy of "The Alaska Highway Milepost" rested in between the seats. It described each bend of the 1392-mile-long route from Canada through the Yukon Territories and into Alaska. It already had worn marks as I had thumbed through it daily, yearning for the pioneering and sparse territory it described. I pre-read about the towns, the nooks, the odd and industrious settlements, and indigenous peoples we were set out to meet.

DAT. DAT. DAT. DAT. The washboard dirt portions of the road were enduring. And worse, the undulating pavement from frost heaves had no set rhythm to them. We bounced in our seats erratically. To keep circulation and to flee the jackhammering, I ran right next to the truck as often as I could. I would jog along in the slow sections of the weather-torn route they called the Alaska Highway, as my husband navigated potholes. I was just relieved to be outside. It was a long, slow journey to even get through Canada to the border of Alaska.

I have heard it is a much better road now, but in 1986, it was the adventure we boldly set out to find. We were still newlyweds and each bend, each vast view, each settlement we tempered to meet made life feel so worth living. So worth exploring. The purple of fireweed. The horizon of the mountains. The dwarfed pine trees that endure seventy percent of their existence in severe winter conditions. We were meeting people willing to pioneer in a land that stunted the growth of trees. They were proving to be as gnarled, survivors with hearty roots, like the trees.

My husband had story after story about his time in Alaska with his grandfather. As we passed the faded signs for sparse towns along the way, my husband pointed out how his grandfather had excitedly explained to him that they would soon be approaching this wild town or that. His grandfather described what he still thought would be bustling gold rush towns with a lively salon, prospectors picking up supplies, and jobs to be had.

In 1964, the year he chose to return with my husband, the largest earthquake recorded in US history occurred. It had a magnitude of 9.2 on the Richter scale in the gulf region of Alaska. Many lives were lost from the quake, but many more from the tidal waves it caused. The tectonic uplifts and subsidence were substantial. The fishing towns of Valdez and Cordova shifted by 5 to 7 feet. One rose, the other fell, causing the ocean and tides to be instantly changed.

My husband and his grandfather stood in shock, gaping at Valdez in the summer of 1964. They were witnessing what shock waves could do. Stores still had all their goods scattered off the shelves. And the mostly wooden buildings were toppled in all directions. My husband said the earth looked like chunks of ice on a moving glacier. And roads were still ripped apart. While some things change over time, some things can change in a moment.

My husband explained that even as shallow as sixteen years old seem to be, he knew the weight of disappointment his grandfather had when they drove into a town in Alaska that once was the heart of his grandfather's youth. His grandfather, a once-upon-a-time teen, ran away from his living situation at the age of 14 and stowed away on a ship bound for Alaska. When found, he rowed ashore to the Aleutian Islands and lived like a native Indian until the age of seventeen. He enlisted in the army and lived through a war and the Great Depression, surviving on skills he learned in Alaska. But now, instead of vitality, he and my husband found a deserted, dilapidated ghost town.

―⁂―

Our hearts are asked to summon courage to go through times that are catastrophic, as well as plain old, time-ticking change. Just being around my husband's family of pioneers and their lived-out history taught me a lot about that. His grandfather, a once-upon-a-time teen, turned Indian, turned prospector had lived through a lot of upheaval, inside and out. He lived through a war and the Great Depression, surviving on skills he learned in Alaska. And he had lived long enough to live through a lot of change. He never seemed to get past being left on a doorstep as an abandoned baby. And there was a sadness that followed him and caused him to drink a lot around Christmas.

My husband was now getting to share his Alaska with me, some sixteen years later. It was also much different for him than when he experienced it as a teenager. We got to see Valdez restored and bustling in 1986, no longer knocked down by a quake. We sat at a Halibut Fish and Chips shop, and I watched his eyes drift to memories. Experiences he got to have as a boy with his grandfather…outside. I knew he was thinking about the impact it had because there was a softness in his face as he was far off in thought. He held a calmness, and a competency in being self-sufficient in the outdoors. It was a large part of who he was. It had been gifted to him by his grandfather, a lot of it here in Alaska.

I knew we were not going to stay sitting on a bench in a town for long. This was still the Last Frontier. We both stood up without a word, walked to the road's edge, stuck out our thumbs, and started…hitchhiking.

15

It Stung

The road is now paved leading to the Wrangle Mountains.

My husband wanted to attempt something that added the word "bold" to Alaska. He wanted to hike the abandoned Copper River Railroad to Cordova, rather than take the ferry. This turned our trip into an expedition. To do so, we had to ditch our truck in Valdez and hitchhike with backpacks to a cutoff that led down to the Wrangell Mountains. Getting a ride up the highway was no problem.

When we were deposited, the driver asked with concern, "Are you sure you want to be left here?"

We both looked at each other and the long dirt road that dropped across this immense valley, disappearing into the base of the Wrangell mountains. Then we nodded in unison that this was our intention.

We sat on our packs for a few hours and not one car drove by. So, we started walking down toward the valley. Late in the afternoon a rusting pickup truck sped by, blowing dirt in our already sweat-smeared faces. After half a day's walk, we were nearing the bottom of the perpetual descent, and this was the very first vehicle that had come by all day. After passing us, it slammed on its brakes and skidded to an even dustier stop. The clunk of a tired transmission groaned, and the vehicle backed toward us at a high speed. It skidded to another stop, showering us with dust that left us coughing while the driver let it settle.

He had his window down with an elbow resting on it. The arm unmistakably belonged to a Native Indian. A man with handsome features and hair whipping in the wind leaned his head out and wanted to know what in hell's tarnation were two packers doing trying to walk across this valley so late in the day. He added. "You know, it is near sunset, and wherever you think you are going to get to, it will be in the dark." He shook his head.

We told him we were headed to where the Copper River Railroad crosses the road and that we were going to walk the old railroad to Cordova. He laughed out loud.

"Now? This time of year?" More laughing.

"You know, we have a word for you… types. We call you Cheechakos. It's a word for people from the lower forty-eight who do dumb, random things while in Alaska."

We could feel his awareness of our ignorance of his land, but I sensed he respected our quest. In a kind way he conveyed he hoped we would survive. He seemed bemused and grateful for the interest we were adding to his day by being gutsy enough to be passing through this open stretch of under molested wilderness. This was the land he was born and raised on.

"Don't you know the Wrangell mountains are another full day's journey on foot?" he asked, but in a gentle reprimand, as a father would help a child grapple with an error out of lack of experience. Without giving us a choice if we wanted a ride, he ordered us to hop in the back of the truck. We did, throwing our packs in first and climbing on top of them. The look both my husband and I flashed at each other was the one you give each other when you have no idea if this is going to turn out good or bad.

A sense of doom jolted in when, after miles of sitting facing backward atop our packs and watching the valley fade away, the truck turned down a rutted side road and started darting through a thick wooded area. It pulled to a stop abreast of a shanty wood structure with a lot of derelict remains of autos and equipment. The car door opened, and the man stepping out turned into a tall, potentially menacing size. But his voice was soft. "I want you to meet the family."

Two huge beasts snarled toward the vehicle. The man reached out and petted one as its thick gray fur relaxed on the back of its neck. But the yellow eyes of both wild wolves turned to us still seated in the back of the truck and showed us their sharp canine teeth. Both beasts returned to having the hair standing straight up on their backs when they realized their owner had guests.

"These are…" he rattled off two Indian sounding names. "They are wolves. They tend to be very protective of me and the family. Don't wander away. I am not sure what they will do."

All four yellow eyes were piercing us. They were huge. I knew I did not want to find out what they were capable of doing, so I jumped out of the truck bed to trot after the man heading into the shanty. Inside it was dimly lit, but I made out the movement of a handsomely featured lady ruffling her dress and hair. She was in shock that her man had brought visitors.

Young kids were bouncing around asking a dive bomb of questions of who we were, where we were from. They disappeared and I could hear them clamoring into the back of the truck. I suspected they were curiously going through the things in our packs. They were not. They bounded back in, each laboring to carry one of the packs and asked politely if we could show them what we had. They loved the intricacies of the stove and flashlights, pushing buttons and wanting to know how everything worked. The wife thanked us for enduring a barrage of childhood wonder.

As fast as we arrived, the man announced we must go so he could deliver us to our trailhead before dark. The kids escorted us out, shooing the growling wolves away. The larger took a demonstrative snap at us to let us know he was very capable of biting. The man threw our pack in the back and motioned us to squeeze into the bench seat of the small cab. We had somehow graduated to being friends. The kids ran alongside the truck as we sped away. They finally stopped their rapid sprint as they could no longer keep up. We watched waving hands in the rearview mirror and were soon back on the dirt road now known as the Edgerton Highway.

We came into a small settlement called Chitna. I do not remember this gentleman's name who gave us this ride so far out of his way. He talked incessantly, as if he knew this would be the only fleeting opportunity for his life to matter to someone from another world. Alcoholism was the conversation's theme. He shared how much hurt it had done to him and his entire native clan. Even the girls and grandmas were suffering, he grieved. He said that government checks seemed to thwart a desire to make things better. He hoped he could be the one that helped stir change and desire. He said he had been sober for months.

"But," he trailed off. "I think my road will be longer and harder than the trail you are attempting to crawl along."

I wondered why he chose to use the word crawl as his truck rolled to a stop. He pointed to where the railroad had once actively crossed the road. He seemed to have driven slowly as to not want our time together to end. He left the truck parked right on the dirt road and turned to walk to the only building that had cars parked by it. A saloon. Over his shoulder he remarked. "I am going over there to tell them what you are going to try to do. And I am going to start wagering bets as to how many days before we see you come right back out this same start point."

We shouldered our packs and stepped into our trek. We hoped his commitment to stay sober was kept. But we hoped his wagering was wrong. We intended to spend weeks out there, not days. The path immediately became a route of bushwhacking. The railroad rails and ties that had hauled copper at the turn of the century had been pulled up, but their flat imprint was easy to follow. The only problem was that vegetation and tall thin trees had used the turned-up earth as a garden. A worn path was directly in the middle of the removed railing marks, but at the height of a bear. No wonder the Native American had said "crawl."

We bent down and proceeded in a hunched manner that never let up. As I followed my husband's butt, the bending branches whipped me in the face. I had to back away and both of us had to push through the overgrowth in our own misery. We stopped at the first stream and found a sandy spot to pitch a tent as the day grew dark. It was the darkest dark. No starlight or moon could reach into this forest covered canopy. We hunkered into the tent and listened, leery of the unknown sounds creaking in the night.

In the morning, I found my husband studying the shadowy images in the stream. "Spawning salmon," he announced. Though he was teasing them with every kind of fly, dabbling the lure on their lips, none were biting. This seemed like a time-consuming way to get a meal. I rummaged through the tiny tackle box and pulled out a huge hook I had seen that he said was for fishing halibut off ships. Why wait for them to bite? Why not drag the hook through the school and snag one?

It worked and I soon had a huge fish writhing in the sand. He looked over at me in disgust. There is a rule I had unknowingly broken. Fish are to be hooked in the mouth, not "caught." We ate my broken rule for breakfast and found it to be far more meat than any two could consume. My husband had a solid code of conduct and respect for what were gifts of provision. He cooked up the remainder and said we would have it for lunch. We were not ready to leave until he buried the remains of the bones and the skin in a deep hole and left no trace that we had camped there.

Packed up, we began crawling again. There were signs of bear everywhere. A bear, or bears? It was hard to tell. There was fresh scat, huge paw prints, and a rotten odor that drifted too near for comfort. My husband put additional slugs in the shotgun and carried it close. He had tried to teach me how to shoot it, but I missed even the sides of trees. So, the gun handling and protection was left up to him. That was a good thing.

We found travel painstakingly slow. And disturbing. The trestles that had been built to cross streams looked like fallen pick-up-sticks, and it took tight roping and being clipped into our climbing ropes to get across. We feared what we were going to find as the topo map showed the inlet rivers would get larger as we got deeper down the route.

I wanted to be near the gun. But, if I got too close to my husband's hind quarters, his parted foliage slapped me in the face in a battering way. I had to choose between being comforted by the protection of the shotgun or getting whipped by branches. I backed off but was feeling sure that he would flush the grizzly out, and I would be behind enough to get eaten.

Throughout that long day we could hear the roar of the Copper River. It is said to be five times the volume of the Colorado River which carved the Grand Canyon. In rare moments, we could see the river through the trees and the volume of the water was visibly banking as it cornered a bend. We had considered bringing a blow-up raft and taking the river down to Cordova. That was until we researched its capacity, not to mention its glacier fed frigidity. So, hiking through the wilderness was our choice.

We knew emerging gems would be in this overgrowth. The closure of the railroad was so sudden, people were only given a few days' notice to grab their things in the mining town of Kennicott and the train stations along the way. Though super lucrative, the copper mine had either dried up or copper wasn't getting a high market price, so the Copper River Railroad Company pulled up the railroad ties. The last train left, abandoning tools, file cabinets full of papers, furniture, and personal belongings. We were pulling the bushes away from a log cabin and a work building used for the railway. It still had supplies inside. The last date carved on a side log of the cabin was 1939. We hiked on.

The day lingered because we were looking at nothing but thick vegetation and progressing only feeble miles. We were rewarded by the cabin, but that was in the past now. And we had not discovered one plot of open real estate to pitch even the size of a tent on all afternoon. As we now knew how black dark would be, we agreed to retreat to the last railroad tunnel to camp for the night.

It was the only open space to erect our sleeping quarters large enough for two people to flatly lay down inside a tent side by side. We gathered the only wood available and lit the smelly railroad ties as the night sky became as inky as the inside of the tunnel. Though in the land of the midnight sun, these few evening hours of darkness made us feel very vulnerable. The fire we lit was more for fear.

The paw prints were everywhere. Large pads with curved nails that, without even seeing the animal, the respect for the owner of them was primal. The bears were using man's hard labor, the flattened earth of the railroad bed, as a convenient trail link to the creeks. It was their highway to feasting on the salmon arriving to spawn.

Salmon. They wowed me. These incredible aqua beings are anadromous, meaning they hatch in freshwater, migrate to the ocean, then return to fresh water to reproduce. I marveled, observing the strength ingrained in this species of a fish. Swimming so far inland, upstream to return to the creek of their birth. This is incredible to witness. They then die within a few weeks of spawning. A trait known as seme parity. I grappled to accept that this was not sad as the shore of the creeks started filling with the rotting skins of faithful fish. Eagles dived down and tore bites out of the dead remains, and the padded prints of bears told a story of repurposing.

The fire did a good job of illuminating the tent and its crackle felt secure enough to ward off an approaching bear. But from only one end of the tunnel. Again, things began to make noise in the few hours of night, and often, we heard and smelled scurry at the other end of the tunnel. Our tent blocked any trespassing, but we were the true intruders. It was another evening that my listening ear was stuck on over acute. Without saying a word to each other, we both knew that was a bear down there at the other end. Sunrise was a welcomed relief.

We had just crossed another trestle with our ropes and were back to our low army waddle walk. Both of us were doing solo tangos with the weeds and feeling somewhat miserable. But the dullness was interrupted very alarmingly. My husband suddenly let out a war hoot and took off running like a bolt of lightning. Disappearing as the limbs slammed in behind him, I heard him yell, "Get away from 'em."

My head went swinging in all directions in pure frantic. I was not sure on which side the beast would be. I could not see him in the tall grass. I heard my husband's voice again.

A repeated yell, even more frantic. "Get away from 'em."

I stood still. I was trying to think. If I ran, would the bear pounce after me?

I screamed back, "Shoot him. Shoot him."

I could see the outline of my husband crashing back toward me. And while I was riveted to get eye contact with him, it was too late. A black form came from the left side. My brain could not take it in fast enough to flip my misconception. It wasn't a form. It was a swarm, as seen in cartoons, a black pack of wildly angry hornets landed on my face and shoulders. Almost in synchronized harmony, all having the same instinctual intent. I was being stung over and over. As I tried to sweep them off, more dove in the space I left, super charged with more striking stingers.

I was finally running with the hornets all over my face and shoulder. I struggled to get the pack off and plunged into the creek we had just crossed. The shock of the ice melt waters felt as traumatic as the stings, but I kept dunking and dunking until every mad insect was drowned away. I sloshed my way to the dirt bank and flopped in a muddy flood of tears. My husband slid down the embankment toward me.

"I told you to get away from them." The anger in his voice was a way to try and cover up fear.

I looked at him with the sorrowful lip a toddler produces. In tears, I stammered, "I thought you said… him. I thought it was a bear." He was touching and looking over the rising welts with worry.

"We are heading back."

I was in mutual agreement yet said nothing. I fell in behind him, now not caring that the branches were whipping me. I needed him near to comfort both our fears. What if I go into anaphylactic shock? Bee stings can cause the blood pressure to drop suddenly, and the airways narrow, blocking breathing. He was almost running but would swing around all too often and take torpedo glances into my eyes and scan my face. We used the streams we crossed to sooth the welts, but they swelled anyway. I could tell by his reaction my face was taking on a monster appearance. The shotgun did little service to protect us in this situation. It dangled at his side.

We knew that retracing our steps back to the opening at the road in Chitna was days away. We were at the mercy of the outcome. It was another sleepless night in a railroad tunnel. I writhed and the next morning, a burning itching began.

My husband took the first morning's rays to look at me and laughed. "You look like a pin cushion." We believe what helped stave off a poisonous reaction was the plunge into icy waters. It must have helped slow down the spread of venom.

Our pace the next day had less of a panic in it but crawling through this brush for all these days had turned maddening. I spied a sandy bar on the banks of the Copper River. Looking at a topological map, we knew we were about a mile away from the original creek we camped on. We knew with relief that the trail from there became humanly tolerable, as the locals had worn a path to this first creek to catch the spawning salmon. We wanted to get there in the easiest way possible.

I headed down to the sand, announcing I had enough of the bushes. My husband was trying to tell the back of my head that leaving the railroad path was probably not a good idea. I jumped off the side of the forest and onto the sand bar.

It sank. And so did I.

The weight of my pack was pushing me deeper into a mire that had appeared solid. The volume of water in the Copper River had seeped over and was under this sand. I was in quicksand. I thought these bogs were only in movies. As I wiggled to try and free myself, I felt the pressure of suction pulling me deeper. A few movements of twisting had already trapped me waist deep with the bottom of my pack was getting engulfed. My husband had stepped off also. We were both stuck in the same goop.

His voice became very instructive. "Quit moving. Stay still."

I wanted to panic but I could see that flailing was getting me into a worse position. I stopped. I could feel my own weight still sinking me. He reached for the bank and was able to grab ahold of some roots. Pulling at them, he untangled a few twines and tossed some loose ends my way. We both started pulling and pulling and pulling. By barely noticeable inches, we labored to rise on our bellies so we could drag ourselves across the soupy surface toward the side wall of the forest. It took forever.

Once in reach of stronger limbs, we heaved our packs upward and our soiled selves into the thick vegetation. It hurt. Everything we had to grab onto seemed to have a thorn on it. Like rose bushes, twine and branches were fuzzed with thorns. They speared right through our skin and clothing. This lush greenery had the same effect of falling in a patch of cactus. But we could not go back. There was no physical way to return to that faint animal's path that had lured me to follow it to a false promise of open space.

We were now required to scramble upward and over a fallen forest that I am sure had never had a human being in it. For hours. All day. The sun was soon to set when we came to a rock face, sheerly unclimbable. We could visibly spot the canyon we intended to set up camp in, but the chore was getting there. It took more hours and headlamps in the dark. Ouch. Dag nab it. Poke. Trip. Fall with a fully loaded pack. Topple head over heels. By far, one of the more enduring things I have ever had to try and hike. My husband kept helping me right myself. Going only a mile's distance as the eagle could fly had taken us more than 10 hours. We were bleary-eyed.

Finding our original camp spot in the dark, we stuffed up the tent. It flopped lazily, not very taut. Uncaring, we both collapsed into a sleep that had nothing left to give worry that bears might visit in the night. I awoke with the solid light of day. My husband had been up for hours and had a salmon toasting on an open fire.

"Too bad we can only catch one. A fresh school just came in." He called me out of the tent.

Salmon, once they spawn, they stop feeding and are difficult to catch with a pole. The locals build fish wheel contraptions and erect them along the shores of the larger rivers. Powered by the water's current, the blades rotate and scoop the sizable fish wiggling by in the shallows of the edges of the roaring river. He pointed out where a bear had dug up our past meal and devoured the scraps we had so carefully buried. A porcupine waddled right through our camp while we sat on a log enjoying the value of fresh protein baked in oil and salted and peppered.

My husband looked at me and shook his head. "You look like shit." His rare use of profanity assured me the stings had done a good job of temporarily disfiguring my face. They were already starting to itch incessantly. He laughed at the ground. I knew we both felt the satisfaction that comes by being willing to deal with this raw frontier and actually surviving it.

I decided a good bathing would be in order and stripped down to the raw. I was sticking my toe in to convince my body that this plunge would be a good trauma when I heard voices. The sound of kids squealing. Someone singing. Another whistling. I dove for the tent in the nude as a family emerged from the trail. I had seen the tops of their fishing rods first.

As my husband made small talk with the excitement of kids and their parents tying lures, I sat quite vulnerable and motionless in the tent. My clothes lay where I had draped them. Over a limb on the creek's edge. As my husband was busy getting to know these people, he helped tie lures onto the kid's poles. I wondered how long before he would become aware that I would need that pile of clothing to join them. He never did.

This created a rare opportunity for me. I sat in the tent and listened. In the conversations that flowed so effortlessly with fishing in common, I learned that the family was Mennonite. They lived a few miles up the valley. They grew gardens in the summer and trapped in the winter. Their hope was to harvest hay. They offered to home can any salmon my husband could catch if he would pick up mason jars at the Chitina Emporium, the same building that served as the local saloon.

It only took an hour in the morning for this family to fill their rucksacks with fish and the hum of voices disappeared. My husband's voice was talking to the outside of the tent. "Hey, I just met an interesting family. Why didn't you come out and join us?" My husband's head stuck into the tent to find me sitting in the center, fully exposed. He roared. "Oh, my! I had no idea." He chuckled off and on all day.

We decided to enjoy this offer and take advantage, not so much of getting our salmon canned, but the treasure of an opportunity to get acquainted with a family on their homestead. It was a heartfelt invitation for these people to open themselves to complete strangers. The unlock came from our willingness to traverse their rugged terrain. It created an unspoken rite of passage. We were not just passing through, we were experiencing. We were willing to pioneer. And, that action made us feel safe to them.

The Speckles family opened their home and hearts to us and taught us how to can salmon.

Our reappearance at the small town with the Athabascan name created an instant stir. Though early in the day, trucks in conditions of beat up and bent up were already haphazardly parked in front of the Saloon. The truck that originally transported us here was one of them. When we entered past the worn wood door into stale air or years of nicotine vapor and the spilled fermented yeast of alcohol, a rumble of scooting chairs and barstools burst into action. A chorus of excitement surrounded us. All the men in the room seemed to be saying at once. "Are these them?!"

And to the confirmation, "Yes. Yes," the men were pushing past us and filing outside. Our friend, the Native American we had met, grabbed our hands and pulled us out with the group to the side of the building. On the wood wall they had etched bets as to when we would come out the same hole we had crawled into. They knew the wager was that we would never make it to Cordova, but the bet was being the one closest to the number of days and hours it would take us to retreat.

Our Native American was beside himself. He let out a hoot and a holler. Five days by mid-morning had his name by it. He triumphantly won. Green bills were being un-wadded and counted. He offered to take us and our mason jars to the property of the family we had met. Everyone seemed to know the names of those in the entire valley. There could not have been that many.

We drove, squished again into his front seat. He was so immersed in the adrenaline of interest our attempt had offered. "You know," he jabbered. "We never travel through the brush. We wait for the freeze and walk down the streams like sidewalks. You guys are definitely Cheechakos. The bushes are full of stickers, and there are a lot of beehives to disturb in them." He was so pleased that he calculated correctly our retreat that he whistled in between rapid conversation he was having with really no one, but himself. He was so used to not being heard.

He left us at the roadside and pointed for us to walk down a gravel driveway. As we waved goodbye, it was as if an invisible line of comfort was drawn to where a pioneer lived, and a native did not. The moxie of gutting out our kind of travel, meeting people where they are at, had no invisible line. We simply crossed right over and kept walking. And that's how I hope all my travels will be.

16

We Pushed the Gate Open to the Arctic Circle

Prudhoe Bay, Alaska.

We made it as far as we were told we could drive, just above the Arctic Circle, to the last building…the only building between the Yukon River and 215 more miles of open tundra. This was a mere speck on the map, and the map noted it as being called Coldfoot, Alaska. It was a rickety building that served the truckers that were making round trips on the "Haul Road." It is now called the Dalton Highway, though still all gravel. This is one of the world's most remote roads. It runs 415 miles one way from Fairbanks, above the Arctic Circle, to where the Alaska Pipeline starts pumping oil.

The road ends at a settlement, made up of mostly trailers on stilts some called Prudhoe Bay, others named it Deadhorse. Huge caldrons of oil were discovered in 1968 in the Arctic and US President Richard Nixon approved an $8 billion project so the US could produce its own solid oil source. This pipe carries 1.8 million gallons of oil per day all the way to a shipping port. The construction of this engineered pipeline is a wonderous human feat.

The trucking road was an elevated ribbon of gravel spread over a thick layer of insulation for traveling atop the tundra and to prevent melting of the permafrost. As if to have a taunting reason to keep going, the Brooks

Range looms as a daring barrier about halfway on the route. A treacherous line of gravel goes up and over it. We guessed it to be about a 20 percent grade. No switchbacks. Just up and over. Truck carcasses and mangled metals of small aircraft littered the sides of the ravines on the ascent and descent of this wildly remote mountain range.

When my husband and I arrived at Coldfoot, we entered the only building. Two truckers stared us down as they chewed their burgers like someone chews tobacco. We felt like the timid, intrusive tourists we were to them, but we also felt our internal mojo fighting back. We were here to prove to the world that civilians could responsibly be self-sufficient enough to make it all the way to Prudhoe Bay.

We had extra tires, diesel fuel cans, our quiver of canned food with all the labels bounced off. We had the allotted time on our hands to handle however long it would take to bump along a path that reined in a small vehicle, making us go less than 10 miles an hour. That meant driving this road would be equivalent to a 40-hour work week. The big rig work trucks had a chassis of wheels—too many to count as they barreled by. Our mini truck hovered in fear of being overrun if we couldn't find a turnout when the trucks, with an agenda, blasted by.

We had made it so far. We were in Coldfoot. To my delight, I could buy a patch that said, "I have been above the Arctic Circle." Patches were pinned to the wall. They were dusty but had a handwritten for sale sign. One dollar. Yes, you bet I did. I bought the patch to sew on my jacket!

Once we settled at a rocking table that was once a door and on the chairs that were once oil barrels, a vociferous man came in. He first was stomping his boots in the doorway. Then his hyperactivity came straight at us with no true greeting, just a barrage of half sentences to explain his name was Dick Mackey and that he was the owner of the establishment. He pulled up a barrel and was not about to miss an opportunity to drill, not for oil, but what living in the "outside" was like, and what were the likes of us doing by coming up to this forsaken road. Yet, you could tell he was proud to live here.

He shared, as he ordered beers for us without asking, that he lived there so he could raise the best sled dogs in the world. He had won the 1978 Iditarod Dog Sled race to prove it. Once exhausted of all the information about himself, he turned his interest back to us. When we told him we really wanted to keep going even though the information said we would be turned back at a gate up the road he became super animated. He jumped up and his tall, bearded self almost hit the low roof beams. He commanded us to do what we set out to do, to go all the way to Prudhoe Bay.

In doing so, he hoped this would open even a thimble of future tourism to help him keep his establishment and pay for the care and feeding of his dogs. He explained that he had researched the regulations and determined them unenforceable. The "Haul Road" was paid for by taxpayers, so how could the government deny a taxpayer the right to use it? He taunted us to drive on. He said the gate keeper would have to let us through. As we were fixing to leave, we hoped he was right. Either we would be heroes for going, or we would be arrested for trying.

We paid for our patch and meal; a frozen burger patty cooked to the consistency of a tobacco chew. No wonder the truckers were gnawing on their meat. But none of us complained. The vittles offered an excuse to commune with other human beings and shed a candlelight on the heart of solo confinement. Dick Mackey followed us out the door and asked if we wanted to see his dogs. His voice spoke of them like one would speak of their precious children.

He had a collage of dogs. They were all chained on three-foot links outside. Each was sitting erect, next to a makeshift wood igloo in anticipation of the owner approaching. He approached each dog with a name and an array of praise. Tails were all wagging. Dogs were barking. The hillside of igloos seemed uncountable as they disappeared over the rise. He had that many dogs. They all seemed healthy and happy, and obviously linked in respect to their owner.

When we left, shaking the owner's hand, a chorus arose from the beasts made for this terrain. It felt like a scene from Jack London's book *Call of the Wild*. They rang out a howl over our departure, and I think the man, Dick Mackey, felt it, too. "I love these dogs. And they love what I ask them to do. They live for getting to pull sleds." Then he shyly added, "Not many folks have the guts to venture up this far. Thank you for being one of them."

We drove toward the Brooks Range that was still snowcapped and found the gate. A solo gatekeeper was at its base. The man stepped out of his shelter and explained we must turn around. We told him that we were going to proceed forward at our own risk. He rolled his eyes, shoulders, and entire body at us. With a dramatic sweep of his hands, he motioned us to proceed forward… and yelled as we passed through. "At our own risk."

He was just there as a deterrent. The gate was unlocked. As I would find with so many other things in life that I was told were off limits, we just need to go push on the gate. There may be fences erected, but do we check to see if that gate is really locked? Some opportunities are meant to have mojo and the gate to be pushed open. Wide open. And, yet we also need to remember to respect authority and be law abiding. I am not talking about unlawful, disrespectful trespassing. I mean, see if you can be the gutsy one to do the right thing first and let others follow.

We did make it. Oil workers started pouring out of the trailers at Prudhoe Bay when we rolled in. They were looking over our mini truck with the battering ram welded to the front. They had never had a 'tourist' make it this far. We had spent weeks traveling through the summer solstices where the sun just hues but never sets. We were this high above the artic circle now.

We had to ask, "What day is it? And, by the way, what time of day?" Their answer explained why we had been feeling a little fatigued. We had just spent two days fully awake and didn't even realize it!

17

There's a First for Everything

Continent 1: North America – Los Angeles Marathon

Three significant things happened when we returned from Alaska: my husband's grandfather died, I got a new job, and I had a baby.

They called him Daddy Bill. He was 89 years old. Cranky. A loner. Hard to read. Most of his life he had chosen to be aloof. When his kidneys failed, he asked to be taken off the machines and refused to die in a hospital. We took turns, like sailors on a dutiful watch standing guard over him in his home—a humble cabin with a warped floor that made the bed and furniture rock.

He died the day that I accepted a new position working with the City Director of Parks and Recreation. It was a job I enjoyed, and in that position, I made progress merging the outskirts of town into being an active part of the sports programs. Fighting the history of segregation by introducing so many different folks to sports became a theme that began to wind its way through my life.

And now that my life in Southern California was settling down, it was time to set another goal. I decided it was time to run a marathon.

I was a track & field athlete. I didn't run my first road race until my graduating year from college. It did not go so well. I picked the 10K versus a 5K. I had no idea how far a 10K was. It just sounded like a nice round number. Standing with the pack of runners squeezed under a start banner, I pushed to the front for a spot at the lead. I took off with the pop of the starter's pistol like a true sprinter. I made it about 800 yards when the lead pack overtook me at a more relaxed, yet fast pace. I fell further and further back as I ran by a one-mile sign and then a two-mile sign and still no finish line.

I had no idea that I was running six miles and a few hundred yards in change. There was a trick out there called pacing that had not been introduced to me. I had taken off too fast and could not hold that kind of ambition that long. I think I threw up on the third mile, cried on the fourth mile, jogged the fifth, and walked into the finish line after the sixth mile, very much at the back of the pack. Pretty humbling for an athlete used to top scores in the hurdles and Heptathlon in track and field.

But I was now thirty years old, and track competitions were a thing of the past. I hoped I could become wiser in pacing, and I was interested in all this buzz of road races and triathlons. I also was a new mom and anxious to get that layer of excess fat I developed back into proper proportions. Compared to sprinting on the track, marathoning required building an endurance foundation. I had to teach my body to get used to being hot for hours. I was no longer gasping for air. I was having to develop what they call white muscle and teach myself a don't-give-up mindset.

Marathoning sandwiched well with hiking, biking, backpacking, and scaling mountains. I liked it and the excuse it brought to fill up time being outside. It was fun to pick course routes to run. Or people to run with. Sometimes—many times—it would only FIT in time slots I would have to run alone. Doing the mileage consistently was the key. I got disciplined about it. Not like a vice. Not an obsession, but a planned-out goal with purposeful progress. Yet, I really didn't know what I was doing.

At the time, I could only find a handful of runners who didn't think this distance was out of reach. We ran, and ran, and ran. Every other day, we ran until we got strong enough to run six solid days a week. I was careful to honor a rest day. I read too many accounts of people who had not, and who sustained injuries that seem to result from overuse or over ambition. Plus, if God set up his creation week to end with a day of rest, maybe He knew something we didn't know. We need rest.

For months before the marathon day, I ran. I liked the feeling, and I liked the easy flowing relationships that build among runners. It was the same camaraderie I got to experience in high school on the track team. It offered a good reprieve from work, caring for a home, and parenting. On a run, somehow, conversations flowed and could also be comfortable mixed with spans of silence. Natural felt natural. Healthy social interactions flowed with no hang ups on politics, ethnicity, economics, or such. We had a purpose and being with people because we liked running together made running fun. I encourage people to find others to run with. Mix it up and make it fun.

My body had become a composite of standard career-working-woman, starting-a-family. I had given birth to my firstborn son. Of course, biasedly, he was the most beautiful little boy on earth. The toll it took on my body was worth it, but it was time to return it to its former self. I must have already started to be a part of the runner's craze because my baby shower gift from my staff was a combined purchase of a baby jogger.

It was not a rickety stroller that got its wheels stuck in every rut, but a hefty three wheeled contraption with a covered seat and a bar to push it from behind. This tool could turn my excess pounds of weight gained during my pregnancy into firm muscle. No excuses. Could running a distance like this gift back a FIT body? A marathon sounded like the mammoth goal that could do that.

What an indelible morning the start of the marathon ended up being. It was 1991, yet thousands upon thousands of people were in a buzz, bibs on and moving toward corrals at the start. I was in awe as the serpentine of heads started to bob up and down as we all moved forward in a wall of energized humanity. An announcer introduced city officials. I was so far back in the sea of people I never heard a start sound. The announcer was blaring, "And they are off," and we all moved forward, not as thousands of individuals, but one creature called the LA MARATHON. It would take almost thirteen miles before we started finding more space between us and became individual runners.

The streets of Los Angeles were lined with cheering spectators and occasionally they wildly yelled out names of people they recognized. Many were proudly perched on sidewalks and balconies, waving us through their neighborhoods. It was an incredible scene to me. The excitement and commotion made the miles whizz by. In a blur, I was passing the halfway mark—mile 13.1. I felt happy to be here. I felt solid.

They say a marathon is two parts. The first twenty miles and the last six. I had never run this far before. Going back and measuring my training runs in a car, I found out my longest runs were only thirteen miles. That is what my body had become used to, and no further. I did not know to drink or eat anything on those training runs. I didn't even know I needed to. And though people were grabbing cups of water in a frenzy at the water stations posted every two miles, I chose not to bother. I did not feel thirsty. I had no idea that I should fuel or fluid myself in the first miles. If I ate anything the day of a track meet it ended up behind the stadium heaved into a trash barrel or bush, so I never thought about eating something. Becoming hypoglycemic can be serious. In extreme cases, it can induce a coma.

Those that run marathons already know I was making huge first-timer mistakes. Not hydrating and fueling in the first half of a marathon is a formula for struggling in the second half. By the time you 'feel' hungry or thirsty, it is too late.

So, my body started to starve. It started to talk back to me and outright give up on me in those last miles of my first marathon. I had never heard of the word "bonk," which means you have not taken in enough carbohydrates and have exhausted your glycogen stores, leaving you with abnormally low blood glucose levels. It has been found that a body can only store enough glucose for about ninety minutes of moderate activity. A body must be fed during a marathon.

My body started to shake. I broke out in a deep sweat on top of my already sweaty tank top clinging to me. I felt dizzy and very weak. Staggeringly weak. And most irritating was how agitated I was. A person's slapping foot pace next to me bothered me. The way another wheezed got deep into my nerves.

I remember spying a half-eaten, discarded nutrition bar in the gutter around mile eighteen. I was starting to get delirious. I knew my body needed to eat. It was wailing like a baby, "I'm hungry!" Was I really contemplating grabbing that half-unwrapped bar? Clearly, bites had been taken out of it. The slick yellow metallic wrapper shimmered among the gutter trash. Should I do it? I could feel my hand reaching out.

I passed by the temptation, but the hunger did not ease. It consumed me with all kinds of starving thoughts. A deep-rooted memory bubbled up as my focus narrowed to the feeling of being wrongly hungry. I had forgotten how mad I would get inside at my mom. She had a poor habit of splurging my dad's meager food allowance on the first night of the week by taking her three children out to eat at a restaurant. And toward the end of the week, she packed us embarrassing lunch bags that sometimes only held a carrot. I struggled with why she managed like this. We lived in such an upscale house, an upscale neighborhood, yet I feared how harshly we would be teased if the playground knew my siblings and I had lunch bags that occasionally held only that carrot.

I couldn't believe my focus had fallen so internally that I no longer paid attention to the cheery spectators. Only my hunger. I decided this must be how those without food feel. I vowed to remember how bad this really felt. It must be hard to be in a situation where there is not enough food. I made a life note to make sure I did something when I RAN across anyone in true need of the next bite of food.

I started really struggling and wondering how I was going to survive this marathon. I questioned if I could do it. Would I finish? What if I had to give up? I had to decide I was not going to. No matter how whittled to a crawl I was becoming, I was not going to stop. I did try to scheme up the guts to dive into a convenience store on this LA Marathon route and beg for a candy bar, or anything, no matter the food value. Had anyone ever done that before? Did I dare be the first? Should I offer them a $50 bill and beg them a promise I would come back and pay it?

I noticed it was not just me who was starting to creep along. Faces had stricken pain painted on them. Running a marathon can produce some grimacing. But I kept going. I was too afraid to stop. Stopping told me that starting again would be too hard. I could feel every muscle in me wanting to cramp up. People who train and race marathons at athletic paces get this distance done in just over 2 to 3 hours. The back-of-the-packers finish in 4 to 7 hours. Being out there that long is hard on the body. That is the challenge of the marathon. What will your body do? How will you handle it? Can you find those things deep within you—that will to carry on longer than one thought possible? A marathon pits you in a battle to find those extra umphs.

Even if well-trained, prepared, and feeding yourself enough energy, marathons are not always turn-key. My brother, who is an LA City firefighter, says his station has some extra work to do on marathon day. He says, "People can start to show signs of dehydration, heat exhaustion, heat stroke, or hypothermia."

"Hypothermia?!" I questioned.

"Yes. Their body can suddenly not produce its own heat and, regardless of if it is a warm day, they can no longer regulate their temperatures. The scary thing is both symptoms for heat stroke and hypothermia look very similar. If treated wrongly, a person can be thrown into an instant crisis atop their already severe condition. A wrong diagnosis and treatment could make a person worse."

He chided me as brothers are supposed to. "Hey, Sis, are you sure you want to run a marathon?" Then he added. "Doesn't the Greek Mythology legend tell that Pheidippides ran nonstop from the battle at Marathon all the way to Athens to ensure they knew they were the victors of the battle.

He dropped his weapons, and even his clothes along the way to lighten himself. And then he died on the spot?" My brother gave me his sibling smirk.

And yes, that is where the idea of a marathon came from. I bet Pheidippides forgot to hydrate and take in his carbohydrates also.

At mile 24, my back cramped up and I folded over. There was a high school band blaring instruments on the center divider. I was cranky and they sounded very out of tune and not in sync. A very tall man next to me buckled and passed out cold on the pavement. Thankfully, right in front of a water station, so volunteers rushed in. This was miserable. What had I gotten myself into? Here I was. The first 23 miles had been relatively fine. It was these last three. I had done okay and felt almost cocky at the 21, 22, and 23. But now, I was hungry, yet still going.

I just had to keep going. Dig deep. Dig deep. Every step seemed in slow-motion. Finishing that last mile now neared eternity. The last stretch of fencing and clapping clans of families and goodwill farers almost seemed like they were taunting. Sound and color had disappeared. I saw moving hands and mouths but was not able to hear distinguishable words. I was in an echo chamber far, far away. Like in an eerie dream, I was staggering toward a steel arch that read, "LA MARATHON FINISH."

I went under the finish scaffolding and there I was…finished, in more ways than one. A volunteer draped an LA MARATHON finisher medal around my neck. I felt instantly pleased. And relieved. All the agony turned into a gladness to have finished. I took one step and both my calves cramped, pitching me to the pavement. I scooted on hands and knees to the grass and was a little disoriented. It took a long time before I could get up. I staggered searching for my husband and infant son.

My husband was curled up around the stroller. Both he and my son were deeply sound asleep. I guess waiting for 4 hours and 21 minutes is not the most exciting thing you can ask a person to do, especially trying to keep an infant appeased.

But I had finished a big goal I had set. My medal dangled around my neck to prove it. As we drove home, I made a comment about how poorly timed local races were. And how the marathon had somehow captured all our times. I set out on a mission. To create a timing company that utilized all the new immergence of electronics and provided great race service. Thus, began our entrepreneur type livelihood and a dedicated lifestyle to road racing.

18

The Belmont Boys

First experience in the snow.

A small frame. Tattered shoes. His shorts were way too big for him. A gritty grin seemed permanently etched on his face. He had kind eyes and seemed to approach even competition in a jocular manner. I guessed he was possibly twelve or thirteen years old. He was nervously stepping from one foot to the other, but playfully eyeing two world class Kenyan runners, currently in Los Angeles to set records and establish rankings. There was a crowd at this race, there to watch these Kenyans battle it out for a fast road race 5k time. That is why it was so noticeable that his skinny Hispanic boy was standing next to them on that front starting line, eyeballing them like he was potential competition. I liked his boldness.

My heart started to talk to him. "Dear boy, you have no chance against these trained Kenyans. But I like that you dream you can do so. Enough, that you are goading them. I like you," I told myself. I wondered who he was? Where he was from?

Our timing company was scoring this publicized road race in Griffith Park, a huge swath of hills preserved for hiking and running. It is a designated green space for picnicking in the heart of the Los Angeles basin, running distance from downtown Los Angeles, Chinatown, and what I call "the Hood." A fast course was engineered with two out and back loops, meaning it ran to a turnaround and came right past the start line to another turnaround and back to the finish like an elongated oval racetrack. This kind of a course made it spectator friendly. The entire race could be viewed passing by on one side and then returning to the finish on the other. Our timing tent was set out on the center divider, so we were best situated to watch with front row seats.

An air horn blasted at a high shrill, easier heard than formerly used starter's pistols. We activated the timing equipment and set the software in motion, simultaneously. The front line jumped forward and the assembly of over one thousand runners moved as one, a serpentine line that stretched out toward the horizon. Soon, even the stragglers with strollers and walkers disappeared from our view. I was the person standing out in front to activate the timing equipment. Still captivated by this young Hispanic kid, I kept my eye on the front pack.

The young teen was looking like the Looney Tunes cartoon character, the Roadrunner who goes BEEP. BEEP. His legs were wheeling around so fast they appeared blurred as he sped by in those first hundred yards. He was going as fast as any heart could make a frame go. But so were the lanky Kenyans. They had a miraculous cadence. Smooth. Trained. Their heels almost kicked their butts in symmetry. I knew this boy could never keep up his sprint, but at least he would have the experience of a mad dash with the Kenyans for the first part of this race. My chest cheered for him anyway, "Go, young man. Go. At least you can run for a while with the Kenyans."

The announcer had walkie-talkie contact with a camera man, who was riding backwards on the back of the lead scooter. This event was being filmed and televised. He could talk into the mic clipped to his pack and give play-by-play information to the announcer. The announcer, informed of what was soon to be coming back by us, started pumping the crowd that the Kenyans would soon be passing by. The crowd shifted to the other side of the center divider.

Our viewpoint had the advantage of being taped off, so we had a wide width opportunity to see them all go by. My timing crew stood elbow-to-elbow on the curb to watch. The anticipation was exciting. Watching turned to awe as a beautiful pace of legs crested into view. There were six legs churning, not four. And two of them belonged to that scrawny boy.

"Oh, dear boy," I delighted inside. "You are keeping up with them for this long. One mile into the race!" It was so triumphantly impressive. The announcer came running to me with his portable mic asking who the boy was. I looked up his bib number and all the data screen reported back was RAY. No last name. No address. Just RAY. So, the announcer went with it…. mispronouncing long Kenyan names and calling the kid simply… "Ray." That is RAY running with them, folks." And, "Well, look at Ray. He is keeping right there with Olympic level runners."

Admiration inside me smiled at this kid's spunk. I presumed he would not keep this up. No youngster could. As the recreational joggers and walkers were still passing the mile mark on the other side of the road, the announcer started to elevate his pitch to sheer excitement. "Here come your leaders!" he yelled. We could see six pairs of shoes slamming the ground almost abreast of each other. Almost in unison. And that boy, Ray was still right there with them. All three were in a full sprint to be declared champion of this 3.1 mile televised race. All three were on pace to run a 5K course time rarely seen in Los Angeles.

The boy looked side to side, almost smiling with that same etched smirk he had at the starting line. Back and forth, he was sizing up each Kenyan like a taunt. The Kenyans were sunken eyed and intent on one thing, to hit that finish line first. I think they hardly noticed this young competitor was sandwiched between them. Ray hit the line half a stride in between the two of them and the photo finish showed his chest hitting the line as second overall. The Kenyans seemed caught off guard and bodily annoyed, like a fly had shown up to their meal. I could not stop from saying YES inside… repeatedly. This little guy did it. He ran as fast as a trained Kenyan.

Who was he? There had to be more to his story than just the simple name of…Ray. He had given that race his core of what is humanly possible. He staggered out of the chutes, and I expected him to go for a cool down, but he moved up the hillside and disappeared behind a bush. I kept my eye on the shrubs. Minutes later, another boy came out wearing the same shoes and shorts. These swapped items seemed to fit this boy better. He had a strong build about him, and he sauntered down to the 10K starting line with the air of a soccer champion who knew he was good. His hair was trim. He had a set jaw and a handsome way about him. Now, there were two boys.

I felt no one was noticing them but me. There were two thousand people running in both these races. No one took notice that two boys were sharing the same set of shoes, but me. Of course, if my mom was here, she would have noticed as well.

This fresh boy also stood on the front line. He did a few striders and shook the hands of all the competitors warming up, without saying a word. Just a nod of "good luck" by throwing that strong chin in the air and off to the side in a shy, but headstrong way. He stood right over his shoulders, almost at attention. The two Kenyans stood right with him. They were using the 10K as a "warm down" from the 5K. But even their warm down pace would be blistering.

The new boy put one foot on the line and took the stance of a starter's position in a track lane. I could see his eyes narrow, and he meant for this to be a race. The horn sounded. And off all the 6.2 miler 10K runners went until they all trotted, once again, out of sight.

When the lead scooter radioed and let the announcer know the leaders were coming, this same pair of shoes with the different boy wearing them was right with the Kenyans. The announcer ran back to me, rapidly requesting I look up the bib and give him this kid's name. When I looked it up, it said RAY. No last name. No address. The announcer was annoyed.

"What?" he complained. "Come on, there can't be two Rays." He spent a minute berating me with comments. "Don't you have better data than that? What a stupid mistake on a timer's part to have both listed as Ray, with no last name, nor what town they are from."

At the time, we were scanning in No.2 penciled in scan cards for walk up registrants. What was boxed in on the scan card went directly into the computer. This was the only information each provided. The announcer did not bother to announce this kid. He refrained from sounding silly announcing the same RAY name. He used his professional voice to discuss what it takes to train at the level of these Kenyan Olympians. He congratulated the crowd for coming to watch such top caliber finishers. There was prize money for the top three finishers in both these races and the reason why the Kenyans were there. These boys were there for the same prize. They were there to win money.

A solid half hour ahead of most of the runners, the three leaders came racing toward the finish line in almost the same scene as the 5k. This mystery boy, Ray #2, had the look of a racehorse that would drop dead at the finish line rather than lose this race. His stauncher build hit the finish line one foot length behind the two Kenyans, and he came in third overall.

I was walking in circles in a quiet personal victory party for the spunk of these kids. My core got to express more triumphant yeses. These kids had mojo. Who were they? I knew they were on a journey just from the observation that they were sharing shoes.

I got busy timing the rest of the participants when they announced the winners and handed them their prizes. So, I only had the chance to watch out of the corner of my eye. The small, skinny boy who came in second overall in the 5K was grinning ear to ear. He was standing on the second tier between the two Kenyans. When handed his trophy, he held it as high above his head as his little arms could. He threw a smirk to each Kenyan on the higher and lower podiums. He was handed an envelope with his prize money.

When I heard the overall announcement for the 10K, I watched the stage as I coiled extension cords. This Ray #2 popped up on his third-place block and waved to the crowd. He was not waving to anyone he seemed to know. It was a wave to the world to get to know him. Look out, he was saying. I have won the right to wave at success.

As the stage was being dismantled, and we were finally all packed up, I walked toward their bush. My intent was to find out who they were. When they saw me coming, they grabbed their things and fled like wild coyotes. They had been dividing up the prize money into piles. Five boys took off further up the hill and deeper into the Griffith Park brush. Not just two.

Maybe five or six. All about the same ages. There had to be a story behind them. It would take some patient years of love to find out what their lives were really like but running would connect us.

Weeks later, I ran into a coach at a running shoe store. He said he coached kids for the SRLA marathon training program at Belmont High School. He said he had a few "newcomers" that signed up. He was told they were going to be very fast. He showed me a picture of his team and the two RAYS and the other boys were in it. I shared with him how fast these boys could run.

We chatted. He knew as much about them as I did. Which was nothing. He said the shortest, fastest one offered that their motive to come to his program was they heard they could get a coke, a cookie, and a shower after each practice. If this was true, the kid announced on behalf of all the boys, they all wanted to join the SRLA training team. For a coke, a cookie, and a shower.

The coach let out a giggle. "Imagine," he said to me. "What a jokester. Acting like he never had a can of coke before." I asked the coach if he would offer all the boys complimentary entries in a race I was timing in two weeks. It was to be on that same course in Griffith Park. Better yet, I told him, tell them I would buy them each new shoes if they came to the Griffith Park race and helped me set up and tear down the timing equipment before they ran. He agreed to tell them. And I added, "Oh, and tell them they have to be there by 5:00am."

In the frenzy of family life plus business pressures, I had almost forgotten about that pack of boys from Belmont High School. When I arrived at the park gate it was 4am. The rangers had given me an access code for the locks. I swung the huge metal arm open and drove my truck through, parked, relocked the gate, and drove on. My own two children were slumped over in uncomfortable positions with their seat belts on. Asleep, they had their heads on pillows propped against the windows in the passenger seats of the truck's back seat. They really did not like having to get up and come to the races this early.

When my headlights swung in the direction to turn toward the start and finish line area, the beams cast shadows on five silhouettes. I pulled the brake on and stepped out of the truck. The park was tranquil with a deep and dark pre-morning peace. The only sound was my truck engine humming in idle and the night buzz of the 5 Freeway. It felt like a lullaby to me.

Five young men, boys in my heart, were sound asleep on the curb. Each had his head propped on the next boy's shoulders with the two end boys tilting inward to support the pyramid of slumber like book ends. They looked like they had done this many times before.

Standing there, I took in their differences. Some had sweatshirts. Others wore jackets. Some had darker hair, darker skin. All but one had street shoes on. The smallest stature I recognized as Ray #1. He was wearing the torn running shoes. In that speckled hue from my headlights, a light lit in my soul. They became my boys. The Belmont Boys. I looked at my own two kids deep in their peaceful slumber. I looked at these boys, equally in need of that peaceful sleep and said aloud to my kids, "Well, life just got interesting. I just adopted you some brothers."

Those boys worked hard that day. And never stopped working hard. We used proceeds from that timing contract and gifted each a new pair of shoes. A Runner's Circle was a great mom and pop running shoe store in the Los Angeles area. It was located on Los Feliz right before the main entrance into Griffith Park. After we packed up the race, I told the boys to jog over to the store. I would meet them there. They would get to pick a pair of shoes of their choice. Five boys sat on a bench all getting their feet sized. The store was so full of choices, they were overwhelmed and giddy.

Gratefully, the salesclerk was a Spanish speaking runner who enjoyed giving them the RUN down, so to speak, of RUNNING shoes. That day, I was as good as Santa Claus in those boys' eyes. They told me this counted as one of the luckiest days of their lives. Can you imagine? All I did was find a way to buy each of them a pair of running shoes.

I learned that the giver is the one who gets the bigger gift. They were so thrilled with their new shoes that my insides were swelling from their pure happiness. There is something that glows or flows back when a gift is given with true, heartfelt love. I decided I wanted to keep gifting them first time experiences, if possible. Why not keep gifting all lives, when possible, FIRST time experiences?

They learned to ride the Metrolink commuter train to the bottom of my mountain after track practice on Fridays. I learned to pick them up on time. The San Bernardino train station had gangs that would harass my boys because they could not prove they were from the same San Bernardino area. I would pull up right when the train arrived, and the boys would dash for the back seats in my truck cab and all squash in, slamming the door and ducking. They knew something I did not know.

They respected our home. They cleared their dishes, vacuumed after themselves, rolled up their bedrolls and always went out the door at six a.m. for an early morning run to match their afternoon workouts. I never asked them to. They just had that internal drive. It was part of their plan to be winners. And by winning, they were going to do more than survive. They were going to thrive and make something rise beyond their circumstances.

I had no idea that some of these boys were living behind the trash dumpster and washing dishes at a restaurant after closing to feed themselves. Or sleeping in broken vehicles. Or because they were unwanted, being beaten in fights with their moms since their moms had new, more promising "American-born" children. What I did know was they loved the seasons that Lake Arrowhead offered. They especially were exuberant about the snow. This new experience, though teens, let them be the innocent children they did not get to be in Los Angeles. I loved gathering them up at the train station and driving them to an elevation that had white on the ground. They winced if we had to drive in the fog or at the portion of the road that had cliff drop offs. Living on the streets of concrete LA was flat, and where they thought nothing of having to dodge bullets.

They did not offer much information about their lives on the streets of Los Angeles, and I gave up trying to ask. They seemed thrilled to live in the moment and have our home experience. It freed them from having to live that street life constantly. There were rules they had to live by in places like Echo Park and Vermont Avenue. Only after becoming college graduates, would they offer pieces of how intense some of their living had been.

They were loyal and strong to an unspoken family bond. They had to have each other's backs to make it in LA. To them, it hurt in a life-threatening way when a family relationship severed over choices and disagreements. I noticed the bond was between distant cousins and uncles, sometimes sisters, and some mothers. Rarely a dad. There did not seem to be many fathers in any of their lives.

Their situations went something like this. Many young women will cross the border for the states and leave their young children behind to be raised by their grandparents. The moms, once newcomers, make their way to sweat shops to work. They meet new guys and end up with a new set of young children. American children. The grandparents back in Mexico die, leaving the original kids as orphans. Two of my boys knew how to rope cattle by foot. They said they had no horses to ride. And if they could catch cattle, they would get milk and cheese. They also ran for hours every morning to find the cows. There were no fences. And if they could get to the school on time, they were fed rice and beans. If they got there late. The door was locked. So, they sprinted.

What motivated them? This was the way they could find to feed themselves. This is how, they said, they learned to be the natural runners they were. At a race, one of the boys watched a crow land in a tree. He told me that if that had been in Southern Mexico, they would have caught it and eaten it. I do not think he was kidding. He was the one who had never tasted Coke in a can. Something was driving them in a deep way.

I finally figured out one of their biggest hardships was their moms. By the time they each got to the States, their moms were not set up to be able to take them easily in. Some could not provide for additional mouths to feed. As young men of age, they were on the streets, and it was up to them to fend for themselves once again. But now, in unfamiliar surroundings, there were no cows to catch or crows to snare in the trees. Many of these boys outran the border patrol officers. They ran right into an English-speaking world that would take a lot of figuring out. So, they were racing for prize money. They valued any chance for betterment and were willing to work for it.

Running gave them a dream that was full of hope and pursuit. And somehow, it gave them a new family. Ray #2, I would find out years later (and only when he got visas for them to come visit), had a twin sister and a mom in Mexico who loved him very much, but could not get across the border. It was a tear-jerking moment, full of happiness that needed no language, to finally meet Ray #2's mom in person. Just a simple nod, and I knew her appreciation, mom to mom, that her son had my home's opportunity to help him survive.

After the shoes, I asked them if they would help at a race sponsored by a 5-star hotel in downtown Los Angeles. They answered all at once. It was such a responsive set of yeses I jumped. I phoned the manager to see if I could gift my boys each a room since he had offered the entire upper level of the complex. He sponsored us by giving us the upper floor to ourselves. It never hurts to ask. I had a key per boy and presented one to each of them in the hallway. It was Christmas all over again. They were silly and gleeful. Each raced to his own room and slammed the door. I went into my own but kept hearing the doors slamming. Too many times. I marched out into the hall.

"Boys, what is going on here?" I took a sergeant's stance with my arms crossed.

Ray #1 sheepishly filled me in. Not only had he really never tasted a can of Coke before, but he had also never had a room to himself. Each boy was enjoying the ceremony of slamming his own door shut to the tune of, "This is my room. This is my room." Good thing we had the floor to ourselves.

About two weeks after our first hotel room excursion, I got a charge on my credit card for $679 in excess charges. I called the boys together and scolded them for the truth. "Which one of you broke something at the hotel?" They all conferred in rapid Spanish, first among themselves, then Ray #1 stood up to represent them.

"Nada. Nada one of us did somethings wrongs, weez promises," he begged innocently, adding the extra 's' like he always did.

I called the hotel. The charges were for snacks! Each of those boys thought those refrigerators full of sodas, chips, and peanuts were for them. They had a contest to see who could eat the most out of each of their own refrigerators in one night. You know, those fancy snacks they have in fancy hotels with charges like $10 for a tiny bag of chips? I paid for their innocence. And I paid for lots of hardships also, known and unknown. It came with being willing to make them a part of our lives.

Many would question why I would ever do all that for all of them when it cost extra money, time, and commitment. The question bothered me. They were really asking why I would give time and money away that I could be spending on myself. They didn't understand how much more these boys were doing for me than money could ever buy. In some miraculous way, the giver becomes given to in immeasurable ways. We were racing together in life, as a team. Our entire family. The Bible says to give, and it will be given back to you, overflowing. Full of blessing. Don't do it to expect anything in return. But, because you are giving things, things do, almost without noticing, return two fold in ways that may not be in currency.

The Belmont Boys became my timing crew. I made singlets for them. And I paid entry fees for them to run in races we did not time. And of course, they won. They won a lot for a long time. I did not want them to just be winning in running races, I wanted them to win in life. I looked for opportunities to show them that parks and beaches were open to all, that they had the right to explore and roam any place on this earth. I hope I had opened the world to them. They all needed to get accepted to colleges. That would be the start.

Even in college they continued to time races.

19

A Miracle was Brewing

Ray No. 1 graduating from college.

They reminded me that the world really wasn't totally open to them. It was true. They did not have the right papers. They did not have the right skin color for many places. I got called one night at a hotel from the Manhattan Beach Police. They had all five of my boys. They wanted to verify if what they were claiming was true. These officers knew their job was to keep crime from happening in their town and these boys did not belong there. The kids had been seen running in the dark, were reported, and now were apprehended. They were trying to explain in their heavy accents they were just out for a training run. It was 10pm at night and they had been working all day at our race expo.

The officer's voice continued, "Are you really their coach? And were they really running around this neighborhood at 10pm at night training for cross country races?"

I had to drive to the station to release them.

As they got older, they got pulled over many times and had their cars towed away because they did not have the right papers. They were caught in a net of being educated and in high school, but not here legally. It was precarious to be making their way here in the United States, but not free to do so. They weren't even free to travel back to their hometowns. They were also not free from harassment or other gang members or the uncertainties of what a future could really be without the proper papers.

I had run marathons in the USA and was about to do one in France. I had opportunities they did not. I told them I would run a marathon on every continent on their behalf. I would come home with stories and share cultures, pictures, and people with them. I told them I would do this because I never wanted them to give up on their dreams. Somehow, I wanted to be able to open the world for them. They were determined to rise above hardship. And they did. Every single one of them. They ran their hearts out. They worked hard. They learned. They pursued. They put up with a lot of obstacles. But they were not free to roam the world yet.

I drew lots each summer so they could take turns going to Jackson Hole, Wyoming with us on our summer vacations. We only had room for two extra passengers. Like kids in a candy store, this wide-open outdoor experience, with its wonders of rock formations, trees, birds, nature, and live beasts was another best thing that could ever happen to them. Christmas, once again! I knew it would be a healthy, joyous gift for them. And that alone, was a joyous, healthy gift to our family. It was special to share something as personal and epic as exploring the wilderness. And they made instant, healthy backpackers and trail runners.

My "boys" sprinted up trails, tried on day packs, and went on overnight treks with us. They gazed at the mountains and were so in awe. They wondered out loud why they could not see people walking on top of the mountains. Until I hiked them to the top of one and asked them to look down. "Can you see people walking around in the valley from this pinnacle?" It changed their perspective. And taking the opportunity to help "raise" them also changed mine.

One day I had a phone call from the Belmont principal. He politely introduced himself. I answered back, "What have my boys done?"

"Well, nothing," he replied. "We want to know, what have you done?"

I was not sure what he was getting at.

"You see, you have a Guatemalan, a boy from Mexico City, two from Southern Mexico, and one who isn't even Hispanic. He is an indigenous Indian, from Qaxaca."

"Umm, so? Does that mean anything?" I replied. "Are they doing okay in school? You know, they are going to be your next state championship in cross country and track and field!" I proudly added.

"Yes, we all know that. All of Belmont High School knows that. Well, it just is that in this area, none of these groups of kids get along. In my school, El Salvadorians, and Guatemalans, and Hispanics are from different parts of Mexico tend to stay in their own zones, or hoods so to speak. We have not been able to get them to interact with each other. But now, there are "your" boys."

He put a strong emphasis on the word yours.

"They eat lunch together. They sit on the wall and laugh together. And we just wanted to know what you are doing to make them get along so well."

I was not doing anything. Running was. All the miles they charted in the hills of Griffith Park or on my mountain made them life comrades. They knew each other. They felt for one another without speaking, and they had each other's backs. Running became an even stronger bond than flesh and blood family. I watched it and am grateful to have shared the transformation this sport gave them.

It is the heart of what I know sports can do. It can cross right over cultures, oblivious to degrees of skin color, languages, or food choices. These boys were having fun. They were working hard but were also encouraged because life was becoming an adventure. I was having fun with them. It was a kind of miracle.

I felt like we were being introduced to all of Los Angeles. Everyone had cousins, friends, classmates, uncles, siblings, and a cute girl from Boyle Heights. She was so cute that my boys had a fist fight over her. We gave and shared as many opportunities as possible. And they shared back. There was Oscar, who won the Los Angeles Marathon for the 18 and underage category and beat the entire SRLA team. There was Dempsey, who hung with them like family though he was from Guatemala. Somehow, he was the one that ended up marrying the cute girl, but when we attended the ceremony, people showed up in jeans and t-shirts. The ceremony was held at a place much like wedding chapels in Las Vegas where you pull your number and have your allotted 30 minutes and an assigned clergy. But this was in downtown Los Angeles. So, I am not sure if weddings were staged because it helped with proper papers. They both started wearing braces and were divorced in less than two years.

There was Juan Luis. He was a gifted soccer player. He found out his girl was pregnant. Juan was one of the few who had an attentive father.

His dad told him it was his duty to raise his own child and take care of his girlfriend. Juan did not want to do that. He wanted to play soccer. I told him the moment he held his own tiny fingers and feet in his arms he would be different forever. I asked if he would wait until that moment his child was born to decide if he wanted to be a dad or not.

"You have a gift to raise, Juan." I could tell he was disappointed about soccer.

He texted me from the hospital within minutes after the delivery. "You were right" was what the first text said. The next was as beautiful as that newborn. "This little guy is the most beautiful thing on earth." I got pictures for years of the progression of his children. He wasn't just a father, he was a proud dad. It was not easy.

Somewhere along the line, Boxer became a part of us. They never used his real name. He was older than the boys but was already leading the way in champion running. He had taught himself off the streets to do so. To me, he was more on his own and off the streets than any of them. He was exceptional. I believe if he had had the opportunity for focused coaching, he would have been Olympic material. He ran a marathon in just over 2 hours, and he was self-trained. Imagine if he had consistent training! He won almost every 5K or 10K he jumped into for decades, wearing only "boxer" shorts, instead of running shorts.

The YMCA taught him to box almost parallel to the life depicted of Rocky Balboa in the original ROCKY movie. Boxer was our Rocky. Boxer was fit because life was hard. He had amazing cardio strength and because life was hard, he had drive. He rarely looked you in the eyes when he spoke. He smiled a lot. He had a soft heart and a knack for getting into trouble. We all liked having Boxer show up at the races. Sometimes, he would show up with stitches and bruises, and they were no longer from Championship boxing matches. He never offered an explanation. He only offered amazing loyalty to our races.

He always did the hardest jobs and ran even harder. He never seemed to have enough money or a job beyond a day laborer. Later he showed up with kids. He had five of them. That was about all we knew about him. What I did know was that he was the only one who would haul timing gear up to the top of Mt. Baldy, over 10,000 feet just to make sure an event was timed. I relied on him.

Lots about their lives and even intermingling with ours was not easy. Things happened to innocent family members back in Mexico. The drug cartel would board up houses and light the structure on fire with the innocent families trapped in them to produce fear in a community. The "Coyotes" would get others to the border and hold them ransom for more money before they were released to cross. They got jumped when they crossed the wrong sides of invisible lines drawn in Los Angeles between Chinatown and various hoods. Their response—"At least we can outrun them."

But you could not outrun bullets. And when I would pick them up from their places scattered around Vermont Ave., they would have me drive my truck by… slowly. I would have to cell phone each of them when I was exactly out front, and they would dash from the apartment building to my vehicle in a zig zag fashion.

Yet they were afraid to go back out to the car and get their belongings in my mountain home for fear a bear might get them. They were afraid of the dark in the mountains. I told them they had a higher chance of taking a bullet than ever having a bear encounter. It seemed that they were afraid of the wrong things. But what did I know?

It was not just hard for them. Life was hard for me. It was far from easy to make ends meet and meet the demands of running a business. Mostly, what was going on was life, whatever color or shade we were. Life, I have learned, does not slice in smooth portions or fair shakes. It has a little bit of a roll of dice in it. So, we must be willing to accept, deal with, and pave our own roads on our journey.

I purposely never split things in equal portions for my own children. If it was a donut. It got torn into two pieces, one larger and one smaller. A split can of soda into two glasses—one a little more than the other. And with eyes closed, they got handed out. No screaming, "He or she got more than me." My hope was they would learn to be okay when moments of their portions of life were a tad smaller than someone else's.

Being prepared for life to be up and down is super helpful. We need to realize there are hard parts of life and a lot of work going on by all kinds of people of all differing circumstances. My childhood was emotional poverty. Yet, I grew up in a rich looking neighborhood that would be considered wealthy. Would I have traded my plush physical conditions for a sense of security and love? In a world of hurt, the best antidote is to never judge others. We need to be living empathy, reaching out and helping. Love is an action. And love can create…miracles.

A miracle was brewing. The Belmont Boys all ended up in colleges, trade schools, and universities. In high school, Ray #1 was so disappointed he had to miss his senior prom because he qualified to go to the State Championships. But he got to fly for the first time, and he won the championship. With this, he was awarded a full ride scholarship to a university. I think he stopped lamenting that he had missed that hot date. He found plenty of others.

His playful personality was well liked. He used it to survive. He said he used to sprint all the way to the high rises in downtown LA and sell candy bars up and down the elevators to the businesspeople in business suits riding them. They bought them, not because they wanted or needed a candy bar. They were endeared by the boy who was working them over with his fun personality. Ray #1 did this in between classes and on his lunch break, sprinting to and from the campus and back in time for the next class. He gave the money to his mother and helped feed his brother.

He shyly asked me if I would drop him off at his university. I was pleased, as a parent, to do so. As we approached the school, I got off an exit early. He pointed out that I was on the wrong road. I told him we had to do something before I could drop him off. I remembered what it felt like for me to show up at a private university with two shopping bags of my belongings, just like the two of his that were now in my backseat.

We went to Walmart, and I wheeled around a shopping cart. I asked him to put in everything he thought he would need to be able to get set up in his first dorm room–sheets, a pillow, a blanket. I added shampoo, snacks, and a shelf microwave. He picked out towels, a little broom, and speakers for his little radio.

Now I was ready to leave him at the dorms. He jumped out of the passenger side, grabbed his one gym bag with his running shoes tied to it and our new items in plastic Walmart bags. I watched him as he started to walk away. He stopped, dropped the bags on the sidewalk and ran back. He stuck his head back in the window.

"Hey, thanks, mom. See ya."

Off to college he went. I still had four left to go! Plus, my own two children. I was as proud of that boy as the day my heart cheered for him on the front line when he ran between the two Kenyans. As he disappeared into his dorm building, I said quietly in my heart, "Go, young man. Go!"

20

Leaving Legacy

Even my mom knew it was time. My grandmother was so wrung out. She rolled her hands together in a constant twisting fashion. She muddled busily through the rental home asking if my mom wanted a picture hung here or the pillows arranged over there. My mom, looking skeletal, was propped on the couch. Her answer for all inquiries was the same—a gentle, "It really doesn't matter."

I had to speak what was obvious. "It is time for us to take her back to the hospital."

My grandma stiffened. She was so stricken. All the emotions she had been discovering were making her feel the reality of the moment. I knew this thick-shelled woman was feeling many of them, maybe, for the first time. To feel this much of a loss, she was learning she had to allow herself to feel this much love.

Can my words do this rapport between mother and daughter justice? A lifetime of struggle was finally finding its rightful bond. I did not think it could ever happen. Yet, I was witnessing a miracle in my own family. It felt like it was as close as you can get to touching God on earth. Some invisible, but very present force that is larger than us was allowing this mom (my hardcore grandma) bond with her daughter despite all the unmet needs of the past.

My grandma started insisting. "Honey, you need to get your things ready to go."

My mom's eyes rolled to mine and latched on with that look of acceptance. I read her message in them. It was the same acceptance she had when the boat sank. She was talking to me. Her eyes were answering. Instructing. Giving me her life lessons. "What could I possibly take with me?" they said. She smiled at me. Love. That was all she could give and take. We—her children, her mom, her grandchildren—all the children of the earth were her treasures. Nature. Light, hues, angles, colors. Those were her treasures. She opened her hands behind my grandma's back and gave me that shrug. What could any of us take in death besides ourselves? This was real.

"Honey, you need to get your things together," my grandma was overly insistent.

My mom finally asked for help to stand. Once up, she motioned me away as she took staggered steps to the bedroom and shut the door. She was in there for a long time. I am sure she needed time away from our perplexity, gawking at her because we were without power to stop her march to death. My grandma kept busying herself with perfectly arranging my mom's new abode which she would never get to live in.

When the door opened, my mom stepped out with a tiny suitcase, the kind you put photo memories or make up in. Not a traveling one, although it had images of travel stickers and faded images of passports on its surface. Just a toy suitcase.

"I have all I can take with me," she stated and patted the suitcase.

We drove her to the hospital in strained silence. I offered to carry my mom's suitcase as the nursing volunteers helped us get her out of the car and into a wheelchair. She shook her head to say no. She clutched the handle and gave me that smile one last time.

"This is all I can take with me." She seemed satisfied with her decision. She patted the side of the little carrying case.

I totally pushed the suitcase out of my mind because in the next few days she deteriorated alarmingly fast. My grandmother stayed in the hospital chair day in and day out. I begged her to go home and rest. She retorted, "Don't rob me of the mothering I denied her. I am staying right here." And she did, giving her decaying daughter's body warm wash cloths and sips of cranberry juice.

It was my daughter's third birthday, and my kids had learned a lot about being patient. Between managing a business and rushing back and forth to tend to my mom's needs, they had been placed on a life-necessity-hold-button. They decided it was time to go to Disneyland and begged to do so. Not that I like theme parks as an adult, but I knew it would be magical for them. It had been for me as a child. So, my husband and I packed the two kids into the car.

Disneyland can be that kind of place. It was for my dad. As a teen, he got his first job there helping run the magic shop. And later, Disneyland would host Police Days. Once a year, anyone who was a Southern California police officer could bring their families to Disneyland. They closed the entire theme park to the public and only sworn officers and their families were inside. We went every year.

My dad built up the anticipation and set the E-Tickets for rides as good incentives for doing chores. He brought out his puppets and did little shows for us so we could get excited. The puppets were his one safe method for him to show love. We relished this treat. And on the morning to go to Disneyland, he wouldn't set an alarm, but would come into our rooms, sit on the edge of our beds, and gently touch our shoulders and whisper. "It's time to go to Disneyland." It held good memories.

Both my children loved the day at Disneyland. We completely forgot about anything else other than being together. My daughter developed an instant love for Mickey Mouse. As we left the park, she begged for Mickey Mouse ears and a lollipop. We picked a large one, a flat swirl of color on a stick almost as big as her face. It was adorable. The photos, which captured the combination of Mickey ears and the lollipop with my daughter's impish smile and sparkling eyes, make me "ahh" every time I get to look at them.

On the way home I asked my daughter why she wasn't licking the prized candy.

"I'm waiting for 'am ma.' We will lick it too-guther."

Oh, yeah. Grandma. I dropped my husband and son off, but my daughter was not going to let me leave for the hospital without her. She had something better than glow worms to share with her grandma.

The wing that served patients fighting leukemia was on the top floor towards the back. I had to walk a long hall past the children's ward. This was where parents had that look you have when you're battling the worst, but desperately seeking hope for the better. Many times, I placed my eyes to the stark pattern on the sterile floor to avoid eye contact with all those hurting parents. Their kids had cancer.

But with my daughter's hand in mine, and her cute Mickey ears and lollipop I couldn't ignore the raw reality. "Live. Get well. All of you." I silently prayed. I squeezed my precious daughter's hand, maybe too tightly. Hold on.

When I got to my mom's room, I stood at the doorway, and my heart went into an instant grip. The bed was empty and already dressed in new linens. My heart honestly skipped a beat. My toddler stopped also. "Where's am ma?"

The nurses explained they had to rush her to ICU. The simple act of taking an aspirin scratched her throat and blood was seeping into her lungs. Her body was so ravaged, it was going to end this way with something unexpected like an infection. Or this. She was now bleeding to death.

The nurses occupied my daughter at their station, and I entered a maze of wires and machines. Blue gowns were whisking about in urgency. My mom had tubes down her throat, but her eyes were open. She blinked when she saw me, and her hand reached out and squeezed mine. Tight. She mouthed a two-syllable word. I knew exactly what it was.

"Carl." My brother. Her son. She wanted to know where Carl was. I had the nurses call him and they said he was out on a fire call. My brother, the child she sat with every day of his kindergarten year to allow his hyperactivity to work itself into a fine young man. The nurses brought a phone. On the other end was my brother's voice. He asked me to read the numbers on all the machines. I had no idea what I was rattling off to him.

He listened and then answered, "I won't make it in time. She will die before I get there."

I knew my mom's death was inevitable, but does anything really prepare you for something you have no ability to reverse? My mom was still mouthing his name.

"Try." I told my brother. It was all I could ask for.

The clock on the wall ticked so slow and so fast at the same time. Is that possible? About a half hour went by and my mom's breathing got very labored. She had the wild look of someone drowning underwater. Then she stopped breathing. I whirled back to the memory of driving her to the doctor's office when her lung collapsed in the car in the parking lot. I stood again, as helpless as before, my back pressed against the ICU's cold concrete wall. The line on the heart monitor went completely straight.

Suddenly, she sat straight up and opened her eyes. She looked at me and mouthed her son's name again. The line on the monitor squiggled all over the place. I talked to her.

"I know, Mom. I know you want to be with him. I know you want to say goodbye to him. I know, Mom. I know how much you love him. I know how much you have done for him. For all of us kids. For all of us. We know, Mom. We know you love us."

She coded again. And again. It was agonizing. She did this many times and each time I said the same thing. I knew my brother wanted to be there. She did so much for us. We loved her. I felt so anguished. "Lord, just let her have that one parting moment."

The swinging doors to the ICU burst open to reveal my brother, all 6 foot 7 of him. Still in his uniform, the shiny badge, his stature, and his dark hair were striking. This man had his mom's features, and this mom cherished the chance to raise him. He had made it. I stepped aside, and he mentioned the captain came out on the call with his personal vehicle and told Carl to use it to get to the hospital to see his mom. My brother was glancing in all directions at all the machines. I knew the numbers had been falling in the tick tock time it took him to drive here. His shoulders rose and slowly dropped as he let out a long sigh.

"Oh, Mom." He put her face in both his hands and tenderly kissed her forehead and her cheek. My mom looked at him and gave him that smile, and she took her last breath and died. The nurses came rushing in and pushed us out so they could perform last ditch measures. We knew this was unnecessary and would be to no avail. She was gone.

I gathered my daughter from the nurses and headed to our home in Lake Arrowhead. I called my son to come from his room where he was drawing pictures. I sat him down on a stool at the kitchen counter. How do you tell your children their grandmother passed away?

"Honey, grandma could not fight cancer anymore. She died today."

John looked at me and said, "I know. She is with God." He went out on the deck and through the window, I saw him kicking the railings. Our two Labrador dogs bounced around him, and he finally sat with his back against the railings, stroking them and putting his arms around the big black dog. He ruffled its ears. I could see he was crying.

I didn't think my three-year-old would understand, but she did. She looked at me and walked to the kitchen garbage can. It took all her weight, but she stepped on the bar and the lid opened. She took off her Mickey ears and, looking straight at me, dropped the hat in the trash. She went upstairs and came back with her lollipop. She stepped on the bar even harder and dropped the unopened, colorful lollipop on top of the hat. She stepped back and let the weight of the lid slam shut. Grandma was gone.

―∞―

Many months after my mom's death, the hospital called and said I needed to come sign out her belongings.

Belongings? She didn't have any. It was a shallow drive. The battle over her cancer, the intense days of raising a family, running a business, and making ends meet all made me numb and void. I felt lost. A little of God left with my mom. I was feeling the rotten feeling of aftermath.

I had to walk that hall of the parents with their cancer patient children once more. I was mad. Mad at life. Mad at God. I was mad at my dad for being the one to get to live on, somewhere with a new life and the means to live richly. The last thing I wanted to do was step foot back in that hospital. Ever.

I was mulling this around when the nurse handed my mom's glasses and that toy suitcase over the counter. I signed for it. The suitcase had no weight to it. Of course, why would it? I knew it would be empty. The fact that it was empty was the weight of her message. She could not take anything with her. Still, when I shook the luggage, I could hear something faintly sliding around inside. I waited until I got to the privacy of my own vehicle to open it. There was a sheet of typing paper folded in half. It was a handwritten note in my mom's penmanship, albeit, with an extra shaky wobble in the script.

"I cannot take anything with me. All I can leave behind are the lines that I have written on the lives of you, my children. In that way, I live on with you. In the marks you make and leave. "

I found a cardboard box when gathering up her household belongings. I thought it would be full of her professional photos. It was not. Oddly, it was cards. An assortment of greeting cards. Some yellowed and older than others. Bright ones that looked new. She had collected them over the years because of the words inside. She must have made a hobby of looking through the greeting card section and picking words that had meaning to her. And she would probably buy the ones that touched her…for her. The words that life never got to tell her in person. Yet, she in person, still spoke them to others.

My mom loved being a grandma. She loved my children. This is the last picture I have before she lost her hair and her battle with cancer.

21

Stuck in Paradise

I peered past the international customs area to scan the people standing in the arrival waiting area. His bronze arms lead to broad shoulders and down a rippled abdomen. He towered in stature as what movie stars are made of. Or what the likeness of a bronze statue should be molded after. His genuine eye contact, soft voice, and welcoming handshake made him the attractive, gentle giant he was. He was easy to spot. He was a young Tahitian who was making his living in his own kind of show business. He was a Tahitian Polynesian dancer in a tourist show on the island of Mor'ea. His name was John. At least that was the name he went by.

He shared that he had left the islands. Once. He had tried dating a female lawyer in New York City. That flight ticket was reversed within weeks as he fled from the wild land of high rises. He rattled on in stories of not knowing how to operate the elevators and getting lost for days in the subway. He said he returned satisfied to forever remain an 'island boy. He loved his French Polynesian Islands.

Behind him, I could see Tavito. He was tattooed from head to toe in the tradition of his ancient ancestors. These are the islands that originated tattoos. He stuck his tongue out at my kids in a playful greeting. Tavito had also visited the United States. The French tour guide wanted him to experience Venice Beach and Santa Monica in California. Or I think he wanted the Americans to be fully awed and to experience him.

Tavito mesmerized those passing by on Venice Beach, California with his real fire dances and was cited by the county for not having a permit to do so. He nodded in unison that life was meant for him, as with John, to be lived out on the French Polynesian Islands. He packed his duffle bag of firesticks and came back to stay. His desire to experience other countries had been satisfied. This is where he, and his fully landscaped body of tattoos FIT best.

Standing in the back and way off to the side, I spotted Tinato. He was another god of the body. He stood in an erect, but relaxed stance that came from his profession. He was a personal bodyguard, qualified to do so by his highest degree in martial arts. He was encased in the disciplined muscles that come with that kind of training. He was positively gorgeous. The health about all of them made me sense island life was not necessarily easy, yet not a bad place to live. They were strong and healthy.

I am not sure if these gentlemen knew each other but there were all at the airport in Papette, Tahiti for the same reason. We were bringing car parts, electrical fixtures, running shoes, and were even pushing through a very large, and very inconspicuous box that cased an Audi automobile windshield. We had items that were impossible to get. Most would have taken months, if they could get them, and would be charged a hefty shipping taxation most islanders could not afford. The French Polynesian Islands are barely dots noticeable on a globe and sit by themselves in the South Pacific Ocean. Getting supplies was tedious. Being governed by the French, that government wants them filtered from France half a world away.

We tried to ask of the welfare of their families as we scurried for the truck that would take us and our timing equipment to the ferry and onto the island of Mor'ea. We were here to race time an inline skate race associated with the Mor'ea Marathon. I already knew the routine. The generator, emptied of its gas and in a hazardous safety container went in the open back of flatbed first. Followed by the boxes of timing gear and luggage. We scrambled atop of it and held on for dear life as the driver in the truck cab darted on all sides of the partially paved road. He didn't want us to miss that ferry and was barely missing the islanders riding scooters with three to four persons on each.

I look back and am glad I had the guts to pester for such a remote timing contract. In the years that we had been able to time this international event, we had bonded with a lot of Tahitians. Their culture and kindness were as easy and breezy as the islands.

I discovered this timing need while working a portion of the LA MARATHON. We were hired to time a trial year that was adding an inline skating race. To their horror, and ours, over two thousand skaters signed up. It turned into a cluster fluster on the course, with people banging into each other like it was a roller derby. To top it off, there was a conglomerate madhouse dash to the finish line. Good thing they had hay bales. We ended up using a backup video camera and had to rewind it many times to watch the top finishers to determine which skate hit the line first. This was pre-RFID chip timing days. While recreational skaters could barely skate upright, the elite racers were barreling around corners at speeds faster than cars could go.

This crash finish of thousands of skaters fully entertained the usually bored spectators who stand waiting hours and hours for the running marathoners to finish. The elite skaters could out-skate the lead police vehicle going around the corners and all this proved to be too much of a liability. It was the first and only year they allowed inline skating at the LA Marathon. Inline skating had a short flash of popularity as a sport in the USA anyway. I think it was that year.

Yet, inline skating remained popular in France and the French Polynesian Islands. A Tahitian excursion and skate race promotion booth was strategically situated right next to where we were handing out all the skate bibs the one year we timed the LA MARATHON skate race. I listened to the travel guide's spill repeatedly as he peddled, handing a brochure to every skater who signed up for our LA based skate race. The skaters, with their helmets, elbow pads, and bright colored shirts did show interest. He was offering an excuse to travel to a tropical destination with the added perk of skating in an organized event. It spelled adventure.

His brochure said it was in conjunction with a half and full running marathon put on by the Tahitian Sports Management Authorities. So, I pestered the gypsy looking, lanky promoter with questions. Since we had to sit at the expo for three days, it was a lot of pestering. Each of his answers sparked desire for this kind of an experience. In the evenings, I researched what these islands were all about. Traveling to and from them would be complicated. I was a business owner searching for the next meaningful event. This was it. I made a verbal offer. Looking back, I probably was the only one so willing and game to go.

The man stuck out his hand and we shook on it. He introduced me to his wife and two small children. All had the look of living out of their car. But needless, I handed him a business card and said we would time the event in exchange for travel and a chance to stay on one of the island for an extra week.

This glib French guy said he could make that happen. And he did. We flew to the French Polynesian Islands for four straight years to time in-line skate races in conjunction with the islander's marathon. It ended up being an awesomely new and exuberant treat, timing an event and getting to meet a culture so untouched and foreign to concrete Los Angeles or our mountain community of Lake Arrowhead. At the time, these islands were hard to get to and frequented with few flights.

For clarification, Americans seem to call all the islands Tahiti, when in fact, Tahiti is only the main island with the capital city of Papeete, the landing spot for international flights. The cluster of all the islands is properly called the French Polynesian Islands. The French still govern the islands. And the Tahitians speak their dialect and French, and only a smattering of English.

The race was held on the island of Mor'ea. But I told the travel agent, we would come if we went on an extension to a different island each year. I parted weeks on my calendar to spend time on Huahine-Iti, Raiatea, Taha'a, not your typical tourist island like Bora, Bora, but ones in which we would be guests of the islanders. There were even atolls, where the center of the island had sunk back in the sea and only a circle of land was left above the ocean.

To us, it was magical to eat tropical fruit right from the trees and snorkel among the sea life. The stingrays liked to be fed like ducks and be petted like dogs. They swarmed around you if they thought you had a morsel to feed them but watch out if they thought your hand might be food. They have a strong vice grip bite that can crush coral. And they can kill with one swack of that poisonous tail. The islanders seemed far from worried. Rays are mainly docile, they assured. Yet, Steve Irwin, a celebrity wildlife host was pierced and killed by one in another part of the world. We coaxed away from the end of their tails and let them feed like a cackle of chickens.

Paddling around in canoes with the Tahitians to see sea life had a true relax to it. It lacked over regulation as we are so accustomed to in the States. They called their own islands paradise, being among the land, sea, and its creatures. I have not had the opportunity to return to see if it is still the case. I hope tourism hasn't made the islands victim to other world issues like lawsuits and such. It was a foreign concept to them.

On a canoe trip to view the reef sharks, I kicked a shard of live coral with my foot. I did not notice it had burst the skin and I was bleeding spurts under the water. Our hopes were to view darting sharks while dog paddling on the surface and holding onto the canoe ballast in shallow water. I felt strong hands gripping my shoulders and pulling me back into the large canoe. The Tahitian guide said my cut was attracting too many sharks. None of us had noticed a mass of moving fins forming from behind the canoe. The Tahitian Guide ordered everyone back into the tippy canoe.

As the snorkelers started frantically pulling themselves out of the water he apologized and proceeded to do something incredulous. He peed on my wound. I was to learn that coral is a living organism and once embedded in the skin it is prone to nasty infection. The pee was an islander's way of hitting the area with something to sterilize it. The foot is a hard appendage to heal. That coral scrape flared up with infections for months thereafter, and it took a lot of direct care with antibiotics and shots to cure. It left a flesh-marbled scar that I am told could have been worse had it not been peed on. I would notice these marbled scars on many young islanders that surfed.

One of the tourists asked if the Tahitian man was afraid we would sue him if we got bit by a shark. The tall Tahitian let out a belly laugh. "If you want to sue, you will have to fly to the Fiji Islands. There is no US Embassy here. And, besides, if God wanted the shark to bite you, the shark will bite you." He chuckled to himself. And told himself out loud, "How can you sue for life just happening." He was astounded at the thought. He kept chuckling as he gripped the water with strong strokes of his paddle and steered us against the current and back toward shore.

The islands were formed by volcanoes. Mor'ea had one big cone shaped, inactive volcano which spread down to the sea. It's top crust of hardened lava was so thin, a hole formed in its crest. It was daring anyone to climb to it and sit in it like the image of the boy sitting on the crescent moon.

When I heard a group was going, I jumped in and joined. Very ill prepared. It got exceptionally smeltery, like in a pottery kiln, once we hiked away from the lush, overhanging vegetation. I used up my water too quickly. There really was not a trail. We bushwhacked and pulled ourselves up vines, using them like climbers would ropes. It took all day to get to the desired destination, but the reward of seeing the entire circumference of the island and all that open ocean around it was worth mud streaked sweat and raw worn hands from scaling hand over hand to get to this highest viewpoint.

We only had one Tahitian with us. I had thought they were tourists with the skate race but now I was not sure. When I pulled out my lunch, they pulled out something to smoke. The Tahitian teen that went along to guide us grabbed my hand and begged me to get off the volcano with him. He was tumbling down, half sliding, half running and would not release my hand. I was obliged to follow like a rag doll bouncing in the wind. He acted like he had seen a ghost. He knew something those rowdy guests did not. Having illegal substances on an island was highly punishable, and he wanted neither this woman that could have been his mom's age, nor him to be associated with these guests' idea of a lunch break.

We finally made it to the bottom and out to the road. I could see that a roughly paved road went all the way around the island when we were summited. I was told it was about 35 miles around the island.

The young Tahitian motioned me to sit down and wait. We were nowhere near the village we started from. And judging by the setting sun's direction, we were on the far opposite side of the island. That is how far this guy wanted to be away from association to any illegal substance.

After about ten minutes he stood up, looked at the sun now lowering on the horizon and said matter of fact-ly in school learned English words, "We… miss… last… bus."

He started walking. I jumped in behind him and tried to keep pace. What's half of thirty-five miles? That is how far we walked back. It took hours into the evening.

Walking in the dark didn't seem to bother him. He must have been doing it by feel, and I by the sound of his sandals. He walked all the way to the entrance to my bungalow hotel and bid me good-bye with a dutiful nod. He never said a word the entire time we walked, but he hummed and in no way was bothered by the time being used up in having to walk around half his island.

No one had noticed that I was not around for dinner. A twinge in that bothered me. But I even know that my energy, if it doesn't come out in my activity, rattles on with empty words that jabber in nervous spurts like volcanic lava globbing down to the sea. They might have been enjoying the peace of paradise without my energy. And, interestingly, I realized I really enjoyed my talk-less walk with the Tahitian kid.

The next day I decided I wanted to see the entire circumference of the island. I decided it would be much faster on a bike. When presented one from the bungalow resort, it was a rusty beach comber with one speed and flat pedals. I knew from Triathlon training that if I had the ability to clip on, I would get the power of the upswing pull in addition to just the down push on the pedals. I found the same Tahitian kid sitting under a palm tree with a few other teens. I asked him if he would kindly duct tape my shoes to the pedals.

This got wide eyed looks and gave them something for instant excitement. They let me prop myself on the bike and hold onto the palm tree and did an overzealous job of lashing me to the bike. They used the entire roll of adhesive tape. I was not going to pull loose of these pedals! They made sure of that, tickled that I was going to attempt this. One boy had reservations. He asked in mostly hand motions if I knew that there would be rain.

I nodded yes. Rain to me was refreshing. In this tropical area it cooled and was joyously salt free. He shrugged. He made a second plea. His hands were dancing like a crab. "What about the crabs?" Crabs didn't bother me. I shrugged back. More out of ignorance. I had no idea why he would be concerned if I knew what a crab was. They pushed me off and ran with me until I was on the outskirts of the village. "Bravo. Hooray," they yelled.

All was going well. Pedal down, pull up. I could get around this entire island in hours. This was when I finally thought of the predicament I had placed myself in. I couldn't stop. If I did, I would fall over. There was no way to un-tape my own feet. I now, MUST circumvent the island successfully without stopping. It would be another hot day I was getting myself into. But I had the frequent squalls I could look forward to. I could see one ahead.

It was delightful to splatter my face with my now wet hair as I traveled though the squall. But, then I saw movement. A lot of movements. They were drinking the fresh water that pooled in the crevices of the asphalt from the squalls. They were surprised to see me as I was to see so many of them. They put up their one long and short arms and stood upright to fight for their right to the paved territory. I knew if I ran over even one of them, I would have a flat tire and an even longer walk back then I had encountered the day before. I dodged them with the intensity of a race car driver missing cones on sharp curves. This repeated scenario happened many times. I no longer relished the rain.

Somehow, I made it all the way around that island without flatting on the spike back of a misfortunate crab. Those same teens were still sitting under the same palm tree…waiting. They ran out to meet me and showered me with more "bravos and hoorays" and helped me to roll to their tree. They were as into unwrapping my feet as a race car crew is in quickly changing the tires of a race vehicle. And they treated me like I had just won the Tour de France. I think these boys were delighted in this woman who would choose to do such random, active, interesting things on their islands. We all fist bumped each other and did not need to know any language other than fun.

I had no idea there was a reason for the grass-thatched roofs on the islands. I thought it was just to make the tourist feel like they were in paradise. Which, by the way, we felt like we were. Our resort accommodations were bungalows. The shutters opened to views of the lagoon. None had glass panes and I loved that we slept and were housed half outside. The geckos chirped as they freely ranged the ceilings in their lizard ability to grip upside down on surfaces.

I wanted everybody on earth to get to experience being in a grass roofed hut looking at the sea. The explanation they gave me for the roof material was it was plentiful and easily replaced when cyclones come through. We had no clue in the 21st Century we could get stuck on an island during a heavy storm or a cyclone… until one hit.

We were at a restaurant in a village savoring the flavor of coconut sauce mixed with island vanilla. They poured it over blackened Mahi-Mahi, caught only hours prior. Just eating this plate for dinner was a reason to celebrate. But we were also proud of ourselves for coming all this way with all this equipment and faithfully providing the support and timing the skate event needed. A couple that was good friends of ours drew the lot to come on this first year's adventure to see if we could remotely time a race. We had left our children behind on this first venture, just to make sure it was doable first.

The Polynesian restaurant owner appeared and started locking up shutters on the windows before we had even finished the meal. He was motioning us to hurry. It seemed early to be closing, but we thought maybe there was a special holiday we did not know about. The owner kept walking out to the beach and looking down the shore, staring out at it for a long time. As if waiting for a long lost someone to show up walking out of the horizon.

We started the mile walk back to our bungalows, bummed that he had not offered us dessert. Luckily, we had remembered a flashlight. Even with the one among us it seemed darker than any other night. A breeze was blowing. Yet not playfully. It had a bully feel to it.

Suddenly, out of the darkness, a blast of wind struck and kept on blowing, harder and harder to the point I could no longer see well because my hair was wildly being whipped around in all directions. Coconuts started dropping from their lofty attachments high up in the palm trees, hitting the ground like bombs. We knew enough that one blow to the head would not have a good outcome. We ran toward the resort with both hands atop our heads dodging the falling whizzes. We were running like army soldiers being fired upon and felt that same parallel. In a few changing moments, we were in a flight to find better cover.

Even before we got to the complex, we could see fronds of the roofs already blowing off. The sky darkened and hurling rain pounded the island. We got to our huts, but only half the roofs were still intact. Rain was pouring in. And, to my dismay, salty water was starting to rise as the full fury of the storm pressed down on the lagoon and flooded the island with two feet of seawater. We draped the mattress over our timing equipment and hoped for the best. The best was our lives were at least not threatened in the soft roofed abode that was quickly losing its ceiling. We were soggy, but safe. We were riding out a cyclone force storm.

In the morning, after the storm finished tearing through, the islanders sloshed around with bundles of wrapped grass fronds to replace the roofs. They, obviously, lived through this often. Thatched reeds if cut, dried, and layered properly are ninety eight percent waterproof. I guess unless it gets too windy. But good thing these lightweight materials fly away in the wind and do not come crashing down, like wood beams would have done. This emergency rated storm was not life threatening, just inconvenient to travelers. All our clothing, luggage, and equipment were soaked. We threw most of it away.

But a larger problem arose—over four hundred foreigners who had traveled to the running and skating event were now stranded. The seas were still furious, and the ferry could not get back to the main island. Our 747 flew away without us.

The Sports Management Authorities asked us to all meet at our resort. They spelled out the reality of the dilemma. Back then, there was only one flight per week to the islands. The next week's flight was already booked with tourists leaving and only 78 seats available. They declared that the only fair way to choose this was to give them to the first people who got to the airport on the main island to exchange their tickets. They explained that then, each week thereafter, with the arrival of the new airplane, they would have to trickle off the stranded travelers from this marathon on the few seats that were available. They also announced all communication was down and would probably be so for the next week. They thanked us for our patience and walked out. A hum of nervous whispers began in the room with no one knowing quite what to do.

We started to talk in low tones ourselves. The other couple was afraid of the consequences of not returning to a new position in a job in time, and we both had family members watching our kids for a limited time. The spouse we awarded the trip to was a police officer. He needed to show up for his first shift at a newly promoted position. My grandparents had been pre-instructed to drop our kids off for school and leave our mountain community, thinking we were flying in that morning. The roof was blown off our schedule.

We were four people from Southern California who left to time a skate race in Tahiti and did not return on an expected flight. It felt incredulous that we could be stranded in the 21st Century, but we were. A neighbor noticed my kids sitting on the school play yard all afternoon after school. He brought them to their home, and the town started making phone calls to find out what could have happened to four people who left for the South Pacific and did not return. We knew this would be quite a domino scene, so we combed the island for any form of communication and finally got a fax machine to send a notice to our local police station.

All the foreigners on the island went into a tizzy, not just us. The islanders watched in astonishment. Our island friends questioned why people were so panicked just because they would have to stay an extra week or so… in paradise? They thought this a blessing. Stay a month, even a year they offered. My husband volunteered to be the last to leave. I told him we could not. We had the 5k bibs and the contract for the entire portion of the 5k for the LA Marathon that year. I knew there would be reputation and financial consequences should we not show.

I felt for the pressures on shoulders of doctors and lawyers among the marathoners and skaters. They had patients and court cases. Everyone had a valid reason that they must get back, except a handful who had travelers' insurance and were on retirement time…and my husband who liked the islanders' clock better than what the USA was on. A clock linked better to nature. Sunrises and sunsets. Time with people. Most the day spent outdoors. Little did we ever expect that the world would have to experience this in a worldwide reaction from a pandemic.

The islanders decided to try and help the situation and brought delicious food, music, and dancing to the lodge lobby with the sky showing through parts of the ripped away thatch. This is how we got to meet and know John and Tavito. They took it upon themselves to take care of the stranded tourists. To them, time was free. To them, time was as plentiful as the coconuts. They were so puzzled and entertained that the outside world was in such a frenzy over losing a week or so of their schedule. Time was the biggest resource they had. And with it, came no worry of being over-packed with commitment. They couldn't believe we were so hungry for time. It was as astonishing to them as the thought of suing one another.

Our Polynesian friends were disappointed we did not want to stay. They finally shared with us a Chinese cargo ship was leaving the next morning and would take passengers aboard their top deck if we wanted to handle the rough seas and get to that flight with the 78 seats. We felt we had no choice. We had a signed contract to fulfill. We had abandoned children. They were sincerely sad to see us go. They quietly snuck us to the tiny commerce port. A handful of others had discovered the unusual ride across the water also. The ship took waves to the bow, a steel giant, as we battled across the open sea to get back to Tahiti. I knew to stay atop the deck and look straight ahead. And hold on.

We were four of the ones that got on those 78 seats. I heard people took flights to various other countries just to find room on flights off the islands. It ended up taking three weeks to get everyone back to their original destinations. We bumped into a few at the LAX International airport. They had flown to New Zealand and then all the way back to LA and were arriving the same time as we did.

This taught me many things. Traveling was best accompanied with patience, flexibility, and an acceptance of Plan B or C or D. I was learning the art of adjustment and finding options. One does not always know what will happen or what to expect. I vowed in the French Polynesian Islands to be one who could handle the unforeseen, and to remember that we place the pressure of time on ourselves. Nature did not necessarily race to get to a finish line at an exact deadline. The Polynesian Islanders already knew that. We runners sometimes do not.

Years after the skate races no longer took place, a French coach brought some Tahitian boys to stay with us. They fit right in with my Belmont boys and people thought they were Hispanic, yet oddly barefooted, smiled constantly, and bore so many tattoos. They had strange gashes on their skin, like the generations that got polio vaccinations that left a damaged mark. More oddly, they slung inline skates over their shoulders and skated down the streets of Santa Monica and Palm Springs and rock climbed with their bare feet in Joshua Tree. They said it was no challenge. The coconut tree that swayed in the wind were. They took to snowboarding like instant athletes, the ski mountain being just one large white wave because they already surf some of the biggest waves in the world. They had all the coral gouges to prove it.

And, as fast as they soaked up these experiences, they faded into a contentment to get back on a flight and return to their islands…and just be island boys. Living in Paradise. It was okay for them. They were not marooned there. They were born to live their lives there. We asked them to take a bicycle and some brake pads for a truck, and some guitar strings as extra luggage. I pictured John, Tavito, and Tinato standing in the outskirts of the small airport lobby, awaiting their arrival and our awareness of the gift it was for them to get these items.

22

I Ran a Good Time.
He Had a Good Time.

Continent 2: Europe—The Paris Marathon

The year after the races were no longer happening in Tahiti, an envelope came in the mail. It was addressed to Mr. and Mrs. Ware from the French travel agent. In it were two complimentary tickets to the Paris Marathon. Also, there was a letter confirming a hotel room for three days, a rental car, and two airline tickets. I stared in disbelief, like someone had just handed me the keys to a red Ferrari. There was a handwritten note scribbled in a combination of part French, part English. It translated to something along these lines. "This is to thank you for thriving on our kind of travel; the kind that is KIND to people. And being willing to accept the islanders and the circumstances of travel. Thank you for being willing to tackle the races in Tahiti. May you flourish."

They say opposites attract. My husband and I approached this gifted marathon in our own different ways. I was still very un-enlightened that I had been raised to be a trophy child. I thought my drive was just a natural part of me. Embedded in me, I always seemed to make something a competition. Somehow, I made this free gift a pursuit with that part of me that was dialed to not settle for anything less than straight A's. I decided this marathon was a thing to conquer with personal best times. I beefed up the mileage. And, in getting ready to go, I implemented a strategic training schedule that I dutifully kept. The discipline and challenge I set for myself made it fun for me.

My husband preferred walking trails with the dog and sipping a cup of coffee. Why aim? His motto was why add more stress to life than life's stress already had? He did things well, but meticulously well, and in due time. He had been in the Vietnam War. That was enough stress for a lifetime. Best to enjoy it with the overdrive and the competition dial turned back to zero. He was not wired to be in this marathon for the training. He knew he could hike more than 25 miles in a day, so what would one more mile mean? I went after the marathon to at least have a course time that would be considered a marathon runner's time. His approach was to just show up at the starting line and let whatever the day became be the experience.

Picture the iconic Paris Marathon start line. It corrals all 35,000 participants underneath the Arc de Triomphe, one of the most famous landmarks in Paris. When the gun went off, an ocean of participant heads started to bob up and down as they filed past all the famous shops of the Champs-Elysees. The year we ran, the start was delayed by twenty minutes. That was no problem for the Europeans. It gave them a chance to take a smoking break.

I could tell who the Americans were in the crowd. We were rubbernecking. We could not believe how many cigarettes were being lit and casually inhaled and exhaled only moments before a marathon. This was during the hard campaign of the United States to refrain from smoking and statistics were being advertised showing what lung damage smoking caused. I, for one, did not expect smoking to be a habit among so many long-distance participants. I was giving other Americans hand signals in the crowd as we made eye contact. They winked back.

Bang. I had been almost too distracted watching everyone chilling with their nicotine to realize the race was moving forward. It had started to rain, and I was still wearing all the rain gear. My heavy, protective pants started the marathon with me. I must have found some way to extract the long pants and upper jacket because all my marathon course photos have both the pant legs and the arms of the jacket tied tightly around my waist. They were so annoying. Slipping. Coming untied. Slapping me in the legs. But I was unwilling to ditch them. They cost too much. There's a reason people start marathons shawled in plastic garbage bags that can be easily discard. Or they remember to bring their secondhand throwaways.

I was right on target for my planned marathon pace, but so was everyone else. It seemed like the majority of whomever ran a marathon were all running at my pace. We were packed, sandwiched in on the cobblestone streets, stumbling and twisting ankles because we could not see ahead of the backs or moving arms beside us. I never lost this crowd, nor did it ever thin out the entire marathon. At my pace, when we came to turn abouts where the fountain or the statues were, we body slammed into each other as the wall of runners in front of us bottlenecked. It was a people traffic jam as the course narrowed into any of these turn abouts.

The water stations were a nightmare of grabbing arms, and slipping on wet, waxed and smashed cups on the cobbles. They had an ample line of tables, but this crowd, the one I had seen smoking, was stopping at the first and last tables and doing what American freeways are famous for, backing up after a car wreck. Many Americans had discovered each other while rubbernecking at the start or hearing someone in the pack speaking English. We seemed to work in one accord. We dove for the middle section of water bottles that seemed less crowded. We did not know the language.

Those middle bottles were not water, but vitamin water. As the miles piled up, so did the toxins from too many nutrients. I read that a few Americans had to be taken off the course by medics because of stomach cramps. It pays to know the products on the course, especially a race that is foreign to you. I smelled like a carrot when I sweated for almost two weeks after running this marathon with a language that was foreign to me.

I did bring my own nutrient bars this time. I wasn't going to repeat my mistake at my first marathon and go hungry, though each would have new things to learn like what happens if you drink too much fortified water. Not quite midway through the race, though many runner's elbows had been jarring me all along, one elbow swing caught my forearm. My dearly clutched Clif bar was sent airborne, flinging behind me. By instinct, I turned around and crouched to pick it up.

Suddenly, I was no longer in France, but felt like I was in Spain in the Running of the Bulls. I got knocked down instantly and trampled by countless feet. Not on purpose. But they could not see me sprawled on the ground. Every single foot crunched down upon me had a verbal reaction of "Pardon" or some explicit in French. I crawled on my belly…ugh… to the curb. It was quite humbling. My Clif bar was visible on the cobblestones in the middle of the street. I left it there and did what any marathoner would do. I got up and ran on and on until I finished.

The Gortex jacket and pants tied at my waist the entire marathon were annoying. I was so spent by the time I kept up my pace to the finish, there was no motivation left to untie the dangles and turn them back into the protective shell of pants and jacket material that would warm my wet and sweaty body. The mylar wrapper they handed me at the finish was so nourishing and necessary that I almost forgot to allow them to drape the PARIS MARATHON finisher medal around my head. The clock's red display numbers testified that I had crossed the line in a personal best (PR) time for me. I had to walk back and ask for a medal before I exited. I still had to find my way back to the hotel room.

I Ran a Good Time. He Had a Good Time.

I accomplished my goal. My heart was full. I knew I needed to find my way back to the little hotel room up the rickety stairs and up to the sixth floor before I could collapse. The tiny room with one bed filling the entire small space so that one had to crawl across it to get to the toilet, now seemed like a heavenly haven. The shower, the size of a closet, seemed glorious. It was the carrot to keep focused on getting back to the rented room.

Where was that stop on the subway again? I had drilled its name into my noggin, but my drained body could not find those brain cells to remember the address. I should have written it on my arm in permanent ink. I ended up on the subway on the very opposite side of Paris, and it took a marathon amount of time to FIND my way back. I heard steps coming up the stairwell as I was sitting on a step halfway to the 6th floor. I was having to rest every flight to even get this far. The head tilted up, and it was my husband. He was whistling to himself and smiling. He pulled me up to my feet and shouldered one of my arms so I could finish the last few switchbacks of stairs, pushed open the door, and let me be the one that flopped on the bed.

"That was fun," he jabbered. "Did you see the Eiffel Tower? And wasn't it nice to be going along the Seine River for all that while? How about all those citizens along the way serving cheese and wine?! What a treat!" He was so pumped with endorphins.

"By the way, I met so and so. And so and so." He, who was predominantly quiet, was chattering away quite excitedly.

He was talking away about the value of his first marathon experience and his medal dangled in excited metronome motion from his neck as he spoke. He hardly looked sweaty. He reminisced aloud about how interesting this marathon made this day. And I was so tired that for once, he got the full stage to talk… uninterrupted.

He shared that he had walked and jogged almost all of it, and most likely was in the last pack to cross the finish line. But did that matter to him? Not in the least. Did he have an amazing, life enhancing experience? You bet he did. I may have gotten a PR and *produced* a good time, but he *had* a good time. Both were awarded the same finisher medal. And both were award winning experiences.

There is more than one way to do many things. There is more than one way to experience a goal, life, something to finish, something to do. There is more than one road that leads to the same place. And ways of doing things have a lot to do with allowing each other to be who each other is. Sometimes, that means we each do it very differently. My husband and I did this marathon in the ways that suited each of us… best. I got a good time, and he had a good time. What a life lesson to allow it to be that way.

Allow the differences. It felt beautiful to let experience be what it needed to be for each other, as uniquely divine individuals that we were. Hard to do sometimes. Differences may feel wrong or annoying. Or feel threatening to our own esteems, challenging our way of doing things. What a mature thing to do, to allow yourself to do it your way, but not force that upon another person. We both had a finisher medal to prove we did it… our way.

23

What Pets, Sports, and Having Children Can Teach You

My husband and I raised our family with two dogs, a black Labrador and a blond Labrador. We named the black Labrador, Tar. He had a long pedigree name after a long line of top breed Labrador dogs from Newfoundland. He was the most handsome black puppy. My son scooped up the bundle of big eyes and nicknamed him Black as Tar. It stuck. This strong headed, stout animal grew to be over 110 lbs. He had a majestic face that resembled a Newfoundland, but his body was true Labrador features.

His fur was so thick that even when a bully Pitbull tried to grab him by the neck, the bites only produced a mouth full of hair. The attacking dog gave up and walked away. Tar, in his fashion was uninterested in returning a fight. Being his own giant in his own right he walked this earth's turf on his own terms. He did not obey anyone. He obliged. Or he outright refused. Gently, yet determinedly. If you were in his way, he would come up and ram you, not aggressively, but purposefully. Move aside, I am coming through was his everyday attitude.

Tar had two outstanding flaws. He did not swim. It is rare for a Labrador to dislike water. From the onset, as a little puppy, he tolerated the shoreline and only dabbled in exploring water to his belly level. We tried to teach him to dog paddle and he resisted like a madman. He spent his life in panicked mode if happenstance put him in liquid out of reach of a bottom.

People would not know this truth about him. Goofing around, teenagers once pushed him off a dock because Tar was dutifully barking at their swimming party, but not joining them. I dove in right after him. I knew he would barely be able to keep his head above the terrified splashes his overreaching attempts at pawing would produce. Which is worse? Trying to save a drowning person or a 110-pound beast? Those unsuspected kids did not fathom a Labrador dog would not be able to swim and gawked at my lifeguard trained rescue as I hauled the dog to shore in an arm grip keeping his nose above the water line.

Tar was a beefy, slow moving, handsome dog. His dependable, consistent character bonded as my son's comrade. They were personality suited. Both quietly intelligent, taking the world in as an observer, offering watchful, sound friendships to humanity. Loyalty was so notably noble in both my son and the dog.

Tar not only hated water he held a disdain to running. 'Why would I want to exert myself?!' was the look he always gave me. Tar learned to trot along dutifully until he reached his done point. This was typically right at the trailhead. He would find a shady spot and sit it out. He figured out that this trail I ran on had loops and that I always came out the same trailhead I entered in on. He would swing his big head at me as if to say, I will just wait here for you. And he would.

My son would have to play every sport in his small private school just so there would be enough kids to form a team. In all three: Cross country, basketball, and baseball, he would tolerate the running portion much like his pet. Dutifully, but it was not his passion. In cross country, he ran so there were enough for a team and so the other guys who felt their sport was running could compete. He was a team player and pushed himself in something he really did not like to do. He thought basketball was a waste of energy. My son found more value in the outdoors, rather than competition. Weightlifting, water sports, hiking and snowboarding were more rewarding. It does not have to be competitive to have enhancement value. Sometimes enjoying the activity for the fun of the activity out experiences beating competition.

I told my son sport was important and that I wanted him to learn from it, but it did not matter which sport. It did not matter if he won. I, of all people, knew the ruinous pressure of being the Trophy Child. It was his choice, I told him, but I wanted him to make a pick and participate in a sport because of the internal opportunity it held in building character. It helps one get to know oneself.

He decided baseball and fencing. There is so much sport options out there, I think there is one that can be FOUND for every unique body and every personality. Not to dominate the heart out of another being, but to learn some of the depths of who one is, who one can become, and build the confidence to be active.

Sports can be a great teacher. If your life does not have a hobby sport in it, add it in. You will thank me. Find yours! Even failure at something or FINDING out you do not like it is a great lesson. Eventually, you will FIND what FITS for you! It adds a freshness that helps make life interesting. Many people got cut off valuing sports in childhood. Maybe by being cut from a team or hearing poorly executed coaching comments. If you gave up at a young age, ignite again. Explore your likes and FIND your enjoyments.

Fencing! Who would have ever known? My son choose fencing. It is an intense sport that finds a spot in the Olympics. On an elementary level, just learning micro movements and being willing to enter in an arena fully uniformed with a sport specific sword was intimidating, at first. But, with practice, it became a known. He worked past fear to accomplishment. There were three forms of fencing: foil, epee, and saber. My son enjoyed learning all three. I benefited in getting to know my son better in time spent driving to practices and competitions.

The sport does not have to be running. In FINDING YOUR FIT, you need to FIND the sport that FITS you. For me, the beautiful one was running. Running is simple. It takes willingness and a pair of shoes. It can be done anywhere. It can be done any time of the day.

So, since Tar was neither a swimmer or runner, we explored breeders and picked Sandy.

He was a thin haired yellow puppy from a breeder in the high desert. In the car bringing him home, he was all over us. Licking, jumping, sniffing, knocking everything over in the car. Tar ignored him. My daughter latched on and tumbled with him in a ball of shrilling glee. There was laughter plus commotion in our home from the day we picked this pup up.

My daughter and Sandy were linked in spirit. My daughter was overjoyed at this Tasmanian devil style of interruption. Sandy was constant entertainment for her, dragging her across gravel on her belly as she tried to keep hold of him lunging on the leash. I learned to like this dog. This dog loved to run. And he was an exceptional swimmer. We could not keep him from running and swimming. If there was water nearby, this dog was in it. He never sauntered to anything. He zipped. He had to run.

The dog had no fear. But he had no impulse control either. He would leap off and out of anything. Cliffs, boats, out the moving car window. And he disregarded that leash. That was something to break loose from, get entangled on bush branches, or wrapped around legs of people he dashed between. A constant chorus of, "Sandy. No, Sandy. Come back, Sandy. Stop, Sandy. Stop. "filled the air. Those of you who had to or are raising a hyperactivity child know that sound. We had a hyperactivity dog. And my daughter was right in chorus with him. Both had equal gumption and guts. Both were out to touch, taste, knock over, and explore the world at an energetic pace.

Hard to keep pace with that! Sandy would dart through the trees, bounding over stumps and boulders, splashing through every puddle or pond. He would run three miles for every one of mine. Good thing I was raising both children and this dog in the mountains of Lake Arrowhead, California. You could not run him on a leash. Even the professional trainer we paid admitted that among all the dogs he worked with this one was a lost cause.

But I loved him. He kept me company on my runs. And I could relate to his "out of the blocks" enthusiasm. He was really an exceptional, agile athlete. He did have at his core, what a good human sprinter possesses... speed. Luckily, Tar knew to nip Sandy hard to keep Sandy from bothering his noble meander demeaner, being the older gentleman of a dog.

The dogs afforded me the opportunity to explore and find all kinds of places to run up in our mountains. I had a favorite one. It was a great looped trail I could let the super charged yellow pup go unleashed. It was almost my own private backwoods. Rarely, did I run across another person. One time, the dogs took off in full pursuit. I am sure they were chasing a bear that was rumored to be occasionally spotted. The crashing in front of them was heavy and loud.

This trail was only a few miles from our home. It weaved through pine trees and fallen leaves on a dirt path that was part of the forest service land. I was always grateful for the accompaniment of the dog brigade. If a mountain lion or coyotes were in the area, I was sure these two would chase them away. They always protected me.

One day I had the two dogs down on the trail that traversed across a dry pond. This is where Tar usually slumped and slept, and I took off with Sandy. Sandy was just over a year old. He was constantly darting in front of my feet. My stride would get interrupted as I tried not to be tripped by his sporadic path. But this day, Tar took off. That was very uncommon. His black body was loping toward the center of the mud cracked basin and in it stood a lone coyote. I was told later that the female plays bait for the pack. You do not hear of coyotes attacking humans. Something in them has warned them to stay clear. But something in them tells them to hunt other beasts. And do so in a pack.

As Tar approached the female, I saw movement in the trees. Lots of slinking shadows running at a slightly faster speed then Tar. They dove in from both sides, coming and into the opening from behind. It was a pack of coyotes. Tar never sensed, scented, or knew they were overtaking him. He was eyeing the lone bait. He never turned around.

The first two brown and grey furs to reach him grabbed his hind legs with their sharp teeth they pulled that huge dog down to the ground. The next two jumped and sank their teeth right into his neck and hind quarters. These predators were skilled at ripping past the fur in one bite and getting to the flesh. I was horrified and incredulous. I had run with these dogs here for a year and never seen a coyote. They were going to kill him, and quickly.

They had him pinned to the ground, and I was running as fast as human legs could take me. The ravenous pack paid no attention to my voiced yells. They were so intent on their mission. They broke into that unnerving cackle you hear when they are going in for a kill. In among that horrendous sound were Tar's surprised yelps. He knew he was in trouble.

But, like superman, superhero, super spider, super something, our yellow puppy blurred right past me like a bullet at rescue speed.

"What's this game? I want to play it! Bet I can beat you at it," the pup seemed to be thinking.

The golden youngster went diving into the pack, nipping back at their legs like they had done to Tar. All of them. All at the same time. Like a ninja warrior, that puppy was seeing how many coyotes he could capture landing bites in a millisecond. Sandy pulled the one on Tar's neck off first. And then went about nipping as many as he could until all the coyotes began backing off. He forced the pack on the retreat. I screamed at the top of my lungs. "SANDY, NO!" as the puppy went chasing them, nipping at their hindquarters right into the woods.

I could see him proving to the wild creatures he could easily keep up with them. Take that. Nip. Nip. He was playing a 'tag, you are it' game with them. My hero was making sure these coyotes were really on their way. Soon, the puppy sprinted out of the forest and back to me. He proceeded to jump all over me. "Did I do good? Well, that was fun. What next, mom?" his wagging tail seemed to be saying.

I tried to brush him away. Tar was not getting up. He was stunned, lying where the coyotes had taken him down. His 110 pounds was too heavy for me to carry. I knew if I left him, that pack might return. I had to coax my injured pet back up the hill and to the car. We took a fast route to the mountain vet, and Tar received some shots and sutures.

We nursed Tar back to health, and I think Sandy proved too much for the coyotes. I never witnessed another pack, or even a coyote, any other time I ran the trails with Sandy the Super dog, or more like Sandy the super, super-hyperactive-Super dog.

Tar and Sandy, my son and daughter, taught me so much about differences, as the Paris Marathon had. There are so many preferences, and interesting ways of choosing to live and navigate life by. It is a beautiful part of our journey to allow differences. Variety makes life color filled. We accepted the difference in our animals. It let us let each other be individually different. Yellow, black, champion, or loyal. Observer. Doer. Taster. Fast. Slow. Even over talker, hyper, vigilante me. Let's all be who we authentically are. It may be somewhat cliché, but it's also a solid truth—one that is harder to do than I think it should be. Envision the freedom and release from so much wasted energy if we all just flourished as ourselves and put that energy into wholehearted living. We would live lives that thrived, not just survived. We would be flourishing, instead of floundering. We would FIT together some puzzle piece so much more fluidly if we accepted, enjoyed, and cherished differences.

―⚏―

My daughter loved expression, testing rules, being in motion and the performing arts. She would go on to be a gifted singer, at ease in conversation, and a very good writer. Of course, I think she is stunningly beautiful. And yet, spunky. As she worked through her undergraduate studies, she signed up for the hard internships. She walked right into Chino Men's State prison and effectively took on inmates and their issues. And, never stopped in her diligence to received higher degrees or required licensing to be a leader in her profession. Proud of her, and my son. And, I saw that, to her, music and the arts were a sport. One she trained for and fully enjoyed.

When my son went off to college, each time he returned, Tar would follow him around with his grey muzzle and his take-it-easy sway. He was still a beautiful, powerful beast, even as he aged. Tar being around made you feel like life was solid. I can say the same about my son. He was handsome, strong, quietly determined, and so easy-going and relaxing to be around. My son impressed me with how much he could bench press. And more so, with the type of character of man he was becoming.

He hoped to pursue being a police officer. To protect and serve our citizens and the innocent rights of innocent people. He enjoyed everything about the great outdoors and moved to Wyoming. I started making it a tradition that mom and son would find a challenging mountain trail to hike on my birthday. That would be his gift to me. Way better than anything bought was time spent together. The most awesome gift ever. Learning about his life and bonding happens better while walking a path than talking on a phone. He strongly, steadily, easily out hikes me to the top these days. The easy flow of conversation and pace of a day with him spent outdoors is like gold inside a treasure chest held in the heart of this mom. These are the moments I get to know my children.

As time took them to adulthood, and time took us through a recession, the business demanded to be operated at a higher volume. I was gone a lot. And our marriage was taking a turn. We had to find a place for Sandy. Googling a Labrador dog rescue placement organization, we knew our dog needed special space and outdoors. This agency said they found the perfect place, a ranch in Temecula that had a water pond. The owner did a sport I did not know existed–Dock Diving. It was introduced in 1997 by Purina Dog Food. Competitions were springing up and measuring how high and how far a dog could jump. I heard in the wind that Sandy went on to be a National Champion Platform Jumper and could out jump the best of the best. Sandy's niche ability rewarded his new owner with a National Champion dog able to excel in a rare stunt, and an actual competitive dog sport.

When my son was told that Tar was struggling with his hips, as many Labradors do, and was going to have to be put down, he said, "No. It is not time yet. I will be the one that tells you when it's time. I will be the one that takes him."

And he did. Picture a young, college-aged man, taking on the strength to let his good friend go. The little black wad of fur he named Tar. The dog that reminded my son that it is okay not to race through life. That to butt it and knock it down occasionally is a good thing to get you to where you need to go. To have kindness, but inner strength. That taking life at a comfortable pace allows a lot of wiser things in, the quieter things of life. My son called me crying. He rarely does that. "It's done, mom. Tar is gone."

What Tar was to him and taught him will never be lost. I pushed the phone to off and cried also. I am glad, son, we got to have this gentle giant in our lives. I am also glad we had a hyper, exuberant wild puppy that ran my trails with me. Neither was better than the other. They were best being who they so naturally were. I feel the same about my children. I thrill in their beautiful differences.

My highest honor and elation in this world has been to have raised the son and daughter God gifted me with. Elation means extreme, exhilarating joy. This does not mean it was easy. It means all the personality, circumstances, and opportunities it allowed for my life, especially my life as a mom, is forever treasured with satisfaction. Whether a black dog or a yellow lab, whether fast or slow, whether expressive or introverted, it is all to be treasured. Variances and variables. Contrast is a beautiful experience, and despite our differences, we can still FIT together. Like puzzle pieces, sometimes our differences are what help us FIND that our odd shape FITS into another's just as odd…shape. And, somehow we FIT together to make a complete and beautiful picture.

24

Only Silhouettes

A book explanation here. I make mention of my children in only selected stories in respect to their adulthood and privacy. This is not to be taken as that they are not massively important to me. I am a mom. I will always be a mom. There will never be grander, more miraculous days in my life than the days my children were born. Tiny fingers, precious toes, temporary gifts from God with whom I took as the most important job of my life—to feed, clothe, guide, direct, and build character in them. How great a call it is to be a mom?! Or a dad?!

I chose to leave them out of my book so they can continue to grow and develop in their own individual ways and be able to write their own life stories. I am so very proud of who they are, on the inside and out.

This is a blog post I wrote after the Australian Outback Marathon.

My children have no idea how deep my hurt is from my own untold childhood. I do not even know its depths. They have no idea the different upbringing they got than me. As floundered as my parenting was, it was with intent, devotion, zeal, and love I tried to give them something I did not get. I am something, maybe my teens think has not been enough. It would be good for me to listen, but also remember there is a natural struggle between personalities at this age. Leave it to a teen to let you know your every flaw.

But I can only hope my provision and motherly tasks for my kids speaks loudly and my blundered attempts at devoted parenting will be felt through their lifetimes despite my self-protection, distance, wonky vibes; and wrongful, needy decisions I have made. I, too, am a work in process. A person in progress.

So, this book, my past, and what I write about in this book is about blundering, impulsive, explorative me. I write in hope that we all FIND A LITTLE BIT OF OURSELVES in all of this. And the permission for it to be a journey.

25

Using Miles to Heal

(The Midnight Sun Marathon, Alaska)

I was running. And running. Deep in thought and deep in the woods. The Midnight Sun Marathon out of Anchorage, Alaska had a route that started at a high school in Anchorage, Alaska. It turned out of town along a path that was part bike path, part dirt. It was pitted with ravines. Ineffective planks had been tossed across creeks to look like we could cross them. The better choice was to scramble down each embankment and trudge through the chilly cascades. A bull moose with a full rack stepped out onto the trail to show how upset he was at the random flow of people running through his part of the woods. It is what we expected. We were in Alaska. It was the summer Solstice, the longest day of the year, and we were running through wild woods.

In mid-June, in a state where a third of its territory is above the Arctic Circle, the sun never sets. It just skirts across the horizon. But this also means that in the heart of winter, the sun never rises. Therefore, Alaskans soak up the sun when they can. And the Midnight Sun Marathon was soaking me with sweat. It was a surprisingly hot day, and yet clouds were billowing. We were midway through the year 2000 and the world had not ended as many had predicted. But it had proven to have its challenges.

I was bemusing myself with the thoughts of my children. We made the long journey into the interior of Alaska and let them stay on the hay farm of the Mennonite family my husband and I had met on our original Alaskan escapade. My daughter had purchased a bonnet and denim dress from Knotts Berry Farm and was in full stage of playing Little House on the Prairie with this pioneer family. My son was disappointed they had no horses. No bother, he figured out how to ride their aging dairy cow.

As I tried to pay attention to the undulating earth beneath my feet, my thoughts were on the image of my son on that cow. He had tied a bunch of grass to a stick and was steering the dutiful cow by dangling the tease of feed in front of its nose. It walked in the direction my son steered by turning the cow's head toward the lure of a bite.

The quiver of children the homestead now housed were silly with excitement at the new entertainment my Southern Californian offspring brought. New kids, with so many interestingly bizarre habits to them. It was mutually interesting for my own children. My kids were not seeing color or race, but the chance to make amazing play out of all this diversity. I knew this was an important opportunity. After all, this was a Mennonite family who had three of their own children and were willing to adopt a child from India, a half black, half white child from the states, and a brother and sister from Romania.

My son's first question was, "What's that?" as he pointed to an ingress hole in the side of one of the boy's calves and then pointed an interrogating finger at the exit hole on the other side. I eavesdropped on the answer.

"Oh, that? We were on restriction to carry the rifle. I fell when we were running to shoot at targets and accidently shot my brother."

My son stood fixated. The Alaskan raised kids delivered those sentences like it was just a normal day in living on this raw land. Standing, talking about a bullet wound was a waste of time. In seconds, all the kids regardless of age, race, or color were in a game of hide-and-seek under the eaves of a barn cover and among hundreds of bales of hay. The bullet wound was healing nicely. The boy with it bounded like a gazelle from wired bushel to bushel.

Thinking about my son was my way of trying to keep my thoughts away from grimacing. Pain was twisting and it was hard to untwine. The intensity of marathon miles inflicts a body. Endurance becomes necessary somewhere along the route. Yet, I was feeling weary of already enduring so much. Marathon running, in fact, running in general, has been described as worthy therapy. It does somehow help. Somehow, for me, it tires the body so the inside can rest with it. Running mixes what life throws at you with your own choice to throw even more at yourself. The grind rewards you with the satisfactory proof that you know you have what it takes. It somehow invigorates at the same time it's depleting. Sounds like an oxymoron, but it's true. It teaches you that you can take more than you think you can. And, that you can rise above and overcome some seemingly insurmountable foes. I was hoping it could bury pain. The kind of pain that I could not bury with dirt.

People in purple singlets occasionally passed me and I sped up and surged past them. With knowing nods, we were bonding in a camaraderie that supported a cause we all seemed involved in too brutally to talk about. This endurance running gave our cause, our pain… action. On the front and backs of the purple tank tops read "Leukemia Team in Training."

I thought the marathon would gift me some release as I had scribbled three letters on my back. MOM. It welled up in double fury. I found it hard to run and cry at the same time. Gasping for the meaning of life itself, I could not hold back the tears. Unfair. I did not want to feel that, but that is what was screaming in shear fist pumps to the heavens. I wanted the physical pain to punish away the heart pain. Both intensified instead of dissipated. I felt it all. It is good to let it feel, and I could think of no other place to grind it out than miles of a grueling marathon.

I had taken the mileage and divided it by 26 miles to come up with exact mile splits so that I would finish under four hours. I felt by creating this magical motivational barrier that the marathon would have a purpose. I had determined that under four hours would classify my effort as reaching an estimable goal. If I could run under a four-hour marathon, I could label myself a distance runner. All my training and experience had rarely been far from a track, and it was about speed, not endurance.

When the neighborhoods started to reappear, I could hear the garbled amplified speaker and a voice announcing each name as it approached the finish line. As I rounded onto the Anchorage High School track and only a few hundred feet to go to the finish arch, the clock flipped to 4:00:00. I stopped in my stride, only 100 feet from the finish and looked at the calculations scrawled on my forearm in disappointment. I was devastated. I had missed going under the four-hour mark. I had kept right on pace. How could this be? I had ignorantly thought a marathon was 26 miles, not 26.2. I finished in 4:00:39 seconds, the time it takes me to jog a 200.

I felt like there were so many things that grabbed me by surprise. So many things I did not seem to know about. I felt small and unprepared. I felt deflated and battle beaten. Of all things, who would have known I would be running with the pain of the name MOM written on my back? I had hoped to leave some sadness out there on that marathon route, but, as many who have had to live past sorrow and loss, the pain passed right with me under the finish banner and followed with me right out of the finish chute.

26

Touching the Void

If you know anything about crevasses, they are feared in the adventure world. Glaciers can melt from the bottom out, leaving chasms so deep, slick, and frozen that if you end up falling into one, it is equated with sure death. It would be an agonizing, slow death where you might incur massive injuries from the fall but end up freezing to death.

Another fearful situation in mountain climbing is punching through or caving off while atop a cornice. A cornice forms, usually on the summit, as snow sticks to it and then shifts over the edge. It gives the false appearance that there is rock underneath when it is really suspended in air. Dangerous and deadly falls can happen on a cornice.

Touching the Void is a book made into a documentary that tells the true story of two climbers who successfully summit a snowy mountain in the Andes. However, they get in trouble as they descend from their climb. One climber punches through the cornice and free falls, crashing into a rock ledge and breaking his leg. In the documentary, the camera zeros in on the face of the other climber. He glares in disbelief. Everyone knows getting a broken leg this high on a mountain is a fatal mistake.

These two climbers are in a grave situation. They must get down. Having someone with a broken leg is surely going to make descending difficult. And to boot, a storm is closing in. The able-bodied climber puts the injured climber on belay and starts rapidly lowering him down. The injured climber can feel the lack of empathy as the rope is let out. He screams out in pain as he is bounced down the snowy slopes, but the other climber is hell bent on getting out of the situation as fast as he can. They make a beeline drop right down the side of the mountain. There is no route, no plan, except to let the rope go in the direction the body is dangling. On it goes. It starts to snow, and they are in a white out condition. They can no longer see each other. Both are getting too cold.

The able-bodied climber whizzes the injured man down like he is a dead body. At the end of each rope length, the injured man has to anchor in, and the able-bodied guy slides and skids down to him, then starts the next rope length of lowering him over and over again. He doesn't take the time to talk or even ask the injured partner how he is doing. They are in a storm. He just wants out, alive. And yet, he is being held by the responsibility of getting this other injured guy out. He resents the situation. You can sense he almost wishes the other climber were dead.

And then it happens. In the white out, the injured climber feels himself sliding faster and faster. He tries to scream to the other climber to stop belaying. His frantic voice is whisked away in the wind. The rope never goes taut and soon the belayed man falls right over a cliff. His body jolts violently when he comes to the end of the rope and is tied to the knot. He is hanging with nothing but air around him, spinning on his sit harness that is clipped to the tied end.

Picture him, arms and legs sprawled backward as the knot on the seat harness is the only thing holding him. He has been lowered over a sheer wall and is swinging wildly in midair, suspended over one hundred feet above the glacier. He finally comes to a hanging stillness, dizzy and out of breath. He starts to drift in a counterclockwise rotation caused by the storm's wind blasts. He slowly drifts in circles for the longest time, as the dead man he most assuredly is going to be.

The rope tugs many times. This is a signal the belaying climber gives to the other climber to anchor in and get off the rope. How could he? He is hanging in midair.

So, here the two climbers are in the worst of ways. The able-bodied climber on the top is being pulled from his perch in tiny tugs, an inch at a time. Eventually, he will either freeze to death in just holding the dangling climber, or he will be pulled from the belay spot he has dug in the snow. In this case, both climbers will careen to the glacier below. Time is ticking toward both dying.

The injured climber doesn't just passively give up. He tries to save himself. He gets out a prusik cord. This is a small cord carried for survival situations. When coiled twice it can grip the larger rope. With two of them, a climber can make foot loops and step on them, inching themselves up a rope in what climbers call Jumaring. Eventually, a climber could arrive back up with the belayer if it all worked out.

The climber bites his gloves off and with frozen, unworking fingers tries painstakingly to do the loops with his teeth. He gets one on and fumbles with his forearms to press the second cord on the rope. His fingers no longer bend and are useless in the cold. The prusik cord is in his teeth. He is squeezing with all his might trying to press that cord close enough to the rope. And then it drops. It twirls out of the scene and his limbs slump back in failure and the inevitable.

My husband and I had summited. We had two great, aspiring kids. We had influenced the inner-city Hispanics, and all were in colleges. We had a successful business with a solid reputation. We worked hard to get to this peak. But we had not planned for the route down. We had not prepped for life after children, for one, nor for clear retirement retention, or to build good margins. We were too busy making our work…work for others.

I still did not know that my decisions were not made for the betterment of myself or my family. My actions were in hopes of keeping everybody pleased or fixed. I tolerated too much, put others' needs ahead of ours, and raced around validating myself to the point that my catch line, "Racing through life", made my husband say it made him want to puke. Rightfully so. The pace my life was spinning would have done that to anyone. I was trained to be the trophy child. I was a sprinter. I could take life at a speed most would never try.

I ran our family, with all the freeze-framed pictures of adventure tacked on the walls of our home, at such a piercing pace. I am a World Champion sprinter! I never even sensed that my own childhood left my adulthood bomb shelled. I didn't see the pits to fall in, and, by possessing zeal and an overabundance of energy, I could merrily go round and round not realizing that the spinning could possibly make others feel dizzy. My husband backed away, disengaged, disconnected, and put his head down. He began to fight his own battles with energy levels and focus while I tried to teach myself to relax and reintroduce play from a wrongful source. It was an unraveling with significant magnitude.

My husband and I spiraled into our situations like a poorly executed descent. We were a marriage, but we were also a business. I didn't even know we were having a recession. I just knew our finances were coming up short, so I took on a full-time job, already having the full-time business. That alone took a toll on a marriage and sent it off route and right across a cornice. But I added another hazard. I walked across a thin crust and punched through with the one thing that was sure to break any marriage. I got entangled in another relationship. It got called an affair. It got used as the reason for a lot of things. It gave others a reason to label and diagnose our injured marriage with a tangible outcome. I broke the bone.

I had, through the course of years of running like a lone soldier, befriended a massage specialist who kept me literally up and running. I was able to perform injury free at a high performance, very demanding level. But the sports therapist was an addict and addicts need to have someone support their habits. I, the boundary-less life navigator who wants to make life better for anybody, got finagled into a very confusing mix of healthy and unhealthy needs being met. I found out too late that I was a sucker, probably labeled with that SUCK word because I got sucked along. And the outcome eventually led to sucking consequences. A good thing to remember. There are rarely any real victims. They are mostly volunteers. And tampering with a relationship that over impacts your own marriage and family is going to get you in a big situation. It becomes too big of a storm to survive.

—⚍—

Our business of timing races was evolving into electronic chip timing. Training people to know these systems and the cost of all these new electronics required us to double the number of timing contracts while I juggled that second full-time position just to pay their wages. An equity line of credit was taken out on the house. And money was missing.

It started out as a trickle, but at the end of a year, there was close to $3,000 a month that did not balance. I couldn't find the culprit or the leak. So very damaging blame and growing mistrust of each other as spouses began. I was accused of lavishly running off to all these world and national meets when I was flying on sport sponsored flights and sleeping on crinkly dorm mattresses at college campuses, spending preciously little. I blamed my husband who I felt didn't respect how hard money was to make. I accused him of not keeping track of his spending. I ridiculed him as using the business as an open ATM. Lack of additional trust destroyed us further. Emotional bullets flew in all directions. Decisions were made and everyone started grabbing what they thought was rightfully theirs. We could no longer see each other. We were in a fierce white out storm and only concerned about our own survival.

I poured out my wailings to someone else who had just gone through this scenario of missing money in a divorce. He helped me comb through my bank accounts for painstaking hours, well into the middle of many nights. We searched computer history. We lined up every expense and revenue. Everything seemed above board. Until his eye spotted a signature on a check. He made a copy of it and blew it up. There was a signature and a faint line atop the signature. Someone was forging my signature on checks.

We scrambled through the check sequences and sure enough, entire boxes of checks were missing. But who? Who would be writing these checks?

We started going backward through the year. The checks started out in small, unnoticeable amounts. $50 here. $100 there. And they increased with boldness. To the tune of $33,000 in one year. The year was 2009. It was a hard recession business year already. Now add embezzlement to it. No wonder I was working two jobs. And in working two jobs I had been too busy to notice.

We tracked the deposits of the check to a bank and had to wait for a police clearance for surveillance on the bank to capture our crook. It shocked me when the sheriff named the red-handed culprit. He was charming, suave. We knew him. We loved him. His humor, his athletic hope to be an Olympic track star someday. I helped him through hard times and supplemented his schooling with this job. I liked his personality so much I told my daughter she should marry someone with that kind of personality. So, to be taken by someone I trusted was a painful blow. Yet wasn't that the kind of blow I had given my own husband? We were battling in freezing conditions. Though our embezzler was caught, the tearing apart of our business and the ripping of trust was like that torn piece of paper, twice over. The damage had already been done. We were ripped to pieces.

This is where my husband and I ended up. He had ahold of an injured person who had broken the marriage. I had him in a position where he determined that he would die if he did not cut me loose. What to do in this kind of situation? It is not an easy decision to cut loose so much that has been tethered together. To let go of 25 years of life bonding, and the kids you raised together…it is a life-or-death decision. How can you decide to let all of that die? But, to cut loose means you are free to live past something you're already too injured to survive.

I put us in counseling. My husband felt I manipulated the counselor and the conversation. Behind closed doors, she was asking me if I was safe. She felt his contempt was high enough that I should stay clear and near protection. I knew him better than that. So, a second counselor was sought. She told me I deserved to fly like an eagle, be the empowered businesswoman I was being held back from. She said my husband was the problem and worthy of leaving. I think she said that to make me feel good because everything was already so broken. It was poor advice and the prusik cord slipped out of my teeth and any sort of rescuing the marriage dropped out of sight.

Decisions about divorce are confusing. And it was confusing counsel. I see so many struggling people end their relationships in divorce at this same midlife point because they are sold the culture song and dance that we should go out and find ourselves. And they believe that the other person they are tethered to could be the reason that they are being held back. I am not so sure if that is good advice. Good advice to me is "look within yourself." Because guess what? You take yourself with you. You are, more than likely, the culprit that is holding your own self under. Other people enhance life more than they get in our way of our self-pursuits. I dropped the prusik cord trying to save a desperate situation. I didn't gather good counsel.

Counseling and getting professional input in your life is valuable and can be the best gift you give yourself. I received other great counsel in my life. And I account the years of summit success in my marriage to the good, guided input and direction of a professional, long-term relationship I had with a great marriage and family counselor. I sought feedback long before I needed it. I went to hear how I wanted my own family to be different from my past. I think it is one of the healthiest things we can do. Seek GOOD counsel. Learn. Grow. Discover. Delve in. But be so cautious of letting go too easily or of the wrong things. Consider the ramifications of such a fall.

Another issue that left us in this death hold in a subzero temperature—lawyers. Since we had a business together, our livelihoods and our home made the stakes of dividing it very heightened. Because it was during a recession and we had been embezzled from, neither of us could afford a suitable lawyer. I think we both picked them from the yellow pages. And the craziness of tit-for-tat, the court dates being postponed, more material and information needing to be accumulated, it started to feel like stall tactics. There was no *Divorce for Dummies* book, nor a clear-cut way to do this. The severing went on for years. And we were frozen in this scene of two climbers holding onto each other because we didn't know how to get out of the bad, injured scene we were in. We were freezing to death.

I had to go to the San Bernardino County building to renew a business permit. Just to be flippant, I asked the guard that was having to search my purse for firearms and pass me through a metal detector to get in the building. "Sir, what do the poor people do when they have to get divorced?" He didn't even look up from his job of pretending to be interested in what was in my purse. "They go to room 502. fifth floor." He pointed to the elevator. So, I went to it and pushed the number five. Room 502 was half full of subdued people looking like they were seated in a doctor's office waiting room. I saw a number counter like they have in ice cream shops. I took my number and waited for it to be called. The guy behind the plexiglass treated me like the number I was.

"Can you check on case number so and so. We have been trying to get divorced."

His answer. "It has come up five times for review in the past two years."

My question. "What does that mean?"

His reply, "It means your lawyers have been collaborating to keep it out of court. It makes them make more money."

There is a stove in backpacking called a Jet Boil. It is valued because it boils water in seconds. That is what my blood did. I went to Jet Boil. I walked into the hall and called my lawyer and fired her. I called my husband and explained to him what had been happening. The 502-counter guide said since all the paperwork had been filled out and properly filed long ago, all we needed to do was come in together and give him our driver's license and sign the final document. And that is what we did.

It was surreal. I was seated, waiting. He arrived. We both heard our number, walked to the window, handed over our identification, signed a paper, and were no longer "until death do us part."

I signed the divorce papers, even though I didn't want to. The grief of the situation was immeasurable. I did not know how to live on. I knew I must fight toward upward mobility, and against all odds. I was totally alone. And it would be up to me, within me, to drag myself toward life. I didn't know why I let go or if I even wanted off the merry-go-round of marriage. I do not believe I did. Marriage is the God given gift of so much bonding, protection, interaction, and life living. It is the place for life learning. It has a protective hedge I think God intended. And it carries with it a reason and purpose to work so hard. I had to muster a new, wholly solo situation. I was left alone, and I was going to have to survive.

No words were exchanged. The hallway ricocheted the sounds of our footsteps, each trying to beat the other to the door. He hit the double doors first. I was right behind him.

Once outside, we were blasted with the full force effects of the Santa Ana winds. These happen when hot air rises in the desert and cold air rushes in to take its place. The wind funnels through a pass between two mountain ranges and torments Southern California. San Bernardino is known to be the blast tunnel as winds come through the pass between the mountains off the high desert. It buffeted me in circles, and my mind flashed to the scene of that injured climber just dangling in the worst of situations imaginable. I was that climber.

In *Touching the Void*, the able-bodied climber finally gets the knife out and cuts the rope. The dangling climber free falls, smashing into snow and ice and disappears deep into a crevasse. Silence. Who could now feel the summit victory in this turn of circumstances? Consequences. Irreversible. Harshest decision. The impact. The "how could you?" The "how could this have happened this way?"

Though the wind was whipping the outside of my body, there was no sound. The world went silent. And though it was an arid wind, my life chilled. We had just cut each other loose. Who cuts the rope of their climbing partner?! Divorce does. I have heard of amiable and congenial divorces. That was not our experience. I was free falling, standing on the sidewalk in front of a San Bernardino County Court Building, touching the void. The business, the kids, the memories and great successes and experiences were falling with me into a deep crevasse. Having the equity of the house used up for current equipment were scrapes and bruises on top of the additional emotional bones broken.

I sustained major injuries to my soul in this fall. I was in the deepest of darkest places and I feared that I could not and would not survive this. When the intense weight of your own body slams down in ice, you wedge into a cold coffin. Was there even a way out of this? FIND a way out, dear Caren. You have had to already survive so much. What purpose on earth did I even have to continue living for?

In the documentary, the impossible happens. The injured climber does not die in the fall. He survives against all odds. At first, he sits waiting for his sure death while fingering the frays of the obviously cut rope, deep in a dark, icy cauldron. But then, instead of climbing up because that was not an option, he courageously goes deeper into the chasm to search and possibly find a way out.

Who would have ever thought that the way out was to go deeper in? That is miraculous. It is a story of tenacity, and grit. And it is the story of how we find our own selves. By going deeper in.

That is where I had to go to get back out into the light. Deeper in to FIND my way to wholeheartedly living with joy and a simple acceptance of myself and life's mysterious bends and flows. I had to hunker in and find the will to dive deep into my own self and create my own passion to spur that will to survive.

The climber in the movie attributes his own cockiness to his reason for surviving. He just determined not to die. I decided my stronger comeback strength would be to include God in my purpose and to look for true friends and mentors to help me live again. I knew I needed to FIND a way to accomplish a real way to help others. We all need that spark. That reason. A purpose. Something deep in us that gives us the will to rescue ourselves and to get ourselves on to better living.

In the climbing scenario, the able climber digs a snow cave and hunkers into his survival bag to live through the storm. I watched the back of my husband round the corner in a race to get away from me. It would be the last time I saw him for a long time. What was I going to do?

Oddly, I determined I would finish the 7 continent marathons I had started to do. That I would finish my oath to myself to see if I could earn a World Championship medal. Not to prove anything to anyone else. To do it for myself. To finish the climb I had started, I would make myself climb another mountain. Just because this climb had not turned out anything like I had expected didn't mean I wasn't a climber. But first, I had to survive this fall.

Once the injured climber gets himself out of the crevasse, you would think the story ends there. But it doesn't. He ends up finding himself on the far side of the glacier. He must drag his broken body across its entirety with no water. Once he accomplishes days of crawling and miraculously ends up back at the basecamp, he is met with shear surprise by the other climber, who knew with almost certainty that his climbing partner had died.

Now flurries a new situation. The climber that had been belaying was loading up to leave and had already burned all his buddy's belongings because he couldn't carry them out. What does it feel like to have everything you own burned? And to be given up on before you really died? The level for needed forgiveness in this real story is acute. This is also true of divorce. It took years for the climbers to reconcile and more years—almost a decade—for my divorce to even find tiny finger holds and foot placements of forgiveness.

I did not realize my journey from divorce to completing the 7 continent marathons would be equivalent to a crawl across a glacier with the injuries I was dragging with me. I had already determined that my quest to do remote marathons on each continent with indigenous people and their stories would be funded, not by my established business, but by money I earned the hard-working way. Delivering packages for UPS at Christmas time. Coaching high school track teams. Getting cast as extras in commercials. Working at a coffee roasters shop making sandwiches.

My journey to run those last marathons, compete on all 7 continents, and stand on a World Competition podium would require endurance, setbacks, some pain, yet many grand joys. Finding a stream of melting water to quench a much needed thirst or finding a stick to help walk and prop up a broken leg would be required of me. It is about overcoming and using the only things you have. Mainly, yourself.

So, when you read the remaining chapters know this…that I had not only touched the void, but I was also taking the VOID with me. Life has its extreme survival moments, but there are a range of summits out there to master. And that is what FINIDING FIT is all about. It is hunkering into a will to make it…happen. Make your life survive to be able to thrive.

I had already signed up for the Outback Marathon in Australia and was corresponding with a man in the Galapagos Islands who hosted a marathon. How remote? Sometimes survival comes in FINDING a way to fill the void with something that wills a will. Sometimes you need to get lost, in order to be found.

27

Can the Earth be Orange?
Continent 3: Australia—The Outback Marathon

The earth was orange. Their dark skin and light clothing shimmered. It etched beauty with the brush and this effervescent sand. So vast was the landscape, the Australian outback likened to the open sea. There was one lone rock formation on the entire horizon known as Uluru or Ayers Rock. The land looked like an entire ocean with only one cargo ship. A circle of women came to squat, then slowly roll to a sitting position on the sand. They circled in a private enclosure of tribal unity. They were conversing in a click, clutch type of dialect.

The men had gone into the shanty with the sign STORE etched by hand on the eave. I started to walk toward the women. My teenage daughter and my college age son were horrified. I ignored their whispered pleas.

"Mom…noooo!" I left them on the path.

The enclosed women ignored my presence until I approached close enough to cast my shadow in their midst. This made them jump into practiced reaction. They scooted closer. In a deliberate act to communicate that I was not welcome, they shifted in movement to have all their backs turned to me. My shadow fell far past them and stood in sight beyond their backs. It didn't move. They didn't move. It was as if we were in a western showdown, hands on guns at the ready. I heard another faint whispered plea from my children on the trail. "Ahh. Mooommm?" I knew what they were trying to tell me. Just leave this circumstance and situation alone. I couldn't. My own mom wouldn't let me.

We were outside of Alice Springs, Australia in the Outback. I was awaiting the start day of the Outback Marathon. These ladies were Aborigines. When my shadow remained and would not leave, the one lady with grey gracefully weaved in her hair sent me a look over her shoulder. It was a look that had developed over the years. It was trying to protect their culture, family, and some thimble full of self-esteem and worth. I am sure they wanted the look to throw a punch. They wanted it to voice how much harm gawky tourists were to them as pure people trying to live on this earth as they had been born to. I knew what to do.

I uncrumpled a folded postcard and saw my kids out of the corner of my eye. They had thrown their hands in the air and wandered further down the trail to pretend they did not know me. I moved slowly and reached over the black hair heads opposing me. I let go and let the postcard flutter down on the earth in front on them. A very awkward amount of time did go by. Finally, the woman who dared to bullet me with a "go away" glare picked up the postcard and rolled it from front to back.

She pointed to the picture on it with my pod of Hispanic youth and myself, all in the same shirts which showed them we were obviously from some form of the same tribe. I sat down as the fifth body in the row on the ground and crossed my legs. All the women were leaning down the row staring at me. Now the women were cluck clicking and pointing at the picture of dark skin and at myself, the light skin. And they were pointing at me.

"My children." I pounded on my chest. "I helped get them clothes, food, shoes, and jobs. They are all in college now." I wasn't sure if they understood. I added, "I miss them. But I am so proud of what they are doing. And who they are becoming." I told them I also had two of my own. I pointed to the two patient beings who had now positioned themselves on the crest of a hill, waiting for what they had grown to know their mom just did. I talked to everybody…everybody. There is no beautiful reason not to.

I am not sure how much English they understood. I think a lot. And, again, I believe the language of love is God designed and universal. I hope they were hearing my words. I pointed to them and waved. "Hello, moms. It is nice to meet you. "I knew not to reach out my hand, but as I got up, I patted each of theirs. They seemed stumped but tickled. One was looking at the store building nervously, and I knew that my being in their presence might cause tension with the roles they filled with the men inside. My time with them was up. I winked at them and walked away.

I have no idea if that helps or hurts, but I am willing to be bold enough to at least try. Try and step over lines that somehow, we the world's human beings, have drawn in the sand. I FIND in doing this I meet interesting and incredible lives.

DNA study has found evidence that Aboriginal Australians are the world's oldest civilization. Aborigine comes from the Latin words ab, meaning from, and origine, meaning origin. This name given to them denotes that these people have been here from the beginning of time. There should be respect shown for coming from that kind of lineage. Instead, we tend to shy away from the awkwardness of such a difference…and gawk. Instead, I choose to be in awe.

We walked back to the town, my kids and I talking about all the interesting lives that we were connected to because we were bold enough to step over lines drawn in the sand. We reminisced about the Quechuas high in the Andes. And the antics of the Tahitian boys who had never been off their islands when they got to experience a flight and time in California. I had almost forgotten about all the Japanese exchange students my kids' childhood were filled with. And, we had the inner-city boys to call our brothers and sons. What more was out there? A world full, I reminded them.

At the starting line of the marathon, a native was playing the didgeridoo. This long wooden tube is made from a tree trunk hollowed out by termites. When blown like a trumpet, sounds are made with vocal cords. It is a sound that waffles in my heart like the wooden flute sounds of the Peruvian Andes and the Quechuas.

Finding Fit

When the announcement was made to start running the marathon distance across the orange, soft sand and among the stringy brush, the Aborigines did not run with us. As I headed into the Outback, I looked back to see the group, probably paid to entertain us, walking back toward their village huts. They were most likely shaking their heads in disbelief that these crazy westerners would pay so much investment of time and money just to come all the way there and run in the sand.

This red rock sand and brush has the colloquial name, The Outback. It spans the vast interior of Australia, covering 5.6 million km of land. That is over seventy percent of Australia. It is so arid; it is barely inhabited. And those that have chosen to call it home are as gnarly as the tenacious shrub that somehow grow here. Some ranch. Some just seem to be hanging and baking in the sun. The marathoners were being eyed with suspicion as we milled in that small town of Alice Springs. We were as peculiar a species to them, as their accents and rough cowboy ways were to us. Why would anyone come here to RUN?! That was the eyeing look they were giving us.

As I fumbled with each step forward in that sandy sea of orange softness, I started thinking the same thing. What makes a marathoner possibly be motivated to even traverse 26.2 miles anywhere, let alone here? It's a long, boding way when running on foot, propelled by nothing more than the muscles you have trained and your own will and motivation. But to do so in the Outback would take something out of my back. Finding and refining that will was enough reason for me to be here. Seeing how remote, remote could be, was another reason. I gathered all the others felt the same. We willed on.

There were few enough of us willing to tackle a marathon in the Outback. Soon, we were spread out and dealing with our own thoughts and reasons for running. But marathoners seem to link as comrades. If one was doing it, we willed all would finish. Luckily, the organizers chose the winter months to run us across this expanse. In the summer, things are so arid the flies take advantage of any liquid and land on your skin and carpet you as they lap up your sweat as a water source. We were running at a cool month for this desert.

Your mind wanders when exhausted. I was stuck on a thought. Why do they call this earth red, when it looks so orange, especially when the sun stays directly overhead morning to night? Since I was left to my own thoughts this question with no answer kept popping up. I also had another question popping up. Right before I had headed to the starting line, I had used the lobby's very weak Wi-Fi and sent off a few emails. I checked the business bank accounts. It was blinking a very RED (not orange) warning sign that the account was overdrawn. When I clicked on the red alert button, it was overdrawn by thousands of dollars. The fear and knowledge that something in-house was, and had been, draining our accounts was now obvious. I was not there to tamper with them. Someone else was. I felt this red of a realization the entire time I was running the marathon.

We ran past that sandstone formation called Uluru by the indigenous and Ayers Rock by the tourist maps. The land is so flat this earthen monument looms in view no matter how many miles we ran in the soft sand, giving all of us the sinking sand feeling we were not going anywhere. I felt like we were on a never-ending treadmill of bush and dirt. Yet, somehow, with enough mojo to keep my head down and do it, I ended up at the tacked-up finish banner. When it came in view, my two kids were there, even more patiently waiting for me to finish than when I personally greeted the Aboriginal women.

Didgeridoos were playing. The Aborigines had decided to come hang out at the finish. My kids were patting me on the back. I staggered and almost collapsed. Their faces went from congratulations to looking very alarmed. I didn't realize how dehydrating these hours in an arid land, though winter, had been on me. I am not a natural long-distance runner. My body was more trained to run in bursts of speed around a track. I did not realize how much those miles had taken until I stopped. I felt woozy.

I was hoping this marathon experience would help us be okay with being that torn piece of paper as a family. The one I tried to tape back together to demonstrate to my children what was happening in our home. My kids were giving me the best they could as a sense of support. But I think we all felt like life was getting arid and sapping us into dehydration quicker than we knew how to replenish. We were all staggering. That was the only continent marathon I got to celebrate with my children. They were at that age of college pursuits and starting up their own lives. This led me into living life now as a solo female…which seemed as parched as the Outback was. I would have to muster up a new notch of mojo and, again, use that self-will to will to live and breathe and FIND a new purpose. Doing life alone. It would not be easy. It was not easy.

The stars shone that night as if in a canopy of celebration. The marathoners sat at round tables with linens under the open sky. We toasted champagne to the fact that we were gnarly enough to come all this way and do this thing called a marathon. We toasted to each other's will. And to the beauty of the Outback in shear vastness. We raised our glasses to how hard it really was to run on this sandy, dismal remoteness. I believe each of us was taking inventory that we had what it takes because this kind of marathon took what it had. Marathons teach that hard things can be tackled. Even an overly large, oven baked, arid expanse called the Outback is doable. Even death and divorce. Abuse and neglect. Harm and healing. It can all be tackled with will and fortitude.

I lifted my bubbling glass which I held for celebration and toasted to the stars. I set it down on a side table. Somehow my life was chore enough. I knew to keep it sober. Masking it with a vice would have added another mountain to climb. I am so grateful I didn't have addiction added to my challenges.

So here I was with three continents down. I had run North American marathons in Los Angeles, New York, and Alaska. My Paris Marathon covered the European continent. Australia just finished. The Galapagos Islands would be my next one. I checked to make sure it was considered part of South America. So, how in the world did I end up in Japan?

28

The One that Didn't Count
Continent 4: Asia: The Tokyo Marathon

Who would have ever known how long of a journey it would end up being running my sought after, remotely located marathons on every continent? I did not get to jump on a plane, land at these amazingly remote locations, run the marathon, come home, and hop on another airline and do it over again. A lot of life had to happen in between. Remember, I was making myself earn these marathon trips with money that came from extra jobs and contracts. It was "above and beyond income" like when I was a kid and pulled weeds for our neighbors.

I took on a head coaching position for a high school track team. I photographed weddings. I was an extra in a few commercials. I did get a lead contract in a few photo shoots. The neck they put necklaces on for a jewelry catalog was one of them. Not much fame in that! But here is why I did it this way.

I watched all the cultures I had already RUN into having to work hard, wait, or possibly never get an opportunity to pay for a travel dream. I wanted to value what it took to get to each of these places. Value buying an experience more than a thing. Value purchasing something to do rather than something to buy. Value the people I hoped to meet. It would take a piggy bank kind of approach to accumulate enough money and it would take a lot of patience. I pre decided I should not go on a marathon excursion until the amount was earned and margins were in place to pay for the trip and living expenses when I got back.

So, think, how proud I was of myself when my 'self' earned a travel fund full enough for not just one, but two continent marathons. I was able to prepay for the Galapagos Islands Marathon, but that was not until May. All it took was someone to say, "Hey, want to join us? We are going to run the Tokyo Marathon." And I was all in, sending in the registration, booking a hotel, and buying the airline ticket in a day.

I hastily filled out the entry application. It was required to be couriered and signature signed upon delivery via Fed Ex or some shipping company. I folded the tracking number and slid it into my wallet. I had Expedia find me a flight and hotel…and within a few days, I was flying over the date line. This was to be my Asian Continent marathon. It was almost like gobbling your food too fast. My momentum to drop everything and rush to this marathon had gluttony mucking all around it. I was about to be halted in my haste. Here's an adaptation of the events from some of my Caren. Ware WordPress blog jots from the Tokyo Marathon written in February 2012.

So, I am here in Japan dealing with virtual reality. I am a day ahead of myself. And minutes behind in life. I have just been told my entrance to the marathon arrived 5 hours after the deadline. I am not sure what that means.

I just was told I was not on the registration list to run the Tokyo Marathon. I am standing in the Expo lobby with 30,000 expectant runners, and my name is the only one not on the list. A hand reaches out and hands me an envelope while the head to it never looks up. I hear, in very staccato and practiced English. "Next. In. Line." The packet says, "No entry".

Talk about queues. I am about to be one of those runners that will try and beg myself back into the system. I don't think I have ever been on the registration problem side of the fence. As I am not advancing very quickly in my new line under the solutions sign, I thumbed through the papers in the envelope I got handed. It was just pages and pages of instructions. I admired how organized this marathon was. Get this. Your marathon package tells you when to get up, what to eat, how to stretch, what to pre think about how many minutes prior to the race start…good vibe, positive thoughts, but it also said in bold ink, "If your registration was received after the deadline, it was not accepted."

When I finally got to the front of the solutions sign, I bantered like Americans do with the officials. I gave them a long barrage of information and pleas. They returned with facts. My entry for the marathon arrived at their office on a Japanese holiday and was postmarked a day later….one day too late. This marathon is also the Japanese Olympic trails. Therefore, it is governed strictly by the Japanese military, which governs strictly. What was staring at me, matter of factly, was the Japanese military police. And, they were saying, "You are not on the list."

The answer they unanimously gave me was NO EXCEPTIONS. 335,000 Japanese applied to run this race and only 30,000 were able to be accepted. The marathon committee allows an additional 3,000 entries for internationals. I continued with the American thing as we do not give up easily. I explained my missing entry to every official I could find. Each led me to yet the next higher official and the answer was the same. Your name is not on the list, they all said without feeling. This is how so many people can abide in such a small space. The pressure to have their name on a list for a college, a career, a haircut must be phenomenal.

"NEXT. IN. LINE." There were no more lines to stand in.

I left the buzz of excitement in the Expo and took the busiest route back to the hotel. I returned to my tiny cubicle of allotted space they called a hotel room… contemplating. I finally had time to read a newsletter from the family in the Galapagos Islands. It rambled on as an easy breeze, a life without a pace. Island time. I longed to be out of my current dilemma but knew I had so much to experience by being gutsy enough to come.

Tokyo has the busiest intersection in the world, Shibuya Crossing, which means scramble. I had just witnessed what appeared to be zillions of people crossing in all directions when the lights change. I had stuffed myself into a subway train during rush hour, just to experience it. I think someone with a broom handle with foam on the end had the job of pressing us in even further. I was glad to be hiding in this closet of a space they called a hotel room to try and recoup from all that. And figure out what I was going to do.

The phone rang and I was asked to join a group of marathoners for a lunch and a tour. While waiting in the lobby, I spotted an office center with a color copy machine. English speaking marathoners were arriving back from the expo and had their race bibs and colorful custom chips to affix to their shoes in hand. They almost all thought the same thing as I was retelling the story of not being on the list of registrants.

I followed all eyes to the color copier. Without even talking it out, one was putting their number under the lid and pressing the button. The other took a *pair of scissors and some scotch tape. The two cut and pasted a new sequence of a runner's bib number and put it back under the lid with a crafty smile. Color photos of the chip were taken and pasted to a small piece of cardboard we cut to the same size and thickness of the chip that would be affixed to the shoe. And, before the tour van arrived, I was a bootlegged bib number 1823. The justification. "Just run along the same route and run the same distance. Don't take a medal. Dive off the course right before the finish. And you will get to be a legitimate marathoner and, at least, will have a legitimate marathon experience. You are already here. You have to."*

The Japanese tour guides asked us to take off our shoes, sit on pillows behind a low table, relax, and enjoy a meal with them. I was chewing slowly. And not sure I could swallow either one. Not doing the marathon at all. Or doing it with a fake bib.

This was my first day ever in Japan. It had been overwhelming to be in a sea of structures. So well designed, was the view of retrofitted concrete and steel buildings, yet miles and miles of them. Over 10 million people were working and living in them. That over-boggled my mind. I was puny in this forest of engineering. I am glad there was a tour guide and a tour vehicle to take me further than just walking the busiest intersections and subways. It could get disorienting and be, for me, easy to get lost in.

The skinny tourist van slimmed into parking places that latched up and imprisoned the belly of the vehicle until the electronic meter was paid to leave. Slick. Slick also were the vending machines that popped out hot coffee and warm soup. There were orderly lined bicycles with their baskets. The traffic was not obtrusive because everyone and everything is somehow…orderly. Very few drove vehicles. Most took the subway.

Noticeable was the fact there was no trash, nor a sense of crime. Just a hoard of well-mannered, groomed people squishing past each other on their way to something that must be very important. Our Japanese host laughed a lot and did an excellent job translating in English. He communicated well

The One that Didn't Count

with his choice words. He said he worked for a company that catered to the Golfing industry. He was interested in what new products were emerging from the running craze, because, he shared, "What sets trends in Japan becomes the fashion for the world. I was surprised to find Japan was the influencer for colors, molds, and fashions for so many things, including running shoes.

Our guide takes us to a traditional part of Tokyo with a temple. We lunch in a view of the ancient wood pagoda. We sit on pillows, cross legged, enjoying rice and deep-fried tempura, but mainly their hospitable and friendly company. I tell them my son likes Japanese Anime art and video games and they take us on a train to a section pulsing with electronics and a feel of Time Square in New York. This area is known as Akihabara. This seems like a birthplace for video games. We returned over Rainbow Bridge at night. The view of lights and shaped geometry over the water was eerily moving. Like a sunset casting color on a mountain lake...but not.

A marathon, to me, is the way to see a city. When would you otherwise be afforded the privilege to run down the middle of the street past shops, temples, towers, and the 10,000,000 people that live here...traffic free? One gets to take in more of a city than any double decker bus tour, for sure. I leave feeling like I got to high five a major metropolitan area. It felt as if all of Tokyo was out on this 26.2 mile route. I guess I decided to run the marathon. Bandit bib and all.

It intrigued me that the Japanese love costumes on marathon day. The runners came in all creative themes...men in business suits with briefcases with their bibs pinned on front. I saw Santa with a helium balloon sack of gifts and even an Elvis Presley impersonator. The spectators clowned even more. The entire 26.2 miles was lined with people who were equally as adored and creative and sincere into cheering us on. I think I even saw someone dressed up like the Statue of Liberty. And rocket ships. And the Sun and the Moon.

The day prior to the marathon, a 'Friendship Fun Run" was staged to welcome the foreigners. I was at least on that list. It gave school age children a chance to greet us. The day was wet and cold. Rain and bitter wind shrouded

Tokyo. I went to the hotel lobby and …heard an exuberant group of pre marathoners willing to spite the weather. Most of the "noise" was coming from one person, a man from Singapore. He was tooting on a whistle as he snatched everyone's names, some instant information about them, and introduced everyone to everyone…creating an instant family in his whirlwind. There were some from the Hawaiian Islands. A group from Russia. Singaporeans. Americans and more. Mohan was a character on purpose. He must have as many friends around the world as there are people.

He shared with me that he had tried to be an ultra-runner. One serious race he was unable to finish and had to be shamefully driven back in the sag car. Since he was unable to finish, he decided to change the mood and went to the finish line and cheered in every last runner. He said the 'cheer' that cheering gave him flooded him with more energy that he could ever muster personally through hard core training. Since then, he has been all about meeting people and energizing them to have fun and fulfill their goal to just finish a marathon.

When asked how fast he runs a marathon? His answer is 'As long as it takes to help someone along the way get to the finish. I saw him the first few miles of the marathon running up and down, back, and forth, among the runners, and the spectators, tooting his whistle, and everyone was laughing. He was contagious. I was enthralled by the effect his non-competitiveness actions had on people. It was like sprinkling magic dust that was making people remember to enjoy themselves.

As the miles wore on, though, so did I. I started to wear out. I survived by the beat of my iPod. Music is too rare in my life, so I reveled with the concert in my ears. But I kept the sound down so I could hear the cheering and be aware of the runners around me. I was surprised how thankful for the company of the iPod. When a marathon starts to demand a toll, it can get very lonely even among so many people. It can become a quiet, self-fight that turns inward.

It seemed to be that the Japanese are a quiet people that say very little unless prompted. The marathon seemed an exception that gave some Japanese spectators an excuse for fun, noisily motioning us on. But the runners seemed deeply into their quests and themselves. Especially at the start. We stood in formation for nearly a half hour and no one, except the foreigners, were talking. The Japanese stood in respect; each giving the next person just the right amount of room to fit properly into each start corral. It seemed too formal.

I had sat down cross-legged on the pavement right in the middle of the thousands. This became a meditational position of examining running shoes that were as varied as the number of people. Yet not one shoe was moving. No stretching. No stomping feet. No jumping up and down. They just stood in place, quietly waiting for the prompt to start forward.

When the cannons finally went off and my corral's turn came to move forward it was 14 minutes into the start. Everyone did so politely. No pushing and shoving. Not one properly positioned person bumped into the next. The system was so efficient it lacked personality, but somehow had character in the way of respect. I wasn't sure what I felt. I started to feel guilty that I had a fake bib number neatly pinned, partially hidden, behind my running jacket. I was shifting my weight from foot to foot.

26.2 miles is a long way no matter the opportunity to tour a city and its people. I fell into survival mode about the 32K mark and dug deeply into my survival shuffle and the iPod. I was impressed by the water stations. The Japanese runners were politely bowing as the cup was handed to them. They stopped, sipped, folded the wrappers of their snack breads, folded the paper water cup, and placed them in the trash bins. Then began running again. I had never seen this courtesy out of marathoners.

A marathon is a race. In most the world, people grab the cups, splashing half the contents on themselves, making the ground slick with all the squeezed and discarded waxed paper cups thrown down atop the water spills. It's almost part of the marathon's atmosphere, running past volunteers pushing big brooms and rakes to pick them all up. But here, trash etiquette was part of the culture and in doing the marathon…properly.

Though I was so enthralled by witnessing how a marathon in Japan ran, I was having a hard time with the mileage. I felt irritated and squished in with a crowd that didn't seem bothered by it being so squished. And then I remembered Mohan. I was watching the people and sights along the way but doing so from the center divider lane. I was with all these people trying to stay away from them. How does that work? I was missing a great opportunity.

I moved to the curb and stuck my hand out. The spectators roared. And a line of hands playfully slapped back. The hand owners giggled as I slapped each one of them, especially the little kids who had politely stood on the sidelines all morning. The spectators down the row anticipated my arrival and created individualistic cheers and handshakes. Miles went by, and I hardly noticed the cramping in my shins, screaming in my cement pounded arches, and the knot in my glute. I ran Mohan style.

A larger crescendo of cheering told me I was close to the finish line. I dove out at the 26.05 mile and stepped right into the crowd lining the street. No one noticed. But it was the oddest, most anti-climactic way to end a marathon distance. I pushed through throngs of spectators like it was an above ground subway and ended up back at the hotel room to shower in the smaller closet of my closet space. My fake paper bib number had partially disintegrated from my sweat. I looked at it in the mirror.

How many have had that feeling of grave disappointment in not being able to officially finish something you started? Did this entire marathon effort even count? It had that low lying fog I felt about my dissolved marriage. How did I not get to that finish line…officially?

—⁂—

A girlfriend and I took to the outskirts of Tokyo for a few days recovery from running. We were welcomed by a Japanese woman living in Yokohama. As a single mom, she had raised her daughter in Hawaii, but returned to nurse her dying mother. Misako was our English translator to every day Japanese life. She shared that it was a hardship for her and her daughter in this country that valued conformity. She took her daughter to a school in the States because she was so painfully picked on in Japanese schools. I am not sure what the social casts are here, but I sensed there must be some. None were blatantly visible to me, but the lifetime of hurt on this mom and her daughter was.

Her self-esteem seemed to cry out for love and acceptance in a place that was so well put together and orderly, but not demonstrative. I thanked Misako for being so candid with us. I could tell that was hard for her to do. As if to keep the subject off personal pain she bundled us up and took us for more touring. Up escalators, across train stations, on packed subways, and to the top of the Landmark Tower. Its view was even grander of a never-ending horizon of never-ending buildings. Mt. Fuji was somewhere out there shrouded in brown smog.

This matched the look of Los Angeles when I was growing up. I felt lost and my own pain seeped in. How to replace significance? I was no longer able to label myself as a wife. My kids were growing into the adults I hoped them to be. Where in the world could I go to hide from life kicking me around. Nowhere. Remorse went with me.

Gazing at structures beyond the reach of an eye, it almost had curvature to it. I felt more lost and aloof in this forest of endless buildings than the miles of woods in Alaska at the Midnight Sun Marathon. Staring out across what I was told was 10,000,000 people, I felt an aloneness, like even God was not with me. It was an aloneness even throngs of people could not eradicate. All those miles of flying and running and being here was vaporizing. Something gnawing in me was telling me I was trying to outrun my feelings. What was it? It was grief.

I could not get over how clean Japan was. The people were clean. The streets were clean. The buildings were clean. We stopped to examine bulletin boards advertising restaurants that one could pay to eat with a cat in a lap or pet rabbits. Both types of pets are not allowed in personal homes. Tokyo is no place for bunnies to hop and cats to wander. So, if you want a cat experience, you go to a restaurant and rent one for your lap. And get this. People PAY to get to walk someone else's dog. It made me giggle. The thought of someone paying me to walk the personality of my unleashable, hyperactive Labrador named Sandy.

It was starting to snow. Good thing this rarity did not happen on marathon day. People were whispering of a potential earthquake because it was February 29…leap year. I thought I would like to skip the earthquake experience in this ocean of buildings. Our Japanese single mom thrilled in any souvenir movie knickknack and was buying bottles of Pepsi because they had Star Wars figurines attached. Sponge Bob, Snoopy, and Puss 'n Boots seemed to be highly important to her and a lot of others were willing to stand in the same long lines for them.

I unglued from the gelatin press of people in the transit van that shuttled me to the airport. I placed one foot on the curb, gingerly. The sidewalks and a tunnel toward the subway were packed. But wait. Yes. The ground was shaking. We were experiencing an earthquake. My thoughts raced. Is this localized in Tokyo or a larger shaker somewhere else on the island? Is this one going to get stronger?

Everyone stopped for a split moment. They all glanced down at their phones. It was just a mild, regular occurrence. A 5.8er. A split moment later, the phones went away, and all were rushing to something that must be very important. I wasn't sure if I just saw what I saw. It was like a completely synchronized step in a dance. 10,000,000 people in Tokyo all just looked at their phones at the same time because Japan has a synchronized national alert system.

I squished my way in among them and on to the boarding gates. Did this marathon count? If not, the experience did.

29

Evolving Inward

Continent 5: South America—
The Galapagos Islands Marathon

After the Australian Outback Marathon, I began googling what other continent marathons I could drum up that would be in a remote place. My browser landed on a well written monthly newsletter entitled, "Come to the Galapagos Islands." I paged back through past months' issues and read them like a sponge. Loving them like they were a solid novel, I was enthralled. I signed up for the author's Galapagos Islands Marathon. He was an American married to a native Galapagos woman.

Being over 600 miles off the coast of Ecuador, this constituted remote. Many of the species on the Galapagos Islands are endemic, meaning they are not found anywhere else in the world. The islands are so cut off from any other influence it has land and marine iguanas, giant tortoises, Darwin finches, flightless cormorants, blue-footed birds called Blue Bobbies that are found no other place than on these islands. Over time, these animals have adapted to this solo environment and became different than those on the mainland. It is not a place on any beaten path.

Getting there is a challenge. I felt my choosing to go would help prove to me that I could figure out a way to do this world, or this thing called life, for that matter, as Caren Ware—the person I was trying to FIND. Would the going teach me? I knew it would. Plus, I think I was feeling as isolated and cut off as these islands were. Maybe, that was the draw.

Taken from Journal Jots
WordPress: Caren Ware Blog, May 2012

"I am in Miami eating Cuban food from an airport stand, charging my netbook computer and phone, and hoping I can get a message off to you all that I am on my way to the Galapagos Islands. I am embracing one of those remote Marathons I proposed to run, as remote as I can get on each continent. I sincerely had an hour to pack after returning from four straight days of expos and runs. I am reading that Ecuador converted to the US dollar to their demise and have no coins, and no change for hundreds, and no ability to accept foreign atm cards. So, I will be on the budget of the cash I carry. Yet, I am also reading so many expansive, remote things about the islands, the race, and the reason the race director is hosting this marathon. There will be less than 200 of us bold enough to venture to do it.

Here I go. I do this so you can venture with me. Who knows if I will find internet access? PS. I dropped weight this week. Cramped up on the shortest of runs. I am dehydrated even before leaving for an equator humidified heat, and possibly struggling with low levels of iron. HELP, my insides are trying to tell me."

This seems to be something my body experiences when pushing up the training mileage. I was not a good hydrator, and I didn't want to crack open yet another thin layer of my childhood eggshell to admit why. Maybe I will have the guts to include something in this book about bed wetting. I spent a childhood trying not to drink too much water. And now, heading to the equator, my surviving the marathon might depend on it.

I read Rick's instruction newsletter. It shared the weather report: Ocean temp. 87 degrees, Air temp. 97 degrees, Humidity 87%. Partial clouds, mostly sun on the coast. The sun feels like it's arriving through a magnifying glass. The ocean doesn't cool you off, particularly if you are doing any aerobic activities, swimming, surfing, etc. You either want to be in the water floating, in front of a fan or in some air-conditioned room. The bank is one of the nicest, 68 degrees, very low humidity."

Doubts crept in. This did not sound like IDEAL marathon running conditions to me. This sounded like I was about to get sizzled.

Good thing I had grabbed books to read. My flight did not connect in Guayaquil, Ecuador. I had arrived one day too early. I slid my back to the wall and sat on the concrete floor of the basic airport and finished reading some self-help advice I needed to know. I finished both books waiting for the next day. I had been told that this town was not one to walk the streets at night. I sat crossed legged in my running pants and a zip up jogging jacket. And I learned a lot.

"There is nothing inherently wrong or unhealthy about high standards in various arenas of life. However, striving for perfection is a demoralizing and *guaranteed formula for failure. Striving for excellence, on the other hand, is motivating because reaching it is attainable."* The Disease to Please by Harriet B. Brailer, Ph.D. I wasn't sure why I was reading a book on what happens if you try to please too much, but my exhaustion knew it wanted answers. I employed my travel time to read these personal growth books. I only semi understood that I was being drained by my own drive to please.

I also had a book with me entitled Boundaries, written by Dr. Henry Cloud & Dr. John Townsend. Its subtitle was "When to say YES and when to say No to take back control of your Life". This book had very helpful and needed instruction. It helped me put some healthy boundaries on my willingness to please. In an overcompensation to being loving and unselfish, I was failing to set good limitations on my own resources and well-being. I had let myself be too responsible for other people's problems. And their needs could knock mine right over. That's one sure formula for exhaustion and a whole lot of other chaos.

Once done with my books, I still had to sit there. It gave me no choice but to think. To think that if I had better boundaries, I would not have let so much be encroached upon. You can only dive deep and ponder the depths of yourself for so long. That can also turn into a different form of exhaustion. I start thinking about the marathon. The distance I would ask my body to do. And the hot conditions the islands would present to make it more challenging. I looked at the clothes I had been wearing for almost two days, and I started to self-talk self-doubt into my soul. Did I have what it would take to conquer this physical endeavor I had signed up to do?

It was an almost fake it till you make it. Was I pretending to be an endurance marathon runner, or was I one? I bought shoes, running singlets for the tropics, a runner's cap, suntan lotion, and kept reading the newsletters. It took a solid year to earn the money to get to come to the islands. In that year of wearing the clothes and running the mileage, I, at least, started looking like a marathon runner. Over time, a mini miracle was happening. Because I decided to start being one, somehow, I became one... is the point. You don't have to be able to *run to start being a runner. Just start running and you become one! That is true about almost anything. Choose to be it, and you become it in the process.*

Island waiting area for an airplane.

Yes, I decided on that barren floor on that barren day as I awaited a flight. I was a marathoner. I told those self-doubt thoughts to take their own flight. I realized I was able to evolve into the active person wearing the running uniform...over time. Maybe to get through some of the hardest fights in life, we might have to dress ourselves up to match what we want life to become. In a realm or realness, not deceit. Just start doing and being what you want your life to look like. Take wise, decisive, and winning action to win the wars that want to kill your joys, momentum, sense of purpose, or direction.

At this moment in my life, I was running to just keep going. To stay in motion. Everything felt like it wanted to topple me. Drown me. Hold to a deadness almost equal to death. Take me down that low. Basically, because it was. Divorcing has a way of putting you on a raft, where you feel adrift, and are very much out to sea. Running has a way of putting the ground back underneath you. I was about to test my own evolution on the islands that were known to inspire Darwin's theory. Had I made myself metamorphose into a marathon runner? The heat would bake me through a sort of self-kiln.

Graciously, my arriving one day too early was humored. The airlines gave me an open first-class seat to fly to the Galapagos. I flew right over the dingy industry and shanties of Guayaquil and out over the Pacific being served appetizers on a real plate. If I wasn't a marathon runner, at least I was getting to experience first class for the first time! I could feel the Galapagos was a world away from the Ecuadorian mainland. I felt it in the attentive airline crew. I felt the relaxed, meandering spirit of the residents that were boarding. I knew I was going to FIND something unique by being willing to go to such a remote place as the Galapagos Islands.

I took a deep solid breath for the first time in…well, in months. Maybe a year. I felt all the divorce and upheaval cracking apart in the weight it had held in my lungs. I had been experiencing wind-induced or activity-induced asthma, but even I knew it was from the pending spiral of so many changes and unknowns. It had been taking my breath away. I had to heave hard. I had to inwardly and fortuitously tell fear of the unknown to take a backseat. This would be a needed skill at almost all new adventure. To do something never experienced before is foreboding, though thrilling. And I learned to just take a deep breath and just do it.

I felt a twinge of gratitude that I was gutsy enough to try. Disembarking out of the small, pleasant plane and walking across the runway seemed so island arrival style. It felt like a movie scene. A great breeze swirled the oven air as I met Rick from "Come to the Galapagos." He was the gentle, friendly handshake I already knew he would be just by reading his newsletters. He writes these journal thoughts to help the guests break a mindset that time here should be a 'Wally world' week that appeases appetites for packaged and predictable vacations. His hope was that the marathoners would come to really experience the islands.

A dog sniffs efficiently through our luggage for shark fins and sea cucumbers. Rick whispers, "They discovered they were being snuck through pretend tourists who then sold them to the Chinese."

Rick had me side saddle his quad runner with my luggage in my lap, riding in the same style as Dorothy in the Wizard of Oz made her dog Toto do in the front basket of her bicycle. Rick served me lunch at his home to orientate me. He did this with each new arrival to set the stage for what to do while here and what was in store for us in running this island organized marathon route. His young son chopped and played construction man on the porch as we chatted.

I spent the rest of the day trotting out to a beach, getting the army of seals to bare their teeth at me, watching a sunset, and smiling at the tracks the waddling iguana tails left in the sand. My accommodation was on a roof top studio at Casa De Nelly overlooking the bay. The pleasant mom-type "Nelly" asked what time I would like her to make my breakfast. She is literally welcoming me into her home.

The small town is meant to stroll. I book a day of snorkeling and am told that Roscia is a great place to eat. My grilled shrimp atop marinated pasta is served just as all the lights in the entire island go out. Not an ounce of urgency. Candles are lit. A battery backup light weakly illuminates the eating patio. No one is concerned that it might take hours to come back on. I try to follow suit. Another unforced deep breath freely fills my lungs. It is let out slowly, matching the island's lazy breeze and the pace of its people.

I found an internet cafe…slash… ice cream place…slash… coffee place. I can send pictures for the price of a piece of homemade chocolate cake. The electricity almost unnoticeable had come back on. Internet access here sure beat the trouble I encountered in the Australian Outback where it had cost $25 for three minutes that never went through. I am still very concerned about my body's ability to do this marathon. I had a hamstring cramp up on me just walking around and I am winded at the least of hills. I have arrived here very life tired. And it is very hot.

The snorkel boat excursion headed out to a Gibraltar looking rock sticking out of the sea. Dolphins frolicked around the boat, spouting and unabashed. Not in a hurry, nor harried by our presence. The snorkel guide had us jump in the deep, dark waters and swim to the sheer faced, towering rock. There was a narrow opening that opted a chance to follow what they call Eagle Rays. We floated above a school of spotted sting rays the size of small whales, flapping in synchronized slow motion through the shadowy waters. The current became too strong so the snorkel/naturalist had us return to the boat so we could approach the crevasse from the other side.

As very typical of me, I was yakking out some story to the boat crew and had not noticed the snorkel pod had jumped in and was approaching the new entrance. I grabbed a hold of my mask and plunged in after them in a flurry, like I was trying to make up the distance in a triathlon. The dark sea reminded me of the bleak, see-nothing ocean swim during my St. Croix Half Ironman attempt. But, here in the Pacific Ocean this darkness was placid. Until something even darker than the sea darted by the tiny view I got from my mask. And then another. My head didn't need to guess what my heart pounded out. Sharks. What is there about the presence of a predator that we so instinctively give elevated heart rate to?

"Sh…. Sharks!" I screamed.

It sounded like "SPIII…EK…AR..K…SAW out the end of the snorkel, but the shriek got the attention of all the other snorkelers who were now furiously swimming toward me. But not because they wanted to save me. They WANTED to see the sharks. Galapagos sharks, I am told, don't seem to disturb snorkelers. Knowing me, I'd be the first one they would like to try.

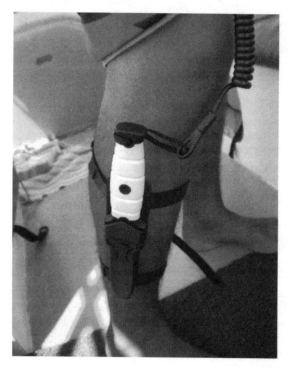

The guide's knife to protect against island sharks…that don't bite.

The boat takes us to emerald glimmering bays, to sandy solo beaches with lines drawn in the sand that led to the iguana tails that made them. They desalinize sea water in their bodies and spit out the left-over salt water. There were Frigate birds that were choosing mates by blowing up huge red balloons from their throats and sea turtles bobbing for breath.

The names of the rocks, bays, and beaches are presented in Spanish adding to the mystic. I don't bother to remember their names.

There are fish, and fish, and fish in the waters off the Galapagos Islands. It's fertile feeding grounds for anything that needs to eat fish. No wonder there is a carpet of coughing sea lions all over the islands. Clearing their throats sounds so human you want to say "God bless you" all day long. And I did just that. At the end of the evening, after a very pleasant dish of coconut prawns on the porch of THE PLAYA, I could hear a Wednesday evening church service singing worship songs. They sang in Spanish, but my heart recognized the melody in English. God bless each and every one of us.

Galapagos Islands has an 's' to it, so Rick sent me on the smallest of planes to another Island to experience more than one island. Four of us crawled through the window and sat behind the pilot who was putting duct tape on an instrument panel made around WW11. We bumped through rain and clouds to finally soar over the open ocean in this prop plane. It was thrilling and unsettling in one emotion. The pilot and plane seemed routine at this. Or simply resolved for the outcome of functioning when missing some screws.

We finally came out of the clouds and onto a postage stamp runway. It took such little time in flight to be on another… more amazing, more remote… island. Isabela has one town. Dirt roads were lined with a few open-air restaurants that lead to the hotel that was right on the beach. The Albemarle hotel was surprisingly pristine and charming. It had large rooms that opened to palm trees, soft sand, and the most inviting opaque blue ocean. The breeze was pleasant. The sun solid. The sound of crashing waves just enough.

As I pulled the doors open to let the beach and breeze tickle, two sentences fought each other in my head. "I wish I wasn't alone. It's good to be alone." How do the two of these settle an argument?

The gal at the front desk gave me the run down that most tours had already left for the day, but I could meander around without a guide down this mile stretch of beach and turn inland along a national park road to other playas, lava tunnels, cactus groves, and tortoise waddling grounds. I spent the morning totally by myself, plodding through shallow surf as warm as bath water. The red crabs must have had good eyesight. Long before I could reach them, they would dive into their sand holes. They seemed to escape as fast as my life was escaping me.

But I didn't feel good that day. Not sick. Just tired. From a lot of days of no sleep and the travel. Plus, it was hot. Really hot. I found some shade from a bush over hanging some tide pools. I rarely afford the opportunity for a nap, but my body was giving me no choice. I heeded the warnings because, for the first time in a long time, I could. Five minutes into the 'rest' an iguana jumped down from his hidden perch in the bush and ran across my leg. That is hard to sleep through. Ten minutes into my attempt to return to removing lactic acid from my limbs, a pelican dives down, snatches a fish from the lagoon and noisily gulps it down. Liking the location, he proceeds to remain and took a long, splashy, noisy, luxurious bath. When a little black crab bit my toe, I gave up. I'm in the Galapagos.

There's a little boat port ten minutes walk out of town. I was told I could get a boat ride out to the brim of the port and see those mixed-up penguins that were supposed to help me decide to stop going north and south and just stay put. Johan, a handsome teen, was willing to take me in his dingy for $20. I rented a mask and snorkel for $5.

I was trying to decide if he really was that excited about the animals and his island or if he was doing so to entertain me…the tourist. I think a little of both. "Look, Look…a baby manta ray. He will be big someday. Look. Look. Look. A turtle. He will take another breathe. Picture. Picture. And look. The penguins. They are happy. So very happy." A couple of penguins were mating on a rock.

He explained his world to me in half Spanish with a few English words. I respond back with my few Spanish words mixed with English…and we communicated. He threw an anchor out and motions for me to get ready to snorkel. He lashes a huge diver's knife to his calf. Catching my eyes, he assures it is only in case a shark approached us. Remember those Galapagos sharks? The ones the other tour said were not supposed to bite!

After snorkeling around, Johan laughingly motions to the boat. The anchor had freed loose. We swam quickly after the getaway dingy. Once aboard, he gets a serious tone and proceeds to tell me how tourism has come to their island and made everything good.

"Mucho dineros." He looks at my left hand without a ring and says I could marry his uncle and build a big house on this island. "Look. Look. And be happy. Happy…like the penguins. My uncle would be happy you built him a big house."

I politely decline the invite. There were some boundaries I appreciated I had fenced.

Two very relieving things happened on the marathon day. It got misty, hiding the baking sun. And I found some ounces of energy. It was probably because I ate TWO dinners the night prior. I ate a dinner of fresh chicken in a coca cola sauce with mashed potatoes and vegetables. Then I turned around and ordered an entire mini pizza…and ate all of both! I also had gotten eight hours of sleep the nights I was on the island of Isabela, which was two more than I was able to get traveling. Someone told me that eight hours of sleep is the difference between hope and despair. Oddly, I felt like all the walking, not running got things pumping. And, yes, a proper night's sleep helps a better perspective.

Isla Isabella had been better for my body than any timed released iron pill or a women's one a day vitamin. I loved being in the room that the doors swung open to the pastel blue of a tropical ocean. I loved wearing summer dresses and flip flops. I loved walking miles and miles around and across an island so uninhabited. I was saddened to leave. I latched the doors shut and stepped out into the heat. A leisurely walk on a dirt path led me to the airstrip. Yet, I had to roll my luggage. The tiny wheels keep getting stuck in the sand. I wrestled with them and the sad fact that I was experiencing something alone. I wanted my kids to do so with me.

The Landing Strip

The duct taped together airplane and pilot!

It appears the duct tape job was holding. The same pilot and plane appeared hours into my reading another book in the open aired cover on the runway. The buzz…buzz of the prop was loud. I was the only passenger. After an hour over the open ocean the pilot deftly brought his faithful plane down onto Cristobal's black tarmac. Rubber squealing. Bounce. Skip. Skid. We putt, putter to the airport building…which was locked. I got my own luggage from the back seat of the airplane and Rick was waiting with his quad runner. How did he keep track of all 200 of us marathoners coming and going? Especially, all the flights that have no exact time to them.

The town of Cristobal was a hub of excitement surrounding the marathon, which, by the way, a "marathon" in south America seems to mean any running event. You then must clarify the distance. 42 kilometers and they all hmmm with respect. ESPN had full cameras set up and crews darting about. They were filming footage and doing interviews. That makes the hub bub even more elevated. It was fun.

I had heard that the landowner at the start of the race…way up in the highlands, where the windmills for electricity were stationed, had decided to hold the marathon start line hostage. He told Rick if he did not give him 50 sacks of concrete that they could not have the start on his property. Since this was an annual event, Rick and his crew decided to not give into a bribe and went about changing the course which would now have some added hills. And…like, I didn't know any exact time my flight was, the marathoners would not know where the exact start was until we assembled, taking turns, on a school bus and were driven to it. Be flexible.

I finally feel like I am living my quest. The Outback in Australia and now the Galapagos Islands. Both such isolated, one-of-a-kind places. I came to be sensitive and learn from the issues, struggles, rewards, and gratifications of the people from these places. I came to become in touch. And to find out what their "against all odds" were. Would I FIND they had a better place? A better pace? A richer way of doing life? More at peace? I was already starting to conclude that life has challenges. On all corners of the earth. But those that struggled for their families were the richest. And, that all of life, everywhere…has its challenges.

I bore a feeling as a castaway, a person no longer with a home, a place to be from. I was riddled by regret. Then I remember to refuse to let life wallow. Each adventure, each breath, each step I was taking on these continent marathons, I vowed to make life anew. I determined to FIND a route that would take me to living a life worth being it. To being a person worth becoming. Keep climbing, Caren, I would have to tell myself. For a long time. Tread the waters until you reach shore. Build a raft to get to a mainland. Walk toward the peaks. And make it to the top of one…or two of them. I was using the continent marathons to keep me going…strong. To teach me not to give up…even when I wanted to.

Come to the Galapagos—Rick and his son.

COME in his business name of "Come to the Galapagos" really meant COME. I thanked Rick and Bere in my heart for the connections and the marathon I was about to experience and that I had COME. I had come! That was a big thing right there. I soaked into my cells all the wonder that had already happened from being on…the Galapagos Islands and decided that I was ready and glad to be doing this marathon. It really was a privilege.

A Saturday night in South America means loud music. I think I was still trying to figure out how to sleep through pulsating walls when the 3:45am alarm went off. The instructions were clear; do not miss the bus to the start. Wherever the start was! Here's a helpful note. I hardly slept the night before any major undertaking. Our bodies can man up and handle it when they must. Just not healthy to make it a habit over many consecutive days. The honest anticipation of what's about to happen is hard to sleep through.

The high part of the island was shrouded in fog and a heavy mist was falling at 'the top'. After bouncing up and down hills for nearly an hour on the bus, we were dropped off by blow-up arch supported by a loud generator. Two holes had been dug in the ground with three sides of plywood leaned against stakes. These were the Galapagos Islands' rendition of porta potties. ESPN was busy capturing the start. Most of the allotted 200 entrants had opted to run the half marathon. I kept hearing 'muy difícil...42 kilometers aqui.'

Starting line in the drizzle. Finish line would be in the egg baking heat.

The Galapagos Island Marathon is everything a remote island marathon should be...and that makes it a little frightening and intimidating. You don't *know what to expect. Is the fog going to lift too soon? Will the extra miles out of town be found in cow pastures, lava trails, dirt roads, daunting up hills, and sheer down hills? Will we run on hot black top near the death zone on the last miles by the airport? Yes, to all the above. But yes, to kilometers. They go by faster. There was a little sign propped by a lava rock and every .62 miles you could measure progress.*

Every five kilometers there were young navy men in uniforms holding out baggies of water and baggies of Gatorade, albeit 97 degrees. But these worked well. You could tear the tiniest hole with your teeth and sip away as you ran. They asked us to drop the little baggies in the middle of the road so they could easily be gleaned. Since parts of the course are out and backs like wings on a grasshopper, I strategically left a few protein bars by the kilometer signs.

I have no idea what happened to them. They were gone on my return loops. Dogs? Who knows. Trash pickup? The rocks had been moved. So, I had to rely on that sweet Gatorade for fuel and a handful of gummy PowerBar gels I had tucked in that running shorts pocket meant for a car key. I knew what starved felt like from my first LA Marathon experience. I was here once again.

The forest in the highlands was picturesque, yet the hills and running past the farms was downright hard work. It is to be noted that islands are not flat. As the fog burned away, the view of the town we were rapidly dropping down to came into view. It was so awing that anyone would be ashamed to complain. It did feel thrilling. The expansive Pacific Ocean rolled off in the horizon. We entered the town and ran past casual bystanders all saying "bravo, bravo." What a tease. We had almost 12 more kilometers to go. We were running a path like the wings of a grasshopper and in that exact design.

Waves crashing against the shore made it durable until we ran all the way out to the airport and beyond. This was on the dreaded black top with the morning sun directly atop our heads. I know for a fact that an egg would have fried on that pavement. I baked into blurry thoughts of "why did I make my son take piano lessons" and "God bless you, again, coughing sea lion." A long, cruel hill on this black top dropped to a lone beach that we all knew we would have to return back upward. This felt cruel this far into a marathon.

I staggered back through town where everyone was taking a Sunday stroll. Again, they would carefreely comment, "Good job. Keep going" in Spanish. I doubted if they really knew what this was feeling like. I wanted to bite them like a sea lion. I vowed to keep running, but it was starting to resemble more of a shuffle. The hill climbs and fast descents were havoc to any legs, trained or not. And the heat was debilitating. Literally. Many of the marathoners were starting to drop out.

And then, there it was. The finish line with a smattering of cheering and interviews being done by the ESPN crew. The overall winner surprised everyone, being a Danish woman 48 years old. For me, I was just glad to survive it. I concluded, again, my body was better suited for track. It did not like this heat. My brain felt hot. But I was proud of myself. I had been afraid, fearing that I would not be able to do it. It took a truthful inventory during all those miles. I let the books I read speak to me in a very self-revealing, yet self-accepting way. I was able to detect some change. Of whom I was becoming. Not who I had been. I congratulated myself for getting to the Galapagos Islands and running a full marathon in it. It felt HOT to have just accomplished it."

My feet are finished.

The moment was so personal to me, I had to move away, even from that quaint of a finish reception. I walked down the sand and plunged into the Pacific Ocean to cool off. Though the water was too warm and the bay murky, I flipped over on my back and basked in shear relief. I had done it. I was my own living proof I could. Evolution was taking shape. Changing outwardly was guiding me to change inwardly.

30

FINDING Myself…
in the Middle of Nowhere

Was I running away from or toward something? I couldn't run away from home because I no longer had a home. So, I took off running toward something. Kind of. I decided to leave Southern California. I figured the war of divorce would stop if it did not have a target to shoot at. I hooked up a 10x10 trailer, packed it and every inch of my truck with enough belongings to recreate a living space in a rented apartment and headed to Jackson Hole, Wyoming. All my kids were off to college. I felt the crumpled need to hit a refresh button with a very real need to find a new place to call home. So, I headed toward Jackson, Wyoming in the remotest of ways, via Yosemite.

I decided to begin a new journey by returning to Yosemite Sierra Summer camp. I was following the advice of a friend after questioning her as to which direction I should go following the divorce. She looked me straight in my face, put her hands on both my shoulders and said, "Where did you lose the sock?"

"Excuse me?" I replied. I didn't get it. "The SOCK? What do you mean?"

"You need to go back to where you think you left your sock in life… and FIND it."

The trailer pitched and bounced behind me as I left the farming valley of Fresno and headed into the parched foothills. It was always stifling hot in the summer in this valley. Soon there would be pines and a smell of mountain freshness that is uniquely crisp to the area of the Sierras I was headed to. I would mark this as the start of a journey in search of the missing sock. I had marathons on continents still left to run. I had kids making their way through colleges. It was time for me to FIND my own way. I had no choice.

I left the truck and trailer down by the road that circled the lake and walked up a familiar path toward the camp complex. The hum of happy campers was better than a hit song from any Broadway play. I passed kids climbing ropes courses, other's shooting bows and arrows. Delight was the lyrics to the song in the air.

A posse of kids dressed in waterski vests and their counselor passed by all whistling a camp tune. I stopped and let them. Another group was returning with paddles from canoeing, sunbaked and enthusiastic. The place buzzed with a multitude of activities. Sara Slevcove, Jim Slevcove's daughter now operated the camp. She just happened to be coming out of the camp office. She gave me a sideways look to take me in and try to register a familiar face. They had so many visitors. Was I a parent or a past camper? Then, she let out a squeal.

"Caren! Well, Caren! How the heck are you? What a pleasure to have you drop in!" With a hug, she threw her arms around me and gave me a genuine squeeze.

I did not stay long. They were in the full swing of a camp session. I just needed a booster shot. This was still the camp of the world's greatest campers and still impacting lives. I smiled, closed my eyes, soaked in the melody of kids at play, and sucked in a breath of that special pine scent. I let the solid memories be like Easy Off sprayed over a stained oven. With a revisit to this place, I was able to wipe back some stains I let build up in my insides.

I passed the parked truck and decided to take a quick dip in the lake. It was hot and driving toward the entrance to Yosemite in wet shorts and a tank top would be refreshing.

I clambered over a boulder and did a cannon ball leap into the lake. The late afternoon sun and a slight breeze cast a dark green shimmer on the surface. There was a clap sound as my knees broke the surface. Followed by a bewildering bang. Instead of the free-spirited wet splendor I anticipated, I was met with instant pain. Right below the water's surface were huge, sharp edged granite boulders. My leap and full body weight hit large rocks. I dragged myself ashore and was not sure if any bones had been broken. Blood was spurting out of punctures in my shins and the tops of my hands which had met with the edges of the immovable submersions. Good thing, I did not dive headfirst. Bad thing, I was bleeding and hurt.

The pain, mixed with the stupidity of plunging in without checking what was below the surface, produced tears with a wasp nest of emotions.

The hurt on the outside magnified my hurt on the inside. The hurt on the outside was a 10 on the 1-10 scale. But so was the hurt on the inside. I rocked and rocked, and my physical pain did not go away. I cried and cried. For a long time.

On the side of the lake that had brought some of the best years of my life, I felt a piercing tattered-ness that wanted to cement me with a feeling of no worth. I had to suck in between sobs. I could hardly catch my breath. My mom's life. My mom's death. My dad's insensitivity. My precious kids and husband. We had enjoyed the rightful, little things. This past year of marital fights. The words rang as harsh as the day they were hurled. My crying turned to sobbing. Every fiber of me felt injured. Lost. Like I was losing the battle, somehow, to living life in the right way.

What had happened? Where did I lose it? Did it get stolen. Did it get taken? Did I let someone have it? Did I just drop it? Did I deserve to have it now missing? What good was one sock? What do I do now? Where the heck was that lost sock? I started out with a pair. Didn't I? Like the ones that get mysteriously eaten in the dryer, it mystified me that I was walking this earth without my marriage.

I began to question everything. It is a very deep and profoundly sad place to experience rock bottom, especially one that has rocks in it. ROCK BOTTOM. I rocked back and forth some more. Sobbing. I had hit rock bottom. It is a place that questions your very existence and I believe it has as much pain in it as open flesh wounds. It makes you fear that you will not be able to take any more pain. It is a place that denounces your own worthiness. It comes with a feeling of being ineligible for future joy. I was at rock bottom.

The sun was going to set. I needed to drive on. I was heading to Yosemite and should get there before dark. I had the running shorts on and a jog bra. I took my tank top off and dipped it in the mossy water and smeared the blood around on my legs. I would clean my wounds later. I limped back to the truck and drove toward the park entrance. Broken.

From Bass Lake, it is a very windy road that takes a long while before the national park gazebo appears. This is where a ranger opens the window and through it takes the park fees like a fast-food drive thru. It is miles from the actual epic Yosemite Valley. If you turn to the right, you are rewarded seeing some of the grandest trees, a Giant Sequoia Redwood grove is there. If you go to the left, you end up down in the valley floor. This is where all the iconic views are of Half Dome, El Capitan, Yosemite Falls, and the meandering Merced River.

The sign said All Campgrounds FULL. The ranger told me I could drive through the park but must pass through and not spend the night. There is positively no overnight parking, he warned. I told him I would head up to Tuolumne Meadows and go over Tiago Pass and spend the night in the little truck stop town of Lee Vining. He agreed that was a good plan. I felt a drop of blood rolling from my knee down into my sock. Another dripped on the floorboard of the truck. I thanked him, paid the entrance fees and he handed me the national park map. Even sitting in the truck smarted.

The sun set and twilight was making its way across the High Sierra meadows as I left the valley and headed toward the pass. The views were stunning. I got out and used a clear, bubbling stream to wash my wounds and treated them with Neosporin I carried in the glovebox. This was a good excuse to stop, get out, and feel that God had done some mastery in this granite place of massive walls and domes. Planets were starting to pop out in a few small bright circles in the sky. Stars appeared and started to twinkle. Though the temperatures were dropping, I felt warmly hugged. Like a mother coddling a small child with a scraped knee, Nature was soothing me.

It was now dark. I must get down the pass and to Lee Vining. I found a few cell service bars on my phone and made a call to reserve a room in one of the few motels at the highway's junction. When asking for availability and cost, the strange sounding voice on the other end asked very slowly, "And, are you.... completely.... traveling.... a.... lone?"

Caution rang through to me. This seemed an odd question to ask, and to boot, such a creepy voice. Of course, I was traveling alone. I was divorced and now had to mark that on every application. Yes, I was traveling alone. I wasn't going to answer that. I slid the phone to off and did not further the reservation.

The truck, the squeaky utility trailer trailing as my temporary locker of belongings, and I descended the steep grade down off the pass. It is so steep, one must gear the engine down to avoid burning up the brakes. After a long haul, Lee Vining was rolling into view. It was almost 11pm. A few dotted rows of lights were coming up on both sides of the Highway. I don't think this town on Hwy 395 even has a population sign.

It was less abandoned than I remembered in earlier years. No longer was it solely a gas station and one motel. Someone had invested in a few bar-b-que eateries, a pizza joint, and there were three motels. Semi-trucks, cars with camping equipment strapped to their roofs, and an assorted array of other vehicles were pointed inward like horses at a watering hole. Three red lights were blinking brightly back at me. No vacancy.

It had been a long few days getting this far. Bruising was starting to color around my cuts. I was done. I was exhausted. And the town was full. My truck was stuffed with my earth's possessions, even the passenger seat. I remained seated in the driver's seat, locked the doors, cracked the window, and laid my head back like you so uncomfortably have to do on an overseas airline flight. This time there were no stewardess or flight restrooms. The cockpit of my truck would have to do.

Possibly less than an hour into my stiff-necked attempt to sleep, a tapping on my driver's side window made me not want to look. But I had to. I turned toward the sound, and a flashlight beam was pointing into my eyes. I could see past it, just enough to make out a shiny badge. I turned the key in the ignition to roll the window down just a crack more. "Yes, officer?"

'Madam. I am so sorry. But you cannot spend the night parked here in your vehicle."

I had no choice but to drive on. I ignited the engine, pulled back onto the highway and drove into the black night and into the wide-open territory of the entirety of the state of Nevada. The squeaky trailer hitched to my circumstances also had no choice but to oblige and follow me. It was one of the darkest nights of my life. Literally. There was no moon. I wondered if the universe knew I had hit rock bottom. Or, more honestly, if it even cared.

For hours it was just the two dim beams of my headlights and my eyes peering past them into nothingness. Somewhere in those hours my phone lost service, and in turn, I lost the GPS signal. I was cutting across the entire state of Nevada, entering territory that hardly had paved roads and very few travelers. A desolation that feels like it has no escape.

This no moon night was equivalent to being in a cave. Black was as black as black could get. My bouncing two truck light beams did little to pierce it. I was encapsulated in my cab seat, peering at nothing for hours with the monotony of bouncing. The road seemed to have changed and no longer felt smooth, but squishy. It had been so for a long period of time. I was too hypnotized to take notice. I opened the window to let some fresh air in and try to get a little more alert. Stay awake, I kept chanting. The sound of the tires was making a crunchy sound. This did not sound like gravel. I stopped and got out.

In the small spread of light from the headlights I could see hardpacked, very white salty dirt. I felt my way around the truck and there was dirt on all sides. I was no longer on a road. Where was I?

I had gotten myself to the middle of NOWHERE.

I couldn't see past the useless reach of the headlights. I reached in and turned the lights off. And instantly felt scared. It was so dark I could not even see the white truck. My heart raced. "F---k." I rarely say a bad word, but the word felt appropriate. Fear felt appropriate. But really, what kind of fear? Okay, this was fear of what I could not see. And currently I could not see any of my future.

I had no choice but to spar with my fears. What was I afraid of anyway? Something or somebody lurking out there that could pounce on me. No. I was afraid of the BIG BAD UNKNOWN. I was afraid of what I couldn't see. I was going down a road I had never been down before. I didn't know what lie ahead. And that was terrifying. I had no other choice, but to just be brave and rely on the confidence that I could handle the unknown. This was harshly that same rawness forming in my life right now. If you think there is greener grass on the other side of a broken marriage you are in for some tough alone times first. You might have to survive a parched desert first.

Then I saw it. My eyes adjusted and across the immense sky was the universe and all its glory. I was staring at the Big Dipper in the company of a zillion stars.

I was not alone. I was lone. I was discovering I was soul-ly okay just by myself. Nothing was going to jump out and grab me. I needed to see the sea of stars and add that to my smells of the pines and the awe I felt driving through, and up and over Yosemite Valley. Something more fathomable had to do with the making of the heavens and the earth. And it really did care about my being a speck in it.

I think this is such a rarely experienced place—gazing solo at the universe in a place where stars meet the horizon. We have created so much metropolitan light that we think we are in the dark and forget to look up with our hearts. I placed my hand on the side of the truck and let it guide me to a better view as I leaned on the hood, like a blind man relies on his walking stick. This was amazing.

I was not alone on my journey. I was meant to be on a journey.

Yet I was afraid. I felt very exposed and obviously lost. Afraid is another emotion. I think we must learn to navigate courageously with it. Afraid to get up and make a speech. Afraid to ask a person to join us in an activity. Being vulnerable. I knew I would have to move afraid aside to continue my journey past divorce. I knew it would take gutsy mojo to start all over. Was I afraid? Yes. But was that going to stop me? Only if I let it.

I palmed the steel frame of the truck until I felt the door handle. Upon opening the door, the doom light came on. It felt like a possible red flare that could warn the enemy I was here. I jumped in, snapped the light off, and locked the doors. I prayed the night would go by quickly. It did not. And I grappled with fear that entire night.

I realized fear had taken on emotional forms and that fear was also barricading positive roads. Fear, I realized was wrongfully robbing me. It had something opposite to the God that made the universe and all those stars out there. It keeps us in the dark, afraid, so we don't even see an amazing starry night in it. God must have known that fear would be one of our challenges. There are so many references to "fear" and "fear not" in the Bible. I had tackled so many fears during my college days already. I did not know there were so many more to spar with.

I prayed. Not really in words, but in need and in feeling. Finally, the night calmed. I calmed. And fear no longer had its grip. Courage did. In this, the darkness wasn't so dark anymore. I finally slept.

When the sun peaked so preciously like a timid wink on the horizon, I stirred in my cramped upright position in the driver's seat. What a welcoming dawn. The steering wheel had annoyingly restrained any opportunity to change sleeping positions. I hit the unlock button and the pop sound it made startled a jump reflex in me. There had not been a sound all night. None. And still, there was no sound. Not even a bird. I cracked the door open and the creak it made, splintered a stillness that felt akin to a sneeze in a morgue. I pushed my rigid limbs out the door and almost fell to the earth.

Catching myself, I had to wake up some circulation in my legs. I righted and stood looking in full view of nothing. Miles and miles of nothing. I turned to take in what was behind me. More miles of nothing. There was just a vast scape of salty, dry earth. In the flatness, as if on an ocean, you could see in all directions for miles. In a faint grey, some far off hills could be spied if you had good eyesight. I squinted to think I was seeing them. I was completely alone on a white, salty sea of dirt. Sincerely, completely, utterly, and fully alone. I had just spent the night parked in the middle of some ancient, evaporated lake. No breeze. No sound. No nothing. Just me.

I began to walk slow laps around the truck and the trailer, trying to comprehend where I was. Gratefully, my tire tracks allowed me to retrace my way back where I had unknowingly driven right off the two-lane road. Somewhere in the middle of that dark night, in the middle of Nevada I had rolled off the road. I knew from looking over a map, there was a town called Jack Pot with a gas station somewhere in the middle of nowhere Nevada. Life looked much more manageable in day light. Once back to the pavement, I hoped taking a right would take me in the right direction.

31

All Who Wander ... Wander

As I pulled up to a trailhead in the Grand Tetons, I saw a sticker on a well-traveled in, very rusty Westfalia camper van. "All who wander are not lost." I smiled and agreed. Right on. That was my mission. I was here to wander. And that was okay. That was my plan. I needed a stretch of time to meander. I was trying to FIND myself in a land so vast.

This mantra felt perfect. I was really trying to lose myself. Almost on purpose, I was trying to get lost. Maybe hide behind that excuse. When trails led in every direction it is so easy to get lost. So easy to feel lost. I felt if I could fade away into something up here, no one would recognize me as ruined. Did the original pioneers head west to flee something? Or were their ventures the rightful hope for a better life? I bet a little of both. It was both for me. I was running from something and hoping to run toward something…new.

I reveled being in Wyoming. I loved the open space, the small-town feel, the wilderness as a backyard. There were so many things to pit myself against. I was not afraid to try. I jumped on an expedition to do an outing they were calling 25 Short. I had no idea what that meant, but I knew we needed a fully loaded day pack with avalanche beacons and our backcountry skis. 25 Short ended up being an all-day ski shuffle up a mountain side that was 25 feet short of 10,000 feet. Being so novice, I ended up knocking one of my skis off the ledge we had painstakingly taken all day to climb up to. We had to peel the seal skins with the sticky glue from the bottoms of the skis, and carefully roll them up, and stash them in our backpacks. While transforming the bindings into downhill skis I looked around and noticed a trail into a ravine over 1500 feet below us. It was my ski. Not having a brake on, it quietly disappeared. Somehow, I had knocked it off the ledge.

While the other adventurers were whooping and hollering and even filmed themselves descending steep vertical powder, I sledded down the precipice on my other ski and spent hours boot kicking my way back up. Though I never got to look like a local in their film footage, I was stamped as an official bad ass for being one of those who had done 25 Short. I think 25 Short had done me. I made it to the truck at dusk utterly exhausted yet, admittedly triumphant. It was so hard, it was fun. Is there such a thing?

I loved the use of the town's Snow King Ski Mountain. They nicknamed it "Jackson Gym." If you wanted to grow hardy, you did not ski down the steepest vertical of any resort in our nation, you skinned up it first. And in the summer, you ran or biked up it. If you wanted the trial of cardio, you went right under the steepest vertical chair lift. This vertical was so steep it was used for snowmobile climbs because none could make it to the top. The thrill of that sport was watching expensive machines roll in splintering pieces back to the bottom as the driver barely jumped aside. Wyoming called that a sport.

My body did that exact tumble one day. Right as I planted my two poles on the summit and took that victory step with my backcountry ski, planting it atop the goal, I popped out of the biddings. I did what Jackson nicknamed "a yard sale." One ski stayed where I last stepped. The other popped off part way. I started to pick up speed and do backward cartwheels. One pole flung off into the trees, and the other I gripped all the way, despite my somersault decent, to the bottom with me. It was Spring and corn snow is hard ice with a sharp edge. I shaved skin as I skidded to a heap. My elbows were bloody.

"Saw ya' yard sale," the townspeople would acknowledge for weeks afterward. Snow King sits as backdrop to anybody walking their dog or for everyone hanging in the town square. Everybody in town seemed to know Caren took a tumble from the top to the bottom. What they did not know was how real a tumble. I was in this town because my life bindings had snapped loose, sending me backwards and skidding downward at a fast pace.

I had been here almost three years, far removed from my young adult children. Giving them healthy space to thrive was one thing, but losing touch with them would be another. It was harder than I wished to admit, making my way into a new community. Jackson Hole, Wyoming was my destination dream town. I had done it. I had courageously left all behind and pioneered my way up to The Grand Tetons. I loved it. Yet, I missed things I could no longer love. With what I could fit in the truck and a few things I had hauled up in a trailer, I was forging a new life.

Or was I? Though the scenery was spell binding, the activities all so strength building (running, biking, hiking, rafting, climbing, skiing in all kinds of forms and places), and the lifestyle hip, I was still a fifty-year-old divorcee, grieving over the loss I had greatly helped cause. What in the world was I doing in a town of post college graduates, ranchers, cowboys, tourists, European J-1 visa workers, and the rarely seen wealthy? What most everyone else was doing: trying to FIND myself. I was hiding out to heal. Sometimes that is a needed tactic. But as my son put it, "Things have an expiration date for a reason."

I found a community church to attend. Or it found me. It was one where they sang the hymns my mom hummed into my soul. A wood sided church was led by an unwavering, gentle southerner. He preached with an accent and a clear perspective. And the church goers were wholesome, hard-working, bedrock community members.

I found an experienced, back country athletic trainer to train me. Poor man, I laid down all these ridiculous boundaries of not getting personally involved. Trying to explain to him the problems I ran myself into came out like a fumbled football in the fourth quarter. He politely nodded, Wyoming style. "No problem, ma'am. I never do." Trying to fine tune fitness kept up my hope to return to competing in future track competitions. I became the high school's assistant track coach. I worked three jobs and countless hours. And I lived through the off seasons, the cold spells, the long winters, and the emerging springs. I hiked. I biked. I skied. I climbed. I delivered packages for UPS. I was a local.

I bet they never thought they would see me hang on, tenaciously, this long. Most moved on seasonally. I was a true blooded pioneer. I was that scrappy kid who climbed Mt. Whitney and chased my dad rim to rim on the Grand Canyon. Dare me to give up?! I dare you back. They started to see I meant it. And finally, enough time was going by, proving to them I could be entrusted as a local. I was here to stick it out. And somewhere along the journey, I was, without words, nodded into acceptance. People would pass me in town and give me a sideward toss of the head. "Hey, Caren. How ya doing?"

But my emotions were still pooling in my eyes. Though the exhaustion had faded, I felt I was a living disconnect. I was FINDING myself getting stronger, more agile, more wilderness savvy, but losing ground financially and growing poorer in self-esteem and the prior self-confidence. I found myself mulling. Grappling. Limping along, hoping for some purpose button to magically pop up. I could not shed that feeling that I had gone through too much. Too much loss to feel world champion anymore. I could bury my mom and all the pain with that. But to let my own marriage implode? Disappoint my children? Myself? Till death do us part? My commitments. My husband. The losses seemed to have collided, like a derailed train wreck. I felt twisted into immovable heaps of heavy debris.

Jackson was still clinging to fibers of the true wild west, where the wild ones and the good guys all hung out together. It was an amazing town I was privileged to be experiencing. I had salvaged up enough equipment and rebranded a new timing company—Itz About Time. Why the Z? Because all my life I had been Caren with a C. I had to tell every single person how to spell my name. This tiny nuisance made me have eye contact and interact with almost every person I met. And it made them remember the name that was different by one letter. My mom always reminded me, "Caren with a C with the word Care in it." So Itz About Time was launched in Wyoming, the business with a Z instead of an S. Nice logo design. Clean website. But there were very few events to time, maybe six in a 300- mile radius. I was without purpose. And "without purpose" slides too close to "without hope."

I RAN into a man named Tim in Jackson. He owned a leadership training company called Grand Dynamics. One day he shoved a book in my hand and said, "Here. Types like us could use this. It's a good read." I rolled the hard copy in my hands. *High Performance Habits* was hand signed by the author, Brendon Burchard. I read the front and back cover. The author had quit his job to write and speak. All he needed was a real purpose and someone else relying on him to make something happen. His life started climbing. The book made needed sense to me.

It was time for me to stop merely existing and get back to existing with a passion and purpose. But what purpose? I felt I had failed and therefore, that I was a failure. I did not realize people are NOT failures. Things fail. Attempts fail. Trying something may fail. But that does not make anybody on this earth a permanent failure. My purpose had been to provide a quality upbringing for my children. I would always be a mom. I had the accolades, the memory, the medal, and USA uniform for being a world champion. I could learn from failures, but I was not a failure.

I was not climbing, and sitting at the bottom because I did not want to have to start over. I had finally let myself be knocked down, and I just stayed down. Sometimes we are so overwhelmed or intimidated to even try to start reclimbing, so we just don't. I had to start from the ground up. I knew that rock wall in front of me. I did not know if I had what it took to do it again. I was waiting for the count down and to be declared knocked out of life. But when I looked around, no one was counting except me.

Most climbs start from the bottom, so I decided to start looking up. FIND the purpose. FIND the cause. DEFINE my passion. To do that, I had to get on my feet. I slapped that book open in my lap and sat on a creek's edge, swatting gnats, and read its entirety. The brook babbled in the background. The exercise of pumping past pages of high-performance habits was like adding spring snow melt to a river. It helped me pick up internal speed. I possessed the habits to be a high performer. We all do.

I was still reading the book as the afternoon sun shifted. I put on a Patagonia hoodie. The author listed six common essentials he found that high performance people were doing. I agreed with them. Yes, this is what it took to go to college, be on a collegiate team, get a master's degree, start a business, raise kids, and win a world competition. *Make these the habits, again*, I thought to myself. They were: Seek clarity, generate energy, raise necessity, be productive, have influence, and demonstrate courage. The book offered a test. I took it, and scribbled X marks in the boxes, still squatting on a rock next to the stream. I could feel the questions revving up the original "me". The high performances of running track, winning scholarships, getting jobs, creating companies, being married, making a house a home. *That* person. *That* person who loved the idea of camp, learned to rock climb and water ski. The one that loved carry a backpack and to trek. *That* person.

It was grief, exhaustion, defeat, and bewilderment that needed the expiration date. It starts out fresh and should be allowed time for healing and restoration, grief and regrouping. But, ding, stay in it too long and mold can grow. I hooked back on my life climbing gear. Wasn't I supposed to be running a marathon on every continent? And writing a book? What happened to those goals. Start there.

"All who wander are not lost," that sticker had said.

"All who wander, wander," I started to realize. And, as my son would put it one day, "Maybe the healthy thing should be to view all of us as lost, some just choose to wander."

As the sunset hues spread out overhead, I finished reading. Gleaning. The author discovered high performers never felt like they were trying to be the person at the top. Instead, they felt confident and relaxed in making things progress, with no doubt that success will happen. Yes, albeit, with already expected setbacks. They built in the ability to fail but keep going. Not me. I felt alone. Lonely. Shot at with arrows of envy and dislike. And I was the one shooting most the arrows, Right into my own flesh. I had been making my value on a platform of accomplishments. And, therefore, that forever tension in me, carried from childhood, would not go away. I wanted to calm down, be confident about my body, myself, my muscles, my self-care. There were so many things I should naturally know about and do at my age, and they were sadly missing.

How do you learn them as an adult? You let yourself. You let yourself learn from your failures. Relaxed. Confidently. And enjoy the process and progress, knowing there will be setbacks. You make and see your life as the journey it can be.

The book had a test. I scored super high on influence. That surprised me. I started asking around. I was stunned to hear replies. People believed in me and my pursuits and WANTED to follow me. They WANTED to emulate and become someone that did things, enjoyed fitness, was kind, and always sincerely concerned. They smirked and offered back that they liked how awkward, jittery, sweet, and involved I was. They were shocked that I would not know that. "Caren, you climb mountains. You have stories. You really go and do real things and come back having met real people. We really like that and live to be you." I didn't know that. I needed to know that.

You do too. Every single one of us has a special self that is only especially us. When we offer that uniquely and sincerely, it bears attraction.

But here is when the book helped me see how I could fall to my rock bottom. The scoring of the habits chart took a devastating dive to near zero on the test for Clarity. I was very unclear who I really was and what I wanted to be doing. I didn't understand that from childhood I was programmed to have no needs, wishes, desires, nor say in anything. I honestly didn't know what I liked, wanted, or should be doing. The roads I intentionally went down in life got derailed as I tried to overhelp and accommodate the wishes and needs of others, over the default of my own needs. How confusing is that? It makes handling life like a dog chasing its own tail.

I think they have labels out there like 'codependent' these days. I didn't understand that what I thought were relationships, were entanglements. It took "three strikes, you are out" for me to see that I was attracted to a wrong, rightly feeling relationship. Or more, they sought to FIND me. I had no clue. But what I realized on that spring day by the river was a big "ah-ha" wake up moment. I was not going anywhere, because I did not have any clear direction to go in. Bill Sumner, one of our nation's great running coaches, confirmed this for me when he said, "Caren, of course you are not going anywhere, but in circles. What is the address? You must know what the address is to get there... Silly."

In town, I bought a card that had a sketched camping tent on it and the pun, "Summer of my intent." Another card had a hammock tied between two pine trees and said, "Reading between the pines." I wanted that to be my new life. And it was. For three years. I worked in an outdoor store, I coached track, I hiked the mountain ranges, biked the backcountry, climbed the rocks, scaled the peaks. At my age. But I started to reword my sticker with a question mark. "All who wander…wander? I think I'm lost."

Wandering did have some value. It lured me to the Wind River Range, an incredible swath of granite mountains that equals, and may surpass, Yosemite in grandeur by its remoteness. It's over an hour and half drive south of the Grand Tetons. The Cirque of the Towers in the Wind River Range are like a legend. Ramblings from climbers and hikers who knew the secret wonders of Wyoming would come into the outdoor shop I was working at in Jackson, Wyoming. They were sunbaked, and their eyes gleamed like they had discovered gold out there. They had just come from what they called "The Winds." One trailhead is at Big Sandy, a solid hour drive from the town of Pinedale, much of it on dirt roads. To reach this mountain range, one must cross high plains where the deer and the antelope really do play. This area is the history of rugged mountain men spending years in this remote region. They trapped beaver for the European need for fancy hats and would bring their furs to a Rendezvous encampment each year to sell them, right here on these high plains.

When I reached the top of Jackass Pass, a towering amphitheater of jagged granite peaks they call the Cirque came into view. It was stunning. All the lines and shadows offered an instant applause inside of me. They were grandiose. Breathtaking. I stood in silent awe and looked face-to-face at the Creator. A welled up feeling of privilege rose in my chest. To see the majesty of nature was breathtaking. It held more wealth than anything monetary. If this was His handiwork, I wanted to be in reverence. I offered a feeble voice of respect for the Artist who had His signature on the corner of this canvas. As I stood and paid respects I knew not to ignore the majestic. I came here for that purpose. This is where wandering is worth it. It was FINDING this.

It takes some stumbling, bouldering, and traversing a solid mile of glacial moraine to get to the top of the pass. Huge boulders. Slippery gravel. This added to the trophy of looking eye level across this range. A rapidly passing cloud spit an early warning of winter approaching as it blew snow flurries into my face. Within minutes, a dusting of white speaks were splattering the panoramic walls, like it was being salted. The wind whipped clouds into dark formation and yet, the sun was shining. It was a beautiful combination of colors. Blue sky peeking through, white falling snow settling in the cracks of tall grey granite. After spending valuable off-season days out there, truly in the wilds, I packed up my tent, shouldered my pack, knew I would return often, and started back over the pass.

It was time for me to move onto a life with clearer purpose. I had started to run a marathon on every continent. I had two to finish. Antarctica and Africa. What was I waiting for? I took a good look at the "yard sale" of my life and shrugged. No more time wasted peering in the rearview mirror. That's called wallow. It was time to lurch forward and FIND a way to these remaining continent marathons.

Only 100 participants are allowed to run the Antarctica Marathon each year, and I had been on the waiting list for over 4 years. It was announced that this next year would finally be my turn to go. Antarctica is a continent! You also know it's cold and frozen. So, I started to train, using all that Wyoming could offer to toughen me up. I finally had an address in my sights, and I was determined to run toward it! It was such a relief to give myself something to aim at. When others were staying indoors during the cold inversion layers that push temperatures below zero in Wyoming, I went out in it.

32

Myself Went with Me
Continent 6: Antarctica — The Antarctica Marathon

I thought I could sign up for the Antarctica marathon and get a vacation… from myself.

Getting to the Antarctica marathon was nothing as I had planned or envisioned. I had put myself on the five-year waiting list and started making the payments in great anticipation. My business was doing well at that time. My family was growing up. And it was time to seek a new adventure. I had no idea in those five years a recession would hit, a divorce would happen, and I would be training solo in the wilderness of Wyoming, pitting myself against the elements in temperatures below zero as a single woman. I also did not know our ship would hit an iceberg.

It did. A month before we were to embark, I received an email informing me that the expedition would have to be postponed thirty days. This made me have to fulfill a race timing contract on the Hawaiian Islands, fly directly to the mainland, and head south. My new flights did not connect well with the rest of the marathoners. I landed in Buenos Aires 15 hours behind the others. I caught a cab to the host hotel and to a room I didn't get to sleep in. It was 6am. We were to gather in the lobby at 10am to head back to the airport and fly to a tiny port town at the tip of South America. I had missed the orientation party and a tour of Buenos Aires the night before, and I felt the pressure of almost missing the flights and the anxiety of my situation. It made me feel the solo that I was. It made me feel like I really needed that vacation away from me.

March 30, 2013

Don't Choose a Life Set on the Spin Cycle

When I was around 4 years old I crawled in the dryer to hide. I made sure I left the door slightly ajar to let light in and so I could peek out. Someone walked by and bumped the door shut. Bam. Activation button on. I got tumbled. I was told our family dog, a little Dachshund, started barking and jumping on the door of the dryer. My mom found me purple, but still breathing. Needless to say, I didn't like crawling into small places for a long time after that. The situation sure changed when that door shut.

> So many things can inadvertently bump the door shut on what we think are our cozy places. Try a terminated marriage! For some reason Antarctica getting postponed sent me tumbling. I like volume. It suits me to do 10 things at once. I liked being in different places, working with different people. I, in hindsight, do not like not having the volume my So Cal calendar of races gave me. Go figure. I worked hard to free myself up for these new adventures and I am fretting over not having the thing that was robbing me of all my time and creativity. I question Jackson, Wyoming. Did I crawl into another dryer in life by venturing to Jackson? It seemed like a cozy place to curl up for a while. Somehow, Antarctica getting postponed has stalled out an additional month and… bam shut the door on my well proposed plans to run on ice, then time an event in Maui, then stage a race in California, and spend Easter Sunday with my kids. Instead, I worked out the race details in California, flew back to Jackson to at least coach a week of High School track, scrambled to get people to cover my race in California, changed a LOT of airline tickets, flew to Maui just to time the race, gave my condo nights to my staff, and connected across South American airports arriving for a few hours in Buenos Aires and in Ushuia only hours before the boat departed. Definitely on the Spin cycle!

Having come from a tropical island, I was still in a sundress and flip flops in the hotel lobby attempting to use the ATM. I had my back turned, but I felt eyes on me. I didn't have time to engage in any meet up conversations. I was trying to access my bank account and get converted cash for the travel to and from Antarctica. I had one $20 bill left in my pocket. What I didn't know was that ATM cards had a protection on them for possibly fraudulent acts. My transaction was denied. I had forgotten to inform them I would be traveling.

I tried to make an international phone call. In a foreign language, the auto response voice was telling me the call couldn't go through. I moved to the lobby computer. The email access to the banks requested I present a valid ID and call during business hours. I was doing a nervous dance from the ATM to the lobby computer. I was running out of time. There was a bus coming to take us to the flight to Ushuaia, and all I had for a three-week expedition was a $20 dollar bill on me.

The entire time I was focused on the problem, I could feel those eyes watching me. I gave a quick glance. A well-dressed man was sitting in a chair, legs crossed, obviously amused by my fluttering around like a hummingbird. He gave me a nod. He had on polished shoes, a polo shirt, and a very expensive watch. My brow furrowed. My time was up. I wasn't going to be able to unlock the freeze on my accounts, and I was going to have to go to Antarctica with only $20.

I ran upstairs to my barren room with the bed still made and took a fast shower with only lukewarm water. No worries. It was hot in Buenos Aires. I picked another sun dress and clambered down the stairs with my expedition bag full of Arctic apparel. I caught the tip of my flip flop shoe on a step and almost went headlong to the bottom of the stairwell. A history of tripping on hurdles gave me the agility to barely land on my feet. The bags beat me to the ground floor. The lobby was packed with energy, all climbing into the shuttle. We were headed for the flight to Ushuaia and a ship to Antarctica. All of us had waited years to be able to do this.

I jumped in the bus and took the only empty seat. I was still deeply focused on only having this $20 bill in my pocket. The man I sat next to happened to be the one watching me race around with no resolution. He introduced himself as being nicknamed the Italian Stallion. He smiled and said it was very entertaining to watch me try to conduct last minute business in the lobby. I did not explain.

Once in Ushuaia, we were ushered off the runway to the ship's plank. At the bottom stood a sailor saluting with one hand and holding a bowl in another. We dropped our passports in it for safe keeping. They literally would be stored in the ship's safe. I wondered if this was a way to keep a log of passengers in case we sank like the Titanic.

Next to the sailor with the bowl stood the owner of One Oceans, our expedition company taking us to Antarctica. He was shaking each of our hands with a sincere and official "Welcome aboard." His eyes were clear. Focused. Friendly. He was comical, business-like, and instantly likable. Yet, there was a distance and determination to him. He seemed full of purpose, well-mannered, yet impressively aloof. A kind of aloof that has the confidence to sail around the world…solo. Or solely build an excursion business that takes guts to finance, develop, market, and execute in one of earth's harshest elements. He did so with stellar perfectionism.

All the equipment, staff, and experiences he offered were top notch. Everything was of the highest quality, well organized, and operated at a level that allowed you to sit back and enjoy one of the most awing experiences of being among frozen icebergs, humpback whales, penguins, and seals. The sunsets and sunrises were so near the sun the hues lasted for hours and were all around you like something an artist's brush could only splash. Marathon

Tours linked with this company, One Ocean Expeditions, because they felt it offered the most attentive trip. It was already organized to be nothing less than an amazing experience. And, luckily for me, all inclusive. My meals and the boat were already paid for.

I moved past the handshake and up the plank, but this man's genuine eye contact slid to my heart. Over the course of the cruise, I was impressed with him. It was the mixture of his ability to be with people and put people at ease yet command an expedition at the ends of the earth and possessed that solo spirit. He valued the unique opportunity of exploring and traveling in this place like no other on earth. And I saw his passion was to share this special place with others. But what was it? His far-off gaze told me he could handle the elements very adeptly, alone. Solo. Comfortable in his own skin.

There were a lot of crew members rushing about the boat, throwing lines, grabbing luggage. But as fast as they rushed about, they all disappeared, like ants into an ant hole, somewhere deep in the belly of our whale called a ship. The huge research vessel, with its specially made steel hull for cutting through ice, moved forward. It was slicing a V mark in the water of the bay. Within the hour we were out to sea. I loved it already. But where did all those sailors go? I was told they were all Russian. My luggage was neatly propped at my berth door. We never saw them again. We were ninety-eight passengers on our way to run the Antarctica Marathon. And only a choice few positions, specifically two Russian ladies, did I see serving above the ant hole opening.

My assigned berth opened its door right next to the One Oceans owner's quarters. Rather than have anything different than his passengers, his accommodations were identical to the rest of ours. Since the ship's routine was all the same, we would bang open our doors at the exact times…on the way to meals or excursions. Bam. Bang. Oops. A shower of apologies. He would be polite and say, "Nice dress." I would blunder and say something that made me groan inside, and then berate myself for how stupid or unintelligent my comments were.

I was giddy around this man. A businessman who was an adventurer at heart. Here, finally, was a real one. I knew they existed. It wasn't like I was trying to put a make on the poor guy. I genuinely and instantly had a crush on who he was, much like a teen would over a movie star. It was because of the out of the box life he was bent toward doing and living it. Being infatuated over him caught me off guard. Here stood a living example and the reality that someone could be all rolled in one; great businessperson, people oriented, and an avid, solo adventurer. It could FIT. I had been berated so many times during the divorce that it was a pipedream, unrealistic, unattainable falsehood…to be these things or trying to do these things.

The first three days on the ship were torture. I was acting so silly and awkward around him. My stammering. His polite answers. I had to do something. I caught him one step out of his door.

"Ah." My eyes hit the floor. I wondered if I could really do this. Head down, "I apologize for my awkwardness. It is just that I am captivated with you, like a teen would be to a movie star."

What?! Did I really blabber that? Did I really just say that?

I was really stammering now. "You are the real deal adventurer. I can hardly talk to you or look you straight in the eye. This is silly. It is just that I revere, well…actually idolize, a person who has really accomplished solo travel. And one whom has this much savvy to put together such a quality business that suits his passion and let's other's experience it also."

My eyes flitted up to his. His hand was still gripping the door handle. He looked like he had stepped in cement. A huge grin spread across his face. His far away eyes came straight to the present. Handsome light eyes. He smirked, "Well, dang. Now, you are making me blush."

Done. I said it. We could move back to adulthood now. I brushed past him and went to the mess hall still feeling a little like the mess high schoolers feel.

He did something I felt took the caliber of who he was. He made his microphone announcements and rather than shy away from my approach, came back to my dining table and sat down to join it. He shared about growing up in Canada, coming from a strong family of sailors and doctors and high expectations. He talked of education and adventure. Winning sailing competitions. And racing a sailboat solo around the world. He told us all how much he loved Antarctica. Exploring Antarctica. Showing other people. He explained that the Russians made the best steel hulled ships and were the more experienced crew. He sat back and described his home in Whistler and what the grass, sky, and flowers would look like when he returned. His eyes always floated from gentle and near, too far off and reaching for something.

He got a pained look on his face. "I was talked into selling the adventure company once. I was told that being a sailor for a lifetime was no life for relationships. Right after I sold my expedition company, I toppled into a loss of purpose. After selling the company, I realized I had sold myself. Expeditions to the ends of the earth is me," he told us. "It is my passion and who I am. I have had to work hard to redevelop this new company. But I know, now, it is me. One Oceans Expeditions is me. My passion is to gift people experiences in a place I treasure as one of the most pristine on earth. And you? What about you, Caren Ware?" He asked me, almost already knowing.

I explained I was in a ditto situation. How I sold my business and with it, I sold myself. I shared that my passion had been for running and using it to cross cultures and connect people, enhance lives, offer hope, and gift camaraderie. He was smiling. He knew I needed to hear his story. He added, "Then, go back and make a new one. A Caren Ware one. An even better one."

And I promised him, and the table full of now friends, at that dinner that I would. I was thankful for his sharing and being an example that we can be a lot of things rolled into one. But to mainly be about our passions.

As we all started to all stand up to leave the mess hall, he interjected to the room. "You know, we really do have only ONE OCEAN. Many think it is a bunch of oceans, but they are all connected." I had read a book I grabbed at the airport called *Moby DUCK*. A man followed a cargo ship container that had slipped overboard and spilled open in the Pacific seas outside of China. It was full of rubber ducks. They literally floated for years all over the world and were found on every continent because the currents and ocean bodies of water were all connected. I understood Andrew's point. He then turned to me and almost shouted to the room. "Caren Ware, we really have only one earth. A lot of cultures, but they are all connected. You already know that. That's your passion. Float among this one world!"

I loved the ship. Exploring its nooks and crannies. I liked my berth. The little port window would open to the salt air. It looked out eye level to the sea. I was glad it did hatch down tightly. When the seas started to roll, waves would smash into it and up and over the seven-story bridge. These were the roughest seas in the world, but once inside the protection of the Antarctica shelf, the boat became a calm floating hotel. Of course, occasionally, I had to peek into hatches that were meant for the crew and open gally way doors. Where were those ants that make this ship operate adeptly through these high seas? Somehow, they functioned below decks. Somewhere.

The experience of running a marathon in Antarctica was more than the one day of picking my way through ice landscapes on a frozen continent. It was the experience of waiting for so long, traveling so far, and successfully returning. It was meeting the people on the ship. It was knowing that even the training and all its lessons were a great part of the marathon. A marathon is not just one morning's activity. It is a quiver of all kinds of experiences spread over many months, and for this marathon, for many years.

I had been training in what Jackson Hole, Wyoming calls the inversion layer. An interesting phenomenon happens when a certain pressure moves over that mountain and valley area. The cold air is pressed to the valley floor, while the tops of the mountains can be 20 to 30 degrees warmer. When this occurs, the town would sit in minus zero conditions for days. And, hard to grapple, but the tops of the mountains were the warmer place to seek.

Those were the days I grabbed my running shoes and went out. It got me the title of "the crazy runner chick" and the local newspaper did a story on my training for a marathon in Antarctica. Running in those cold temperatures trained me to move between warming up my breath in my shirt collar, to sucking cold air through my nose. I learned why there is a saying, "cotton kills."

One day, I ran my mileage out of town on a warmer day. When I turned to head back, I was blasted with a head wind and an unexpected temperature drop. My bra was cotton. The sweat made it wet, and it froze to my body. I had to flag down some ranchers and shivered between them in the cab as they rescued me back to town. I got better at it. I acquired more suitable clothing for layers which included merino wool underpants, bras and socks, Patagonia base layers, a down jacket layer, and solid Gortex outer wear that stopped wind and rain shielded.

I learned a local's winter survival trick in using plastic shopping bags. You know the kind you use to put vegetables in? The cheap, thin ones you pull off the roll in the produce section at a grocery store. When the inversion temperatures hit, the snowboard and ski bums would have these bags sticking out of their boots and gloves. They helped vapor wrap heat in and keep extremities from getting too cold. I decided a handful of bags did not take up much weight and room in my luggage and brought them. Almost as a tease.

When the announcement came that the temperatures were at minus two and that tomorrow's Antarctica Marathon run day could fall to minus twenty-two, I was undaunted. I pulled out my produce baggies. I know it looked ratty, but I also knew it worked. Plastic stuck out from under my socks and at the ends of my gloves like a stuffed scarecrow. I exchanged beauty for the essence of functionality. What's that saying? "Function is the essence of beauty!" I got looks. I shrugged them off. Losing the feeling in my toes and fingers would not be the challenge it could have been.

There were so many interesting and varying people on this ship. But we all had the same goal. To complete this rare stunt of running 26.2 miles on the hardest continent to get to. We took turns being taxied in rubber zodiacs to the shoreline. We were starting and finishing at the Russian research station on King George Island. I think it was the Bellingshausen Station. We were to run in a figure eight configuration so that, if in trouble, we could drop out at a few check points. The course passed by a Chinese Station and crossed over some very frozen, but rutted and rudimentary utility roads before it went out into the white, hilly terrain. We were running on a freeze-framed cork board.

We were pretty much on our own. We were not allowed to bring anything with a wrapper. Rightfully so. If it blew away, it would be out there forever. I took cubes of Cliff bar chews and put them in my pocket. I took the sheath off the protein bar and stuck it in the other pocket. We had to send sealed bottles of replenishment fluid ahead of time to the Chinese station with our name in ink on each bottle. They had agreed to put them out for us. What we didn't know is that is exactly what they did. Put them outside. When we ran by our products, they were lying on the ground, frozen solid. We would have to rely on what we were carrying for fluid.

I had a Camelbak with an insulated tube. Instead of hanging it on my back, I slung it against my stomach. That way it would stay warmed enough to drink. It worked effectively at minus 2. But as the temperatures dropped and the sea water bay could be heard cracking and popping as it froze, so did the insulated tube on my water bladder. Though the water nearest my belly sloshed and sloshed in a cruel, teasing manner, I was unable to get a drink from it. The outer tube was frozen solid.

There was nothing I could do. I put my head down and forged forward, hopping from one rut to another on the frozen ground, slipping and falling and picking myself back up. I decided the event would go to whomever could fall and pick themselves back up the most. I already felt like I was a life champ at doing that. So, I decided I could do this. Fall down and keep going. At least my hands and feet were toasty.

The next biggest challenge was the music in my ears. I rarely run with earphones and a playlist, but a marathon is a long way. And a marathon in Antarctica seemed like an exceptionally long way. There is something that helps pull you through when your body hits lulls and wall moments if you have music. Determination can be encouraged with an upbeat song. I wanted that option.

But somehow, I had pressed a button that is used for playing one song over, and over again. I had no idea there was such a button. The same song. Over and over. I ran the first half of that marathon to the tune of The Black-Eyed Peas' song "I've Got a Feeling." It was energizing at first and a nuisance after a few miles. I finally succeeded in biting the earphone cord in half with my teeth.

Whew. Hear that? Listen. Silence. That has an awesome set of lyrics.

To this day, all I have to hear is a few bars of "I've Got a feeling" and I feel like I am enduring a marathon in the furthest reaches of the most frozen corner of our earth.

Very far off, I could hear the sound of the bay freezing. And underneath me was the crunching of the waffled soles of my Inov8 shoes. My breathing was steady. I took the silence in like a great orchestra in a concert of minimal. The silence was loud. It had a feel. So did this vast expanse of land of ice with a breeze and a horizon that disappeared before the snow did. It has a feel also. And I felt grand in it. The feeling that comes when you know you are such a vulnerable speck in something large and not tailored for your survival. I respected it. Everything felt so much crisper.

A tiny speck was trotting across the valley and taunted me to catch up to its pace. I looked behind me and there was no one in sight. That is how spread out 98 people get running mileage on a frozen continent. It felt rewarding. I felt free. I couldn't have been more grateful to live long enough and work hard enough for the means to do this. My head wandered through all the bays we had already gotten to explore in Zodiacs. The whales had played among our boats, rolling on their backs, poking the black rubber with a purposed fin. Then rising to eyeball our reactions as we squealed. They would breach and slap the water with their tail as they submerged below the surface leaving a circle on the surface called a footprint. And they would follow us back to the ship. We toasted to them from the railings as they would wail, asking us to come back out and play. They would circle the ship for hours in disappointment as we ate a meal and watched them, now from the windows. It was uncanny. Very magical.

With those images in my mind now, I ran along and was overtaking the figure in the valley. It was a penguin. Not a real penguin, but a person who had brought a penguin costume to run in for their experience of the Antarctic Marathon. It gave me comic relief to watch the tail and the arms flap as I passed. The temperatures continued to drop and so did my head. I was alternating between freely breathing and taking breaths in my collar. And I was starting to feel the strain of the miles as they piled on. I had no idea what mile I was at. But I knew I was starting to feel thirsty. I stopped and tried to take the Camelbak out, but it froze solid within seconds of taking it out to try and drink from it. I ran on and could feel a bit of a stagger starting to creep into my steps. I determined I would never stop until I crossed that finish line. I crawled into that world of foggy thought.

Then I heard a man's deep voice calling out to me. I could not make out what he was saying. It sounded like I was in a tunnel, a wind chamber. "Maaaa, ma, ma." The sound came closer. "Maaa, Ma." Strong hands grabbed my shoulders. I fought to get away. "No," I tormented. "No. I am not stopping. I am finishing the race."

I kept running. The hands grabbed me again and the voice said, "Maaa, Ma." This time with more force.

He was forcing my body to turn around. The man put his face in view of my fallen head and pointed with earnest. I looked up. Behind me, in the direction he was pointing was an Antarctica Marathon Finisher Banner and a makeshift structure that flagged the finish line. I had run right under it, and in my fog and determination was continuing to run right back out into the vastness of ice.

A Russian scientist had spotted my head going by and ran out of his research trailer to turn me back. I had finished. I had been so determined to finish I didn't even know I had. I almost collapsed in his arms in triumph. I let out a feeble, "Oh, thank you. I guess I am finished now."

And I was. I had finished a marathon on one of earth's most inhumane terrains. I had finished a task done by only a handful of the entire human population. We celebrated the marathon with an American style bar b que on the back decks of the steel ship. Albeit all of us were wearing expedition jackets with the down hoodies pulled in tight. It was still minus 22 degrees. I was handed a plaque. "The Last Marathon. 1st Place. Female Division 50 to 59. March 30, 2015."

The expedition was only half over. We still had more bays to explore and things left to experience. They wanted to know if anyone wanted to try being left on an iceberg by themselves. I raised my hand and offered. When, on this earth can you sit and be totally by yourself with yourself. You better be a person you like to be with. And if not, turn things around to become one!

Reflecting, I sat on a chunk of ice and threw my arms out in an expanse of victory. I'm not alone. I am with me. I realized that "myself" went everywhere I went. I never got a vacation from "me". And, since I couldn't rid myself of myself, I better become a friend with the person I was going to have to spend the rest of my life with. It was a huge reward of this trip. I accepted myself for who I always was meant to be. Just me. And realized that here was no way to make that fact any different. Myself went everywhere I went.

The silence in Antarctica has a feel, and it was refreshing to be cooled by it. It was a good cool on the inside, too, because for the first time, I felt at peace with myself. Like the beauty of what a refrigerator preserves, loving yourself keeps things from going bad. Coming to terms with this was a medal worth adorning around my neck. It is a crisp feeling to FIND that you GO with YOU no matter where in the reaches of the planet you are. So. You might as well not try and take a vacation from yourself. You might be better off getting to like the person you spend the most time with…you.

It was then they announced the dare. It came over the loudspeaker. Did anyone want to do the polar plunge?

33

SERGEY No. 9

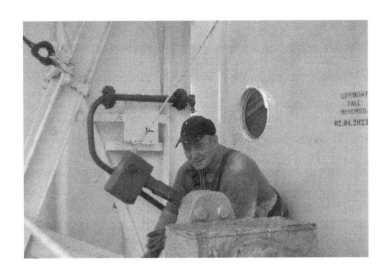

There was a movie when I was a child that captured my imagination—*The Russians are Coming*. This movie probably would not come up on anyone else's radar as influential, but it stirred imagination in me as a child. We were still in the Cold War with Russia. President Reagan must have finally done something to change that because every Eastern bloc country I visited since childhood has thanked me, as an American, for their freedom. Especially Poland. Somehow, he influenced the change and chance for freedoms without a physical war.

But, when I was a child, Russia was still holding countries behind a blockaded wall we called the Iron Curtain. And Russia was a constant themed enemy—the entire country of people pooled into one political label in almost every movie or conversation. I didn't believe it. I decided they had to be just like you and me—citizens trying to survive in the same world under difficult leaders. I didn't know there was a word to describe it. I was too little. It was "oppressed." But I felt it. And the injustice of it. And the need to free all people, like you were letting puppies out of a cage into a sunny backyard. My tiny heart said, *I would like to free the Russians.*

Even as a youth, I was fascinated by the idea of meeting people and cultures especially those estranged, or held back by a barrier, or a government, or economy. I wanted to FIND out who they really were. I knew they would be people just like you and me. I didn't want my conclusions about anybody to be what others labeled them for me. I knew if I met them in person, I would find truer information about them. And I would FIND something to like about them. I wanted them to become a real person to me.

The movie, *The Russians Are Coming,* was supposed to be a funny, fictional account of a Russian submarine that gets stuck on a sandbar off an island near New England. The sailors had to sneak ashore and search for food, parts to fix the submarine, and to try and find the right person that would help them without getting publicly caught. They knew that if the people on the island found out there was a submarine full of Russians submerged and broken so near American soil, they would be reactive instead of helping them.

I decided if I lived on that island and found out about them, I would help. I wouldn't be afraid. Although I was already afraid of a lot of things at my young age, helping people that were feared as different was not one of them. I sat watching that movie in a way most would not. I craved to let them be regular human beings in a scary situation. I was smitten by the idea of helping the Russians. That movie came out in 1966. At the time I watched it, I was only 5 years old.

I decided I would marry a Russian sailor someday at that preciously young age. Smile at the good heart of innocence.

I took the Polar Plunge dare. I had a bikini tucked in my luggage next to the sundresses, packed with me from timing the event on the Hawaiian Islands. It was folded nicely next to my sun dresses. Which, by the way, because the indoor temperature of the boats in Antarctica are nicely heated by the engines, I could wear them to dinner. But the polar plunge would happen on the decks. The challenge was to cannonball into a saltwater tank, the size of a giant jacuzzi, but without the heat. Once fully wet, you then had to dash over to the railings and get a picture taken of your body encased instantly in ice. Then race for the steel door leading to the sauna room to thaw out. I could do that, and I did. I let the other daredevils go first. I noticed, for the first time, Russian crew members were appearing on the deck to watch. They were very entertained by our antics.

It was the chilling experience it dared to be. The encased ice photos were fun to take, but the dash to the sauna was not. I slipped. The water splashed from the plunge had crusted the deck with ice. When the back of my head hit the deck, I was reminded that our ship was made of steel. The impact knocked me out.

I have never been knocked out before and coming to was terrifying. The world just died for a black, unsettling moment. I wanted to throw up. I couldn't remember where I was. The sailors wrapped me in a canvas tarp and were wrestling me down the metal ladders into their ant colony. I didn't care. I was floating in and out of consciousness.

There was a ship's doctor. I could hear the same rhythm of speech the man that had saved me from running back out into Antarctica had. I could tell this doctor was speaking Russian, but I couldn't see clearly. The impact still felt brutal. The doctor rolled the tarp back, and I could only guess his mutterings were, "Why in the world was I in a bikini in Antarctica?"

I was helped to my berth, and once in it, had no appetite. I didn't bother to go to dinner. But as the evening whittled by, I decided staying in a cubicle by myself would not be a good idea. I propped myself on a bench in the lobby entrance and bid goodnight to everyone as they passed to their rooms. Each asked if I was okay. I lied and said, "Yes." Yet, I had a splitting headache. How do prize fighters in a boxing match handle this? I wanted to feel sorry for myself. I went back and got my blanket, like a child does a pacifier. But I knew the best thing for me was to stay awake.

The comfort of the lights and sitting propped up made the spinning world come into better equilibrium. The two Russian ladies on our ship brushed by me at 11pm. They went into a side door down the hall. As it clicked shut, I got up and followed after them. Gingerly, I opened the door and then boldly stepped in. It was the ship's laundromat.

The ladies looked at me perplexed. They were folding laundry. I walked to their counter and started folding with them. They giggled. I smiled back. I learned there is a language of love that can be communicated even though there is no common denominator in a spoken language. I gestured. I inquired. I shared with them my life, loves, and hurts. And they did the same. Time passed quickly, and they were done with their task. We all disappeared back out the hatch.

I joined them many nights that I was on that ship. I learned that they were working to help their families back home. I asked about children and husbands, and their eyes saddened more than they already were. This was no life for children or a husband. I understood. They were sacrificing their own lives so others from their family could live their own. I found subjects to joke with them, and I hoped by doing so, their daily chore of doing hours of laundry was made more fun. At least that first night it kept me from falling asleep. I was sure I had a concussion.

I started wandering the ship well past midnight, after folding laundry with the Russian ladies. I went to the bridge and badgered the captain and co-captain with a barrage of questions. They seemed grateful for the chatter to cover some of the hours of the long and dark night's voyage. The door to where they steered was usually locked all day, but I found it opened at night, and I used the chance to be a student on what it took to be a captain of a ship. I think they felt my sincerity. They seemed to look forward to my next set of questions each night.

"Where did his crew come from?" I asked.

"All over Russia, but mainly from the port town of Kaliningrad." He acted like I should know where that was.

"How many?"

He detailed each crew member's jobs and duties and number per each station. If I added them all together, I think it took 42 crew members to operate this vessel.

"How long were their voyages at sea."

"Typically 9 months."

"How often did they get to get off the ship?"

"Rarely. Maybe one or two times per voyage."

That explained why the dash to Ushuaia had such commotion and held the level of importance as if getting to unwrap gifts at Christmas.

"Did they speak English as well as the captain?" The captain smiled.

"No, we were educated in the States. In fact, my wife loves America and its styles. We end up vacationing there every year." This led to some conversations about America, women, styles, and places. He said, "Thank you. This is very helpful. It will give me things to go and do with my wife when there. But it is also helping me understand my daughter. She is attending an American college."

I remembered to ask again. "Do the sailors know English?"

He explained, "They take English in school, but it is so different than Russian and if not used, it is hard to ever be fluent."

"But, what about the English words on the walls of the weight room?" I asked.

The Captain looked at me with a warm grin. "So, you know about the weight room made out of ship parts?" He was amused.

I had asked the ladies while folding laundry what the clanking noise was beneath us. They giggled and demonstrated lifting weights. They showed me in charade fashion that the gym was made up of balanced out spare parts from the ship. And they wrote pretend words on a wall to tell me that they were trying to learn English. All of the crew put vocabulary words on the walls to study.

The Captain continued, "And that the sailors are trying to teach themselves English. If they can learn English, there is the hope they can work on a cruise liner someday. This is considered a crew ship, a research vessel, not an ocean cruise line. You know, a cruise ship… like the ones that are a floating Disneyland. I prefer this ship. This takes real sailing and real sailors. You have already experienced the temperatures and that this can be the fiercest oceans on earth. But I have the best, dedicated and hardworking crew. Respectful men and women of character." He was sincerely proud.

I liked the way the captain talked about and viewed his crew. He added, "I know everything about this ship. I know everything that goes on… on this ship. I know that you have been going in the laundry room." I was embarrassed at being caught.

"You have made my crew happier."

"How's that?" I couldn't see how. I hadn't even met the crew. I had just been folding linens with the ladies.

"They know you are asking about them. They know you care. And it, somehow, has lifted all the crew's spirits. I am in gratitude for that. It is something I cannot do for them."

How could I have that effect? Maybe it was like that saying, "People don't care how much you know, until they know how much you care." I really did care. I was so interested in what life was really like for these people working most their lives in the walls of steel ladders and grates. And standing in fresh air only from the side catwalks, your front yard and back yard being the ocean. Where the challenge is to teach yourself English out of a textbook and words on a wall. And where a gym was made from spare boat parts to enhance their own situation. These sailors were the real Russians in *The Russians are Coming*.

So, when I physically bumped into Sergey running up the short cut stairs to the top lounge, it was one of those stupid, blunder moments of, "Excuse, me. Pardon me. Sorry." Both of us muttered the same in our own languages. We stood there awkwardly, not knowing who should allow whom to pass. Both of us looked at the floor, then the walls, and finally at each other, straight in the eyes. Light blue eyes with a twinkle of humor stared back at me.

He motioned at his tiny camera and waved up the stairwell. I could tell by sign language he was looking for a cable that would connect his phone to a computer and download pictures. I took the camera and rolled it around to the connector port. I had that cable in my little room with the porthole window. I pointed at myself, then down the stairs and nodded yes. He pointed at his watch. I caught on he had to get to his duty on the ship.

It was funny how fast we could communicate without knowing each other's language. I pointed at his camera. I motioned I would download the pictures on a flash drive and meet him at this same spot the next day at the same time. He nodded yes and handed me the camera. We were already starting to cross the roaring forties to head back to Ushuaia and the sailors were busy sailing. He wanted to take back pictures of Antarctica.

There was a sense of urgency aboard the ship. We would be shifting from the calm bays to crossing the real ocean. I had no idea we were heading into a storm. The sailors knew we were the last passengers they would have on this ship for the season. Their next voyage would be to take this vessel all the way back up to Kaliningrad, service it, and it would begin cruises in the Arctic on a flip season of tours. What a work shift… polar to polar.

Sergey smiled a big ear-to-ear grin and said in eloquent English, "I would very much appreciate that you did this for me." His face twisted with the thought and force of producing each word correctly. I was impressed because I could see how pleased he was to use English. I was trying to stuff down an unexpected girlish shyness. Now this one was a different shyness then that unexpected "teen-ish" crush on the Expedition leader. I knew that was just fun and as shallow as those to a movie screen. I had overheard a radio squelch from the Expedition crew, "Choose the younger one. She can sire a child." That was in response to every single lady on the ship who was smitten by the Expedition owner, like teens are with a movie star. I knew, as wisely as he did, that it was best to be left like camp crushes and to not be acted upon!

But standing here was a real Russian sailor, and of all things, he treasured his photos. He stood there, a solid, but soft soul. I asked him if he used the gym and pointed to the decks below by motioning lifting and curling weights. He chuckled comfortably and looked so bemused that I would know about their ways to live aboard a steel world. As with instant coffee or instant oatmeal, bumping into each other on a stairwell, smirking at each other and our vast differences, we brewed instant friendship despite being from such vastly different worlds.

"Of… yes. We all do. "We…are… Russian… Greco… Wrestlers." And he made a motion of grabbing someone in a hold. I had no idea what Greco Wrestling was, but his sport of choice somehow accounted for why he had such a solid stance and thick neck. Or because he was built that way, that form of wrestling was tailored for his genes. I pointed at my watch and made the motion for tomorrow. He was so appreciative to get his photos in a way he would be able to download on a computer. I was pleased to be able to hand him a loaded flash drive and do it for him.

The last day before we hit open water, the captain announced that he would allow tours of the inside of the ship and to meet the crew. We were going to get to go down into the ant colony! I was told this rarely gets to happen. And even more rare, the Captain agreed to attend a ship supper in honor of himself. It was the Captain who had allowed his crew to come on the decks and watch us silly tourists dunk ourselves in a ship research tank in polar temperatures. Hope and great energy were spreading through the ship.

In the hallway on that last day, it was like a convention. The Captain allowed the sailors to talk with the passengers. Sergey introduced me to other sailors. Come to find out the first name Sergey is like John, or Joe, or Jim in English. Twelve of the 42 crew were named Sergey. This Greco wrestler was Sergey number 9. At dinner, the passengers all talked about how interesting it was to see the inner workings of a vessel and meet the crew. I suggested we should each team up and adopt one crew member's family. There were 99 of us. We could get to know a little about them and their families and send packages and fun things to them. We could be like a pen pal and give them someone to interact with who cared about where in this world they were. I adopted Sergey number 9.

The first open ocean we entered buffeted us with heavy seas, and the ship turned off course to sail in a better direction with the storm. I knew to ride out rough seas facing forward and not rolling inside the bed of a berth. I stayed on the bridge. Every so often, a rogue wave would slam into the ship and red lights and alarms would sound as emergency systems flickered in reserve. Thankfully, none of them ended up turning into a full alert. Seconds later, full electricity would restore. Sergey later shared we were taking on some water with these side hits, and the system was warning them. We were the last boat to come back from the tourist season, a week behind all the others. The storm was trying to blow us backward, requiring "all hands on deck", and focused sailing from the Captain and his crew. They did a very professional job getting us safely to the port in Ushuaia.

Since we arrived later than expected, there was a lot of fast commotion on the deck. Our bags disappeared from in front of our rooms, and we were pushed down the ramp toward our passports with hasty goodbyes. I squeezed back up the descending passengers, scanning frantically, searching for Sergey Number 9 like some movie scene from Titanic. I had a note to give him with a phone number and email address. I found him loading the carts with luggage.

"You don't get to get off the ship?" I surmised correctly. He shook his head with the somber expression that comes from a job like this. Sailors that drew the lucky lots were already past the passengers and I could see them running to the town. "I have a note for you. It's my contact information. Promise you will keep in touch." I squeezed it into his hand. I gave him the cord to keep so he could download his pictures. I gave him a one-armed hug that could only reach halfway around his wide shoulders. He was shaking. I squeezed his hand again.

Somehow, in that short of an exchange, there was a bond. I always wanted to meet a real Russian sailor. He always wanted to practice English with a real English-speaking American. I wanted him to experience more than being within the walls of a ship. What would it be like if he knew someone cared what happened to him on his voyages? To care whether he made it back in time to see his mom before she passed away and got to hug a sister or a newly born nephew?

About a month later, I had an email in my array of event related work. It was from sergey9@bigwhiteship.com. He had told me to receive photos or send them was very expensive when the ships were sailed back to the Russian shipyards in Kaliningrad. It was almost the cost of a week's wages. He shared that it would take months to sail back. They picked up oil cargo or something to help offset costs that tourism did not bring. He said that keeping contact was always difficult for all of them. He told me he would contact me when he arrived back in Russia.

When not sailing, Sergey lived in a homestead, in a wooded village outside of Kaliningrad. When not at sea, he chopped firewood and planted potatoes and a vegetable garden that he shared with his village. He did not have a car to drive. He took a bus to get to town. He had a sister and mother who live in another region, and his first course once back from sea was to get paperwork to travel by train to that region and spend time with his family.

I googled information on the town of Kaliningrad and found out it is a region not connected to Russia. When they divided land after WWII, Russia said it must have an ice-free port. This area is two hundred miles from the Russian border and a section of Poland separates it. It is a strategic shipyard and a military base. It is highly regulated with permits to be able to exit or enter. But there are many wooded villages that surround it.

One day, almost half a year after the Antarctica marathon, the sound of Skype activated on my laptop. It was a request from Sergey. Through Skype, I was able to learn about his wood piles, farming, friends, and village. I was able to show him the perfectly paved roads of California and take him on virtual tours of places like Wyoming. And, he was able to practice his English with me.

One time, I collected gift certificates for shoes from a running sponsor for Sergey and his villagers. Then I handed the store clerk my phone. "Here, let them pick out their own pairs." Sitting in an apartment size dwelling in the woods of a Russian region, Sergey got to virtually shop for shoes. He picked a pair of Nikes. He, again, expressed how fortunate he was to have this link to learn about America. He felt like my Belmont Boys, that he was the luckiest ever with this chance to be treated to Nike shoes. It was as if I was sending him bars of gold. He reminded me that a man of his means does not get to buy Nike shoes. Or lots of things for that matter.

I went to UPS to ship them. They told me that it would be $361 per shoe box. I was flabbergasted. How could it cost that much to send shoes? This must be a mistake. This was long before the rise in prices created by Covid. I bellowed back, "For one box of shoes?"

The cashier in his signature brown uniform nodded and said, "Yes."

I took the shoe box and went down the street to Fed Ex. The price came up the same. The Fed Ex employee explained that Kaliningrad was in a restricted region, whatever that meant. He suggested I take it the US Post office. The post office rang up as $98, almost the value of the shoes. So, I took advantage of the crevasses left in the box and stuffed event shirts and five US $20 bills in the toes. The postal worker said I would have to open the package so he could inventory the contents and that I would not be able to send the cash. Sergey, in an email, agreed. "No, do not ever send cash," he adamantly told me, convincing me that cash in a package would cause consequences. I wasn't sure how or why. The postal worker was candid. He felt the chances of the package getting to a person in that region, even with no cash, was slim. And that it would probably take at least eight to 12 weeks to get there.

I asked Sergey what other things I could put in a box for them. His friend, Yuri, said he ran a makeshift summer camp to entertain kids. He called it Indian Camp and made makeshift bows and arrows, painted their faces like Native American Indians, and they slept in tents. It cost very little to cause so much enjoyment. Yuri wanted a men's and women's Indian headdress for he and his wife to adorn as the camp hosts. Go figure. I had to order them from China. But I got them and squeezed these into each shoe box.

I got a confirmation that the box was delivered months later. Sergey was denied its arrival for weeks thereafter. He would take the bus to town and stand in line at the post office and get a "no" as an answer. Finally, one day when he Skyped, he proudly stood in front of his laptop camera with a SO CAL Caren Ware Events Pirate's Shirt. He pounded on his chest in triumph. "I'm a pie-rite. The sailor is a pirate!" He raised his feet to show off how well his new Nike shoes fit. I am not sure how he got the box.

A picture popped up on my email. Yuri is sitting, Indian style, in the new headdress, heading up his camp for kids for them to have something fun to do in the summer.

It only took shoe boxes and a heart to send it.

34

Getting to Africa

My life was afloat, long after returning from Antarctica though I had experienced an amazing, rare for any, life experience. I had met intriguing and admirable people, but my heart ached after relationships I so loved, but bafflingly walked away from.

Inwardly, I had missed the train. I don't even remember the name of the movie. I think it was an Australian film, but I carry the point and impact. A man did everything to rescue a woman throughout this movie. Though there was no physical closeness in the film, his protective actions were true love. I, the viewer, fell in love with them as a couple, which was the point of the script. But the parting scene was him getting her safely to a train, and her tipping her hat as the train pulled away. Your heart sank. They were meant to be soulmates, bonded by all the acts of love experienced in the movie. They had been through so much. This scene turned heart wrenching. How could they ever part ways? And part this way? My heart wailed.

And then, at the last second possible, the man turned back and grabbed the caboose railing… and stepped onto the parting train. Whew. That's better. Hurray.

We want life to be this way. Love should be this way. So, why, when I had a person in my life rescue me in such a consistent display of help, did I let that train pass into the horizon? I thought I was supposed to carry the load of my life… solo. Therefore, I was carrying my "why did I let that go" question to all the ends of the earth, along with the severed rope of my marriage, the loss of my mom, the "why does my dad get to live such a 'rich' life?" This was frozen solid in an icy region of me that would not defrost. Love lost. Love never had.

What do you do when you miss a train you were most likely meant to be on? I guess you keep going and finish the one track you are already on. I had more continent marathons to run. I had so much more FINDING to do. And, I had left to choose to be the real love I was missing.

Survival, many times, comes down to a good decision. But I didn't know how to clearly make decisions. Most of my life had been conditioned to make decisions based on what would affect someone else, not me. It did not matter that I had ventured to clear my head. I was in a white out because fog came with me. I still did not know I had a pyramid of poor operational life skills. I had spent so much money and time see-sawing back and forth from California to Wyoming, going on potential job interviews and openings, waiting for a full-time job opening in this town or that. Trying to re-community yourself at my age, without the concrete foundation of making good choices is challenging. I was lost in heart.

Plus, I was dealing with the consequences of a recession. Two years passed and nothing had solidified except my waxing bank account as I had tried to secure a recreation position. After making it on panels as the top three candidates in far too many towns, I returned to a director's office without an appointment. When I stepped in and shut the door, I was told the reasons for not choosing a candidate could not be discussed. So, I shot out yes or no questions at the person behind the desk.

"Was it because they already had a candidate in mind, but had to go through the formal process? "

"Yes."

"Would they ever hire anyone over the age of fifty?"

"No."

"So, did I get put on the top three selection so the cards would fall that the best and likely candidate became the in-house person they had already chosen? A person that faithfully worked a lower position for years and deserved this promotion?

The eye contact told me the answer before the word "Yes" was the response.

"Would I ever get hired as a fifty-year-old in these management positions?"

He put his head down. With no eye contact, the answer took a while. "No."

"Then, I thank you. I will stop wasting my time and money going through these interview processes. This would have been good to honestly have known." I turned to walk back out into the world.

He tried to throw an appeasement. "You do interview well. Your resume and life experiences are amazing."

My destination place of the grand outdoors and hunkering around Jackson Hole, Wyoming had allowed me to heal and get healthy physically. But my chances of financial survival, for sure, were in my face. Couple this with the fumbling inability to recognize danger, and I was surrounded by invisible flames, having ignored the smoke. How? My dad had been danger. We couldn't call it that, nor get out of harm's way. My damage alarms were wired to the wrong things because my dad's disorder needed us to be like toy punching bags that are weighed down but always spring back to meet the next punch. I was so used to being anchored in harm's way my feet did not know they could move. My harm alarms were broken.

This created fear that something stealth was out there to get me because I had no defense. Harm lurks. Harm hurts. And I felt like I was supposed to just take it. Like those experiments with the fish in a bowl where they place a clear plexiglass sheet between it and its food. After bashing into the boundary glass, it finally stops trying to get the food. Finally, when the invisible barrier is removed, the fish starves to death with the food floating within reach. Why? Because it has learned to not take care of its needs having to avoid hurt. See how powerful hurt is? It can literally kill you. Starve the life right out of you if you let it. I had been conditioned to not take care of even basic needs. Food, shelter, water…taking the time to pee when needed. Sleep when necessary.

There is value in our pasts. Things to learn from. And, yes, I am convinced we all can FIND good take-aways. So, I credit to myself that I can handle and muster through what most would never do. When real situations arise, like cyclones, forest fires, and car crashes, I can master figuring out how to get through them. What was holding me hostage from living like I think the Creator meant for me to flourish …was, well… me.

I had gone with myself to every continent, and I was still following me everywhere I went. I was the common denominator in my struggles.

Of course, I still had a goal to run a marathon on every continent, and I had one big one left to do. AFRICA. I started to map that out. I knew a company that packaged trips to the Kilimanjaro Marathon. I could tackle two goals there…run and climb.

But how do you get to the poorest continent on the earth when you are so poor yourself? Life had become raw in 2013 for me. I was down to the bottom level of Maslow's Hierarchy of Needs—food, clothing, shelter. I was working at side jobs that came with breakfast and dinner. Coaching track. Delivering packages for UPS. Working retail. The marathon was in February. It was December. I didn't even have money for Christmas decorations. I went to the dollar store and bought one cheap string of lights and a reindeer with a candle in it. I had two dollars to do so.

I implored the company that had packages to the Kilimanjaro Marathon—was there any way I could work a travel spot off? It was a long shot in asking.

"Funny you should ask," the owner, Kathy said. "I know of you and your reputation with your timing company. I am getting older and would like to offer you to help work some races and discuss the option of buying this marathon travel business. Yes, let's make going to the Kilimanjaro Marathon happen."

She wanted my passport number and sent me a list of immunizations I would need and medications for high altitude. "I believe in you," she wrote in an email. "I believe you are going to start up something new and fresh. It is time for your reset button."

I was going to do the Kilimanjaro Marathon in a town called Moshi and then climb the near 20,000-foot beast of a volcano in the following days. That would be a major undertaking. I already knew how to undertake.

The few winter months I had before Kilimanjaro, I gathered what I needed. The little funds I had in my 401K were making payments on my vehicles and health and car insurance premiums. It was a short matter of time before this, also, would run out. So, I poured through each company and all the products at Teton Mountaineering, learning about Marmot, Arc'teryx, Patagonia, Outdoor Research, Icebreaker, etc. I paced out what I could buy in the way of layers: wool, down, Gortex shells. I bought hiking boots I hoped would handle Kilimanjaro. And I trained to be able to run 26.2 miles and then grab a pack and summit an almost 20,000 foot mountain. It could be as cold as in Antarctica. The normal temperature for that time of year was -22 on top the summit of Mt. Kilimanjaro. Almost hard to believe that could be in Africa. I knew I would have to be creative to finally finish this last continent marathon.

I boarded a flight with a tour group like my clothes were on fire. I was broke. I was houseless, which I guess, is considered homeless. It felt like it. I didn't know where to land or call home, so, somehow, I ended up without one. I had wandered long enough to near purposelessness. Yet, my core—the passion and heart of who I was (or who you are)—is infinitely valuable and should be a thread we cling to. This is a wealth that should never be counted as poor. And thereby, none of us should ever fall to the attitude that we are worthless and poor because we do not have the man-driven possessions that we attribute to success. But all that fades to words as the feelings of worthlessness seep in and become so real. They saturate. Bog down. Sog heavily. And tend to tip the soul toward debilitating depression.

Stepping into Africa, I got to see a large portion of population that was one day away, sometimes hours away, from physical starvation. It seemed like they were innocent fish left in a bowl by corrupt governments and wars over power and wealth. A bowl that needed someone to sprinkle fish food on it and help them be able to even eat.

I was relieved to find Tanzania one of the more promising countries in Africa. The flood of people climbing Kilimanjaro and enjoying African Safaris was helping provide economy and hope. Tanzania made commitments to steer away from warring over power and to concentrate on this peaceful tourism as an economy source. They welcomed our marathon touring group with sincere hospitality.

35

It Almost Killed Me

Continent 7: Africa — The Kilimanjaro Marathon

In Africa, feeling as parched as the land.

Tethered inside the tin sided soccer stadium was a huge balloon arch that signified the start and finish of the marathon. It had a colorful picture of a cloud shrouded Mt. Kilimanjaro. On this day, the real mountain loomed in the distance and remained cloudless. It felt like a towering, regal monument. It would be a tormenting figure that never moved. The mountain would stand there like the rock statue it is, almost with its arms crossed, as if to say, "Now, let's just see if you can make it 26.2 miles in the heat."

It was oven hot. Baking hot. My shorts and tank top were sweat soaked just walking from the walled hotel complex to the buzz inside the soccer stadium. Stepping into that arena felt like all of Africa was taking part. The stadium was packed. The marathon was such a happening the entire town of Moshi wanted to be there. African runners from all over were warming up, stretching, and taking this run very seriously. Us handful of foreigners looked childish and poorly trained for this focused of a crowd. Running was a respected and sought-after sport here. All seemed motivated to train for something that flickered into dreams of going to the Olympics. This was the same drive I found in my Belmont boys. It was impressive.

Bang. The sound of a track start gun went off. We ran through the town and then on to another and another. It was Sunday, so the sides of the streets were arrayed with well-dressed women in their Sunday best dresses and men in starched shirts. They politely cheered and were sincerely as cheerful as their Sunday attire.

I had purchased a fanny pack that had three small flasks for hydration and water. I have an insignificant S shaped curve in my spine from teen scoliosis. It rarely bothers me except when I hang a purse or backpack off to one shoulder. For some reason, the bouncing of these three flasks on that belt tugged my back into knots well into the first half of the marathon. I suggest you run with your equipment and trial it a few times before the actual marathon day. I didn't and this pack was bothersome.

I saw a boy holding the hands of his two younger siblings. He was obviously on childcare watch. He was dragging two reluctant sisters so he could get to the side of the street and watch the runners go by. The reason he caught my attention. His eyes. He was thrilled. They danced with ecstasy to see so many runners running. His head was bobbling. He couldn't contain himself. He started to drag the two young girls at a running pace, trying to keep up with us for a moment to feel what it would be like if that was him someday. He had good speed and was abreast with me, even with the dangling sisters. I unsnapped the belt of the fanny pack and handed it to him. His eyes popped right out of his sockets, and he stopped with his prize in hand, rolling it around. I don't think it mattered what it was. I knew it would be a prize to him because it had to do with running.

As I looked back, the two girls were each grabbing a bottle and sucking the delicious sweet from the Nuun juice I was using as hydration. The boy was still looking straight at me. He pumped his new belt in the air and his mouth said something in Swahili. I think he said, "Thank you." At least his eyes did. They relayed, "I won something special today."

I couldn't have been more pleased. For at least the next two miles I got to think about the boy. Then, about 14 miles into the 26.2 miles of the marathon, I began to sense something I hadn't taken notice of. Something important. Water and hydration were missing at every aid station. I ran by a few empty ones. Used playing card tables with nothing on them. There were smashed plastic bottles and empty baggies on the ground. But, by the time my middle of the pack pace was getting to the aid stations, the water and hydration were gone.

I had experienced no hydration in Antarctica before when all the aid station bottles ended up frozen as the temperatures plummeted to minus 22. Even our insulated camel back tubes had frozen. It looked like I was going to have to go without water here also. At least I had gotten some on the first miles. But this was not as cool as Antarctica. We were near the equator. Heat had already proven to be a problem for me. And, I had given away my hydration fanny pack.

Several of us had flown to the islands in the Atlantic and plopped on St. Croix for the St Croix Half Ironman. On the swim portion of the race, several of us got swept past a buoy in a rip tide. It took us twice as long to get back in. By the time we did, all the other bikes were already gone in the transition area.

The St Croix Half Ironman is known for a gnarly, 16% grade hill climb called THE BEAST. I triumphantly started catching up to and passing the other cyclists on the climb. Easterly winds hit us from all directions on the backside of the island, and I started falling back toward the middle of the pack. I was spent and overheating.

In the final leg, I ran like I meant it, determined to get to the podium for my age group. As I approached the last aid station, 2 miles before the finish, my eyesight narrowed. Then disappeared. *That is odd*, my brain said. In the dark, I staggered toward clapping and heard a young voice say, "Lady. Could you use this?" I heard a pop, and a fizz and that unmistakable sound of a can of Coca Cola being poured over ice. Could I?! I felt a Styrofoam cup pushed into my hand. It must have been the sugar, caffeine, and cool temperature because as I sipped, my eyesight lifted, and I ran into the finish.

I made it two steps past the finish and collapsed. Luckily, I had friends there. They grabbed me saying, "You are overheated and dehydrated." They carried me to the kiddie pools that the organizers had filled with ice and water and plunged me in. But there were no ice baths in Moshi.

―⁂―

About the 16th mile, the course took to the foothills of Mount Kilimanjaro. Though the changing terrain was now lusher, the ability to find water on the course was nonexistent. My head was hot. It felt like my brain was burning from the inside. This was not good. And there was no way to communicate medical need on this far part of the course. I just narrowed my vision and listened to the sound my determined steps were making. As long as I kept that sound going, I would eventually make it to the finish line. I commanded myself to go.

Pound, pound, pound. It went on for miles in an excruciating fight to keep going and not burn up. I felt like I had a fever, and I was starting to go in and out of an awareness of where I was. Even who I was. I saw faces and heard people cheering, but it was if I was in a dream, and they were in another room talking.

I went down. I didn't pass out. I just found myself flopping on the blistering pavement like a fish out of water. My legs, arms, and back seemed to be in a flip-flopping flinging match that I could not control. I was cramping all over. All at once. I crawled to a shaded part of the pavement on my hands and knees. My mouth was bone dry, and I felt pasty. Disoriented. I tried to get up and run, but every few feet I would fall to the ground with the same cramping.

I could hear the hum of the stadium, so I knew the end was near. But this might be the end for me. I knew to be alarmed. That was not a good thing. There was no one around to help and the runners passing me were on their own survival pace to get to that finish. I decided I better count to ten. Ten steps and stop. Ten more running steps and stop. And finally, the hum was turning into a roar, and I was in the stadium. Ten steps, cramp. Hop. Ten more steps. More cramps. Stop. Finally, I was under the arch and looking straight into the mountain folding its arms at me. It seemed to be saying, "I told you it was going to be hot."

"But I did it," I told the mountain. "You almost did me. But I did you. I ran around the bottom of your base, and now I am going to scale you and stand up to any arms folded, scolding my life in unseen ways."

I had every reason to be the owner of a good proud. A gentle pride flooded me that I so needed. A lot of poor self-talk had haunted me, following me all the way to Africa. That flooded feeling of no worth because I had no monetary value. No prominently held job title. No significance without a significant other. You can take back all the words about me, bad self-talk. I did this. And, no matter what circumstances surround me, I am proving to myself in these marathon moments I have what it takes.

Something in the entirety of the project—to run a marathon on every continent was in that last step. Life and its setbacks that wanted to get me down on the ground, cramping in anguish. Divorce. Financial setbacks. Misunderstandings and mistrust. Navigating life without skills I should have learned in childhood. The poor choice of letting entanglements do damage. Being embezzled. The wrong relationships. The right ones. Talking too much. Talking too little. I was eating myself alive with my own self dislike. All those things were enough to take every ounce of liquid out of me, but… I counted to ten and kept going. I was facing the mountain that dared me to just try to climb it. I would start for its 19, 341 (5,895 meters) summit tomorrow. But for today, I ran a full marathon in Africa. I was learning to recognize the predators in my own life. I was determined to keep them away like the Maasai beating sticks to flush back approaching lions or leopards.

They placed a tiny medal with a handmade neck ribbon over my head. The medal slid down on my chest and spun, arching in the sun, and sending glimmers. Glimmers of hope. I felt impassioned. It dawned on me; we always have our heart with us. Somehow, in those moments as I walked away from that finish line, it was only the start. I cared. And that, in itself, had beautiful and significant value. I gave myself a smile knowing I was going to be okay. I didn't need any THING or any ONE to make me feel valuable. I could be of value. And I could value myself. And that was value that was not fickle.

I wandered to the refreshment stand and bought myself an ice-cold… Coke.

36

Eaten Alive

I cared. I felt for the children living in the ravine when our tour buses stopped for lunch. Our lunch bags had sandwiches and oranges, cookies and chips, and little boxed drinks. Few ate all that were in them. Few, maybe me alone, noticed the kids trying to crawl closer to the hope for a meal. A security guard was hired to walk the back fence with a stick and keep them at bay. He had the most pained look on his face. He didn't like his job. But he, most certainly, had no other opportunity for income and had to do a job that hurt his heart as much as it was hurting mine to see such need. I discreetly gathered up all the leftovers on the tables and headed toward the fence while the rest of the tour group headed toward the bus.

The guard motioned at me to stop and then our eyes met. We were in a standoff and our hearts won. He darted his eyes to the end of the fence opposite of where he was standing. He turned his back and acted as if he was keeping watch. I raced over to that far corner and waved the bags in the air so the ravine could see. I thought there were a few. There were many. Children of all ages and sizes came sprinting across the opening. I thought it would be chaos. But each took a turn taking a bag, the older kids letting the younger go first. To my delight there were just enough bags with, save one, remaining. And it was meant for someone.

An injured little boy was dragging himself toward the fence using a tree branch as a crutch. It would have taken an agonizing expenditure of energy to get to my far location. I waved the bag and moved back toward the guard. I threw it over the fence as hard as I could, and it landed within reach of him. He curled up on the ground and hugged that bag tightly. The guard looked at me. I barely detected a nod I took as a thank you. I heard the bus diesel engine start and was the last one to get on.

This is the boy I dropped the $20 out the bus window to drift to his feet. His hand wasn't up asking for anything. It was asking the busload not to stare at his circumstance.

I was staring out the window of the bus, when a boy came into view on the side of the road. His clothes were tattered and filthy. I snapped a picture of him and he angrily stuck his hand out to stop my tourist gawking. He was in real need. In real need of something that curbed his hunger, not a staring sightseer in an air-conditioned bus. It was the first $20 I handed out in a foreign country. It was the only $20 I had. I slipped it through the slit in the window and it sucked away and fluttered in a ditch. The boy ran to see what it was and held it up high in a clutch. I only hoped it will help in some, instant way and the message would be that I cared about his struggle.

Before the Kilimanjaro Marathon, we toured as a safari. We flew in tiny airplanes to the Serengeti to watch what someone counted to be over 300,000 zebras and 1.5 million Wildebeest on their yearly migration across the parched plains of Africa, crossing treacherous, crocodile infested rivers and dealing with immense hardships to get to better feeding grounds. This migration we were getting to witness is one of the most epic animal related events on the entire planet. I was in almost unspeakable awe.

Fun fact. Here's the running resume of the Wildebeest. They have a top speed of 50 mph. This once-a-year trek is over 1800 miles. They do it in true cross country track fashion, running most the way over the course of months. The most startling factoid is the Wildebeests' babies are born, and within 7 minutes, get up on their wobbly legs…and start to run, keeping up with the pack. It's a wonder to witness in person. Almost eerie, it's so amazing.

Equally interesting is why they travel together. The zebra has good eyesight, but a poor sense of smell. The wildebeest sniff the air constantly for lions, hyenas, chetahs, and other predators, but cannot see very well. They travel together to protect one another. The zebras were constantly watching the wildebeest. If they all start sniffing, the zebras begin looking and would face the direction they saw danger. In this way, they used each other's strengths to protect them from their weaknesses. We need each other in much the same way.

To best view elephants, a tour company in the Serengeti filled hot air balloons so we could drift over the plains and watch the elephants from on high. Of course, that jet sound when the hot air is released to keep the balloon lifted concerned the alpha elephant. He sent his women into a circle formation, putting all the infants in the center for protection as the pioneers of American did with their wagon trains when under threat. The bull elephants then went on the attack, charging at our passing shadow to chase it away from their brood. Once our balloon drifted far enough, they eased out of formation and went back to enjoying the grass. I liked how they circled up together. That's what family and friends are for. I decided floating in the warm winds of Africa that I was going to circle up runners in much the same way. Create something that helped people feel like we were there for each other.

After flying back to the Moshi area, we toured an extinct volcano teaming with wildlife so massive, prolific, and unique to Africa. There were even more elephants, giraffes, ostrich, rhinos, water buffalo, and birds of all exotic kinds. We were guests roaming through their parading habit. Standing up, we peered out of the roofless, steal sided safari vans and snapped pictures in all directions. Zooming in on wildlife right before our eyes was spell bounding to me. All so spell bounding to me. I was here, among all that I had read so much about throughout my childhood. How could I eat myself up anymore doing this? It threw a needed switch on my mood. As travel and adventure does.

We slept in tents that were already erected when we arrived. And a cook tent was bustling with warm aromas for tasty meals made just for us. I am sure these smells drifted in the winds and tantalized the portion of the animal population that were predictors. They hired a local Maasai tribe to stand watch and beat sticks at night to ward off the lions, tigers, and leopards. This wasn't an Africa Safari in a movie. This was being on one in real time.

I took to the cook tent. I wanted to meet the Tanzanians and this village tribe. They were boiling water for our tent showers and preparing hot towels to wash our faces and hands. They were humming and singing, chanting in a soft verse that connected them all. I fell in love with the land and these hard-working people.

I asked them if I could go on a run. They instructed it was okay to 'run around camp'. Being one to run miles and miles of trails, and back roads, I took to the dirt road we came in on and a little foot path I had seen. When I returned, the Maasai were gone. I had heard them beating sticks far off in the bushes. And even the guides were gone. Our tour group was looking at me with sore faces.

"They are out looking for you. There is a leopard in the area. They didn't want to tell us about it, to scare the tourists. When they said you could run 'around camp', they meant in this tight circle inside the erected tent formation." They chained me to the guide after that, tethered to 200 yards from any vehicle or tent.

I was in the most astounding place on earth, yet I wasn't doing well on the inside. I was so racked with a sense of lost that I could not sleep. And when I did, I would wake up in a sweat not induced by the African heat. I was grieving. Lost. Still bewildered. And carrying that purposelessness that feels like you are standing too close to an edge. It was peeling the weight right off me. It showed in pictures. My weight dropped alarmingly, as if food had no calories for a detached, no home-based person.

I babbled even more than usual. Filling up the air. I was filling up space with stories, clawing for some affirmation of importance. My words were a desperate struggle to stay above the surface. Talking too much is not an endearing way to draw people closer to you. The roommate I was matched with on the first night we arrived in Africa asked to be moved. We hadn't even begun our African Safari.

Since I lay awake at night there was a benefit. I listened to the many sounds of Africa, and they were noisy. The ground crunched, bushes moved, and nocturnal animals were creeping and came around. And there. Unmistakable, the roar of a lion. Many times, he bellowed to make sure the earth knew he was there. King of the Jungle. In many ways, I respect my dad. And later, would get to understand better the core of his own hurts. He rose to be lion because it was the place that would protect him. It's just too bad such a good looking, living thing has a bent to eat you alive.

Kathy, the marathon tour guide owner, reached down a helping heart and lifted me up by my bootstraps with sincere grace. In a figurative way, she pulled me to the side of the pool with a safety hook because she recognized emotional drowning. Instead of telling me I was on my own to learn how to swim again, she offered kind words, a wide-open gate of patience, and the opportunity to make payments to pay the trip off in small increments, even if it took years. She wanted to help nudge me toward finances that at least had margins.

She gently told stories of how it took years for her to rise to become a functioning business again. She shared about the loss of her husband in a motorcycle accident. And, then some devastating accident also happened to a child. I could hardly listen or even grapple with anyone else's story at this point. And she knew that. She knew the place of nothingness, and how courageous and hard it was to climb upward and out of it. To get to the top of any new mountain. Maybe that was why she was drawn to offer experiences to climb Mt. Kilimanjaro and not just come and run a marathon.

This was the second strongest act of real life help a person had done for me. Jim Slevcove and his family at the summer camp had been the first. I was in a place in my life where I really needed a lift up from someone else. It taught me a lot that I hope to pay forward.

37

It's -20°F in Africa?!
Summiting Mount Kilimanjaro

It is -22° on the top of Mt Kilimanjaro in Africa.

Mt. Kilimanjaro is dauntingly 19,341 feet (5,895 meters). It is the one mountain you can trek to the summit without using climbing gear. It is essentially one gigantic cinder cone. Daunting. Not done in a day's journey but scaled with patience. The formula is to do it in no less than five days. It is like an overwhelming Stair Master stepping machine.

"Poley. Poley," the porters and guides would constantly remind us. "Take it steady and slowly," That's how you summit Kilimanjaro. If you sprint or race haphazardly to the top, your heart does not have the ability to acclimate in providing the oxygen needed. You could create a serious and deadly condition called pulmonary edema. This is when fluid accumulates rapidly in your lungs, typically happening when flat landers ascend in high elevations too quickly or stay in high altitudes for too long.

The remedy. Slow rate of ascent, lower heart rate during ascent. So, in summiting Kilimanjaro, or any life mountain for that matter, it usually takes days. Patient days. For me, it took patient years. Charts show that the longer you take to ascend, the better your chances of a summit success without developing altitude sickness. According to ultimatekilimanjaro.com 5 days has a success rate of 27 percent. 6 days 44 percent. 7 days 64 percent. 8 days 85 percent. The math speaks. The longer you allow your body to acclimate, the better it can handle the higher environment and your successes are more likely. This might be a good way to climb life also.

It is in my nature to sprint. And I have sprinted right off many a cliff. The worst plunge was from my marriage. You know that classic scene in Butch Cassidy and the Sundance Kid where Paul Newman and Robert Redford looked at each other with that, "Oh, well" at the edge of cliff over a roaring river? Being chased and not wanting to be caught, they leaped into the unknown to get out of their current situation. Had I done the same?

"Poley. Poley, life! You have a huge mountain to get up. "FINDING about poley, poley was BIG for me. I would need it to climb more that this mountain. I would need it to take life at a better, healthier tempo. I started liking the "I care" pace. And the rhythm it added to my life.

When we arrived at the base of Kilimanjaro, instead of drinking tourist beers on the porch, I wandered down the road to the porter's station. The porters were lined up, standing with their meager gear, hoping…begging with their eyes… to be picked to carry 70-to-80-pound packs up that mountain. They needed the $5 a day of pay that job would bring. Most porters climb the first day hungry, and in anticipation of that first meal. Most take their meager wages and bring it back to their village to spread out for caring for their elderly parents and their children's basic needs.

The porters only get picked to haul tourists garb up the mountain if they are FIT, and have a pair of boots, a hat, gloves, a pack, and a blanket. I saw tattered scraps, baby blankets that probably came from a missionary barrel they were hoping would pass as the blanket. They were strapping, strong men standing at attention in boots taped to their feet, that fell away after they were chosen or not. A lot of them would straddle that weight and walk on tire treads they made into sandals with the façade of a boot taped to the top. We were going up a 20,000 ft mountain, and all they had were hats and gloves woven from cotton. Most with holes in them. A backpack was just a cloth pouch with straps sewn. I knew this must cut into flesh when shouldered with weight.

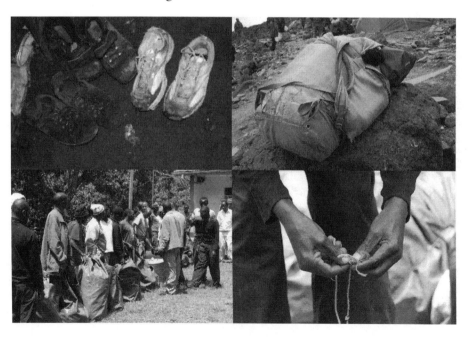

My mom told me to look into faces. See the person behind the eyes. I did. And I saw fortitude and forced perseverance. Soldiers of a different kind of life. I had instant reverence for them and was full of respect. They were impressionable strong because the need warranted it. Some would carry propane tanks. Others heavy canvas meeting tents. Some would fetch water, climbing the trails many times a day. Others had tables and stacks of 10 plastic chairs. Couldn't we sit on a rock?

Finding Fit

Since you have all the days of trekking, you get to know the other tourists as comrades. Our packing group was the marathon runners who chose to remain and summit Africa's tallest mountain. We were worth getting to know. And the guides? They had names like Epaphras, Eric, and Joel. They had families, and dreams, and aspirations to make businesses of themselves. I drilled them on what they were up against trying to provide for their families in Tanzania. They didn't ask for help. They just worked for it. And offered countless stories of how.

I got to know the porters. They had time and togetherness. They talked slow and easy because living at a camp pace was slow and easy. I loved the sound of their language. You didn't need to know the words. But like in Antarctica and with the Russians that crewed the ships there was also an imaginary line drawn. When we camped, the porter's tents were way off to one side and us clients to the other. Like the haves and the have nots. We were the circumstanced, ones living for bucket list check offs, and they were those born into a country that limited their options.

Hearts can cross over that line. I dared to. That bothered some of the trekkers.

In broken English with a melodical accent, the porters shared that gifted items were taxed. Taxed so much they could not afford them. Don't send boxes of used items they begged. A government vehicle would arrive and take a family member away and put them in jail. They would not be released until the tax was paid, forcing the family to pull together all their meager means to give it to the government, leaving them in even more of a dire position. Now with a box of goods that didn't feed them.

But there was a lady. She was from Colorado. She did something. She called it toreturn.com. She bought jackets and supplies and keeps them at the bottom of the mountain for the porters to check them in and out and return them so they could be shared. Practical giving is real heart giving. FINDING a solution that really helps…helps. As we climbed, I visited the other encampments and found corporate groups that came to dig deep wells for clean water supply for villages.

I would come to leave my own down jacket and outer Gortex layers with the guides. Though I had worked hard to earn them, I knew I had better opportunity to replace them than they did to ever buy them. To this day, they take turns wearing my North Face blue down jacket and my red and grey waterproof Patagonia storm jacket. They pop up on random media posts in summit pictures. African guides that had priorly done the summit in layers of cotton sweatshirts. They are smiling.

As the days went by and the climb moved through the jungle to a higher alpine terrain, so my love for these Tanzanians heighten. They were fun and had funny names. They seemed to relax and enjoy their toil. As mankind seems to have this deep need within us, they wanted to work. A desire to have something that defines importance to their life, no matter how hard the task.

Through these remote opportunities to meet so many and so many situations, I am affirmed that every BODY needs to know they are intrinsically valuable, no matter. God claims throughout the Bible that this is so. He reminds us so, as our Creator. But let's admit. We humans are the best at understanding value by labels. Human labels. I run. I play golf. I work as a…? I am good at. Is it helpful to create a few labels that YOU like attributed to your own life and be them. I think I have learned they are important, especially if life is feeling a little lost, hurt, or upheaved, like mine was. Label yourself. Don't wait for others to do so. And be your own best brand! We call people that haul loads up a mountain "porters." They wanted to be one.

I can't remember her first name. Let alone her last name. But I could see the ever-present smile was no longer on her petite face. She was a tiny thing of immense heart, and the travel group loved her. She and I were assigned as tent mates. I had already resolved to stop talking so much, so we got along in a fun way. But this third day out had rained again. We had been stepping up and over steep terrain for days, in a continuous mist or wet, mixed with our sweat. Though, not the cold we would encounter in a few more days at the top, this was dreary and hard hiking.

I loved it. Sadly, yet a good thing, it was one gift my dad did give me. I was hardened for it. Confident in it. She was not. She was scared and overwhelmed on this third day. And as we approached that day's camp after a painstakingly long, all day trek, she was more than spent. She was muttering and not making sense. I grabbed her hand to take her to where the tents would be erected, and it was dead cold. She was shivering. She was hypothermic.

Not waiting for permission, I grabbed our tent out of the pile and slapped the poles together in record time. I pushed her quivering body in and, as a mom with a child, pulled all her wet clothing off. It was soaked. She was soaked. The outer layer she had bought was cute, but not really waterproof. I grabbed both sleeping bags and stuffed her almost delirious body in it. I put the other bag around her shoulders and laid her small frame in my lap. I wrapped as much of my arms and body around her.

I instructed, "I have to get your body temperature back up. You are not keeping your own self warm."

She nods a weak yes. She starts to sob. She is frightened. She knows something is going wrong. I notice her breathing is very slow. I yell out the tent. "We have someone hypothermic. We need hot water, asap. "

I hear the porters jump to the task and light a propane stove for us. Soon a hot mug of tea comes through the flap of the tent. I put sips up to her lips. She can barely take them through the convulsing of her weak face. The fluid does do wonders. My body heat makes the down of the bag effective, and she starts her way back to life. Another mug gets pushed through the flap and we are both able to extract the warmth with both our hands now around each of our cups. That is a good sign. She is holding her own cup. No words pass for the longest time. She tries to revive her smile. "Thank you."

The fight against me with the other guests in camp faded that night. The porters were giving me thumbs up with their eyes. And I earned a place without trying. We were in this climb together. Anything could happen. I was more of a team player than they thought. I was experienced and hyper aware of how to live outdoors. We were far away from the hotel lobby that told me my accounts were again being compromised and frozen. We were elevated to different tasks now, fields away from what I was going to do for a living in the future, or how I was going to re-label my life. Or pay for the boat, cars, and my kids in college. We were in the moment. And at that moment, we were climbing a pinnacle that's its peak would take all our strength, attention, and mojo. We were in this together. Money wasn't going to help us here. Nor was worrying about it.

I heard their shrills and a cluster of excitement. I had to trot over to the group of energetic gals jumping and taking selfie air poses as they made their camp. They were WHOA…Women High on Adventure, the banner said. Two young gals from New York dared each other to climb Kilimanjaro. It was such a life dream of an experience, their Facebook story and photos made other gals they knew want to do it. So, every year, on National Day of the Women, they started bringing a group of giggles to experience each other and the mountain. What fun!

The camp before the summit was somewhere around 16,000 feet. This is as high as the porters go. Even some are left at the camp below. They were trying to keep the consequences at a minimum. They do not have the right clothing and gear to be even up this high.

The tent was shaking with a thick accent. "Time to go." It was midnight. I didn't need to wake up. I had been awake. My heart had fluttered beats in my chest many times that night. And I had to take deep, calm breathes to talk away that panic feeling when you feel like you are being suffocated. Reality of athlete's asthma? Or just reality of altitude? My tentmate was wearing her precious smile. She clambered out of the tent. I followed her and was hit by a blast of wind that sucked my breath away. Oh, no. I pulled back into the tent. It was hellish windy out there.

I started up that last 4,000 feet of that cinder cone, in the dark, in temperatures that dropped to minus 22. And the wind? It felt colder than Antarctica. A deadly cold. Probably, because it was mixed with this high of an altitude. I had on that good down jacket and that expedition grade Gortex Patagonia Jacket. I had brought no wool. It seemed over kill for Africa. I wished I had it now.

But chill was the least of my problems. I was struggling to get air into those tiny lung capillaries. I was having an 'attack', suffocating in the open air without anything but my own body suffocating me. I pulled the parka hood over my head, dropped to my knees, and prayed to live. Honestly. And luckily, I had been in this position before on the GRAND in the Tetons. An African guide was coming to help me. I motioned to him I was okay. I knew what to do. To remain calm. Not panic. Suck. Move the chest barrel. Stay inside that parka cave… find precious straws of oxygen. Bingo. Lungs were now responding again. Triumph for managing myself from my own experience.

It was a hard climb. Step, over step. Sometimes, I felt like I wanted to fall backward. The stars seemed to be below and above us all at the same time. It gave a surreal, disorienting depth perception in the spread of our headlamps. The sun finally started to rise and spread the strongest beam of yellow light across the remains of a glacier and dropped golden hues in the snow divvies. It was spectacular. The rising sun cast a perfect pyramid shadow of the mountain peak across what felt like all of Africa. We could see forever. We could feel forever. We all made it. Together, with our individual struggles.

The summit moments in life are summit moments. Epic. A barrage of all it took to get there. Not just the days of the climb. But each step of the way. It was huge. Higher than this volcano, as if, somehow linked to who we are. Sticking a great label on us, as being able to summit, naming the hardship or task. Emotions filled past what my words could describe.

Pictures were snapped at the huge, iconic summit sign. Prayer flags were flapping in the constant wind I had overcome coming out of the tent to get here. It was cold. Real cold. It was hard to breathe. Words were shared sparingly. Everyone took their moment in front of the sign and quickly started heading down the mountain. I was the last one to leave. Though I had nothing symbolic or material to leave. I put my prayers in the wind with the flags and let my mom be there with me. I had been able to live the summits she never got to make.

Life Worksheet: Picture your life as an African Serengeti

Do you have a LION(s)? What situation, circumstance, or person can harm? Is there a predator that is or can devour your confidence or ability to be who you uniquely are? What can or is pawing at your growth and happiness? Many of us have had or currently have something that roams and stalks our soul. It is the thing that can injure us the most. What is, or can take bites right out of you? Identify and describe the lion or lions and the damage these beasts can do or has done to your life.

_____

_____

_____

If you find no lions. Relish that fact. Identify what could be a lion and make sure they do not wander into your territory.

_____

_____

_____

How about HYENAS? These are the things that pick at your bones. Most of the time, it is our own thoughts, reactions, festerings, grievances, and poor self-talk that dives in and finishes off your own injuries. We want to become our best advocate, not our worst inner enemy. We are not born with poor self-talk. It is taught or inflicted. And so, we must teach ourselves a new language. What hyenas have taught you to pick at your own flesh and bones?

_____

_____

_____

What noise do they make? What do the words sound like? Write them out. Now, turn the cackle into a new sound

___

___

___

Reword it ___

___

___

If you find no Hyenas, think of someone you know that is being eaten alive by learned lower self-esteem or circumstances. Nudge new self-like and self-talk in others. List how and whom you can help.

___

___

___

Think about a lurking LEOPARD. Is there something you are ignorantly or blindly unaware of that wants to, and can, pounce on you? Take the time to think about this. I had no idea there were Leopards when I took off on that dirt road to run.

BUT smile! What about ELEPHANTS? They circle up for you. These are your family and friends that would stand up in times of crisis and be strong when you need protecting. Who are the BIG people in your life and why? _____

_____

What is the best thing about these people? What do you do to ensure they are close enough to know when to circle up? _____

_____

Have you let them know how important they are to you… recently?

_____

_____

What can you do to be an ELEPHANT for others and to whom? _____

_____

_____

Do you travel with ZEBRA and WILDEBEEST? Zebras see things you might not. Wildebeest sniff out dangers you might not be aware of. These are the mentors in your life. Who can travel life with you and look out over your safest direction? Education, knowledge, more experience. Who and what helps open your eyes and lets you smell and see well? _____

_____

_____

How about GIRAFFES? It is good to look up to someone. Someone you want to emulate your life after. Someone you respect their character and values. Who do you look up to? _____

_____

_____

And the GUIDE. It was good to be on a safari with a guide, who knew the terrain and the behavior of the animals. With him, we were able to drive in a steel sided vehicle and be safe in that African jungle. A Higher Power, a God, the Creator, a prophet or parent. Who do you have that best guides your life?

_____

_____

I found Africa to be spellbinding. The rolling hills, rivers, bush, and Serengeti were teeming with wildlife. It can be dangerous. But, as with life, you can make it a safe journey if you identify the things that can eat you or eat at you. Protect yourself by gathering healthy relationships and a good guide. Identify what would be a steel sided exploration vehicle for you and steer your years in an armored car. Journey that way.

Picture walking across parched Africa on foot, alone. Now picture, choosing to do it with a safari, in a guided group with a metal sided vehicle. That is like surrounding yourself with good community. I decided to find a way to pool people together. We need to circle up as the Elephants. I saw sports as the grassy plain this could happen on. And running events could become a community where people could FIND each other in a supportive way. I went home to do something for the porters of Kilimanjaro, the people of Tanzania, and any need around the world I would RUN into. I started Caren Ware Events.

What's your passion project? The thing that would take your life in a direction of true meaning?

_____

_____

_____

_____

_____

_____

_____

38

Enriched is Rich

I tried to tell the guide how grateful I was. I laughed. It came out like I was singing under water. His eyes widened behind his woolen face mask. "Descend," he barked. "You are an athlete. Get down this mountain as fast as you can. You will see the trail. Go. Go. Don't stop at the summit camp. Keep going until you find the lowest camp."

I had the beginnings of pulmonary edema. Liquid was filling my lungs. Somehow, they already knew at summit camp, and all the porters were waving me to keep running. Keep bounding down. My best remedy for keeping this from being an emergency was to descend and do so as quickly as possible. Descend to an altitude that our human bodies do not fight. I was wide-eyed and no longer fatigued by the climb up. Adrenaline was helping me down. And gratefully, a body that had put in a lot of mileage running. It could handle this.

I staged Santa Claus with a Cause to help Epa pay for an accounting degree.

Epa's family in his village.

By headlamp, the others made their way into camp. And the festivities began. The porters sang us cultural songs. We all feasted together. And we thanked our souls for the experiences and the chance to cross continents to do this and be with them. I had nothing to give them, save my down jacket and parka. But I vowed I would FIND a way to help. And I did. I went back to the USA and started a running race called Santa Claus with A Cause. I ordered Santa Suits and claimed we would be the race that GIFTED back. It started small and the proceeds were meager, but so much more than any of the guides I met could earn in weeks. I wired funds, and they were quickly used for their own children's needs. I started helping. And it helped me. There was an address for me to aim my passion toward, and my life started taking this new direction.

The diabetics machine and medicine I sent funds for.

When a child in the village was diagnosed as diabetic, I bought testing equipment and the shots and medicine to keep that child healthy. When another child was dying and there were no funds for a doctor, I paid for the doctor and had pictures sent from a smiling father of his little girl today. I gift money every Christmas so they can spread Christmas to those who can't eat on that special day. And I hope it spreads hope in some simple, singular way.

What would be endless possibilities if each of us gave back to a few people we crossed paths with and helped them when in need? What if we all fulfilled a need when they were not even asking for help? Santa Claus with A Cause has helped send people through college, buy sleeping bags, shoes, and jackets. We even provided a surprise box of toys and teaching materials to a remote village that didn't even think a box could ever get there. And many years later when my own firstborn grandson became ill as in infant, guess who prayed? Guess who reached out through social media with the greatest hearts of concern? The world.

You do not have to count coins or bills to have a rich life. RICH living comes from the heart of ENRICHED living. Any BODY on this earth has the ability to be richer than finances or circumstances. And likewise, by missing the very treasured points of life, be poor though owning a world of possessions, but not a valuable soul. Enriched is the richest rich.

From Epaphras messenger texts, one translates "What an effort you're most congratulated Caren for, this hard work for us as a real community with need. I am so proud of you came to Africa for the adventure but that's not all it meant for you. What it meant was to love to the people… including us."

He also wrote. "You have been such a blessing in my family. I really believe distance is never an obstacle when great hearts conquer all! We thank God for the connection and the loving heart you have. Amen. My son now has medicine, my family got groceries, and we do not take for granted these small helps for betterment. Thank you for helping with schooling and our dreams for the future. We hope to see you as a guest in our own village someday where my wish is to provide a running race for the children."

My hope is to help him get to do that. And to be rich in heart.

I started that long, patient road back to building a new business. Step by step. It began in Africa, of all places. Where I learned to summit something successfully…with a healthy heart.

39

"Hey, Sis. Dad Died." And the Butterfly

"Hey, Sis, Dad died."

"When?"

"I don't know, maybe three weeks ago." My brother was matter-of-fact.

I almost veered off the freeway. It wasn't that I was collapsing into a pile of loss and grief. It was more like a slug I already knew would be coming. It was the bland acceptance in my brother's words that stung with the punch. An announcement coming so casually and after-the-fact for such a big event. Death. I knew my dad had moved on to other things, and even his death, or graveside was something he enforced. His wish was that his kids would not come near his resting place. I sensed he wanted to ensure no one could babble some poor words about him. I was told his current wife and a few close friends were all who were a part of his memorial. I do not know where he is buried.

Death has a sting, no matter. A death like this creates a welt. I didn't know what reactive emotion to have. Is there something like an EpiPen you can stab in your own leg to keep your life breathing with this kind of news? Not in this case. I didn't know how to feel except it felt like being an asthmatic without an inhaler. I had already been on my own in life, rescuing myself. But it pierces deep when finalities do not get to have resolved endings. Just keep on driving, Caren, I instructed myself. I veered back into the lane and headed toward my own destiny.

I was so relieved I had decided to respond like a daughter and had showed up to visit him when I found out he was battling cancer. My dad had moved to be near a main Mayo Clinic. I scrambled for an extra contract and used the income to buy an airline ticket. I reserved a cheap motel on the outskirts of this small Midwest town that almost was the Mayo Clinic. Though I was getting a new running business off the ground, had very little reserves, I flew to Rochester, Minnesota.

This town is often confused with Rochester, New York. Quite a different location. Rochester, Minnesota is a sleepy kind of town. It was just coming into spring. The tree branches were still bare. A few tulips were starting to bloom. I felt like them—in between seasons, and not quite back to spring yet.

Rochester is primarily the Mayo Clinic. It has housing high rises erected for the elderly to live independently but remain very connected to the hospital. The Mayo Hospital has underground, gerbil-like tunnels that lead from each housing complex to the clinic. This allows senior citizens to have stately, regal, activity filled lives, but within reach of medical expertise when critically needed. The high rises offered woodshop, indoor gardening, work outs, and fine dining, yet are within minutes of a fully staffed hospital.

This is where my father and his wife were residing and living out the realities of battling the stage four cancer my father had been diagnosed with. It was in his lungs…and spreading. They had pre-paid into the clinic for this very scenario, in preparation for things that come with age. I think I heard he had to be rushed many times to be treated for a burst appendix, pneumonia, and things that crop up from going through harsh chemo treatments. I think he preferred it this way. That treatment came from professionals and did not require any close family on hand.

I imagine he never thought he would have to use this clinic. But, in the admirable part of his nature, he always worked hard and made sure he was well taken care of. He would not have wanted to end this game of life on the bottom. He would never want to be at the mercy of someone having to take care of him. Picture many of the characters Clint Eastwood, Robert Redford, and Paul Newman played, and you get a visual of my dad. He was perfectly handsome and stately. And feeble was not in his vocabulary.

When I landed, a cab drove me past professional health care workers hurrying about to make it to their appointments and work tasks. Quaint restaurants and artistic coffee shops dotted the downtown area. But the main event of Rochester, Minnesota was this hospital. It was the town. It took blocks to drive past it. We pulled in front of a motel that flashed its name in neon red lights. I can do this, I drudged. I handed the cabdriver his cash and I shouldered my carry-on daypack. In it were my bare essentials to save on luggage fees. My laptop computer. My toothbrush. A brush. A dress and sweater. Dress shoes. Pajamas. And most valuable to me, my running shorts, shirt, socks, and shoes.

My dad had scheduled the appointed time I could visit him which was 10am the next morning. I unlocked the door to my musty room and was met with the stench of stale cigarettes lingering in the drapes. Who comes to Rochester and smokes when they are probably visiting someone dying of cancer? I tossed my pack on the bed, quickly changed into the runner chick and went to the lobby. Did they, by any chance, have a running store in town?

When I searched on the computer, there were three in this one little town. Score. Towns always seem to have at least one! I called to see if there were any weeknight runs with patrons of the store. They all hosted them. I felt uplifted already.

This is the case in most towns I travel to. I can always find a track. But better, yet I can find a running store that offers organized training runs. Relief. This helps fill what would otherwise be just sitting in a motel room, waiting. I trotted in the direction of the closest store. Runners are a community. And the best way I can get to know a new place and people is to RUN around in it with some locals.

When I jogged up to the address of the store, people were already mingled in a cluster. They were stretching and exchanging conversation. I introduced myself and enjoyed their instant camaraderie. We were all interested in each other, linked by the fact that we liked running. Sports can be one of the best surrogate choices if you need to be around people and their support. They were so interested in me joining them from some other place.

The next morning, I left the motel and walked in the direction of the address of my father's high rise. I did so at a pokey, almost sulky walk. Much like a kid who puts off doing a dreaded chore. I poked into a small restaurant. I poked around a plate of breakfast I just didn't feel like eating. I gave up. I left it half eaten and a tip and walked across the street to a funky coffee roaster shop.

Here was another thing that gave me a hug—walking into the aroma of roasted conversations and people doing the various things that WIFI allows. I collect going into as many small-town coffee roaster shops as I can discover. It's almost like a hobby. I don't necessarily drink the specialty coffees, but I like to see the décor, feel the vibe, and experience the atmosphere they created. And I also like to feel the people. It's become one of the things I like to do.

That is when I remembered I had left my computer back at the dumpy motel. I had been filing pictures of the seven continent marathons. The Galapagos Islands and its remote beauty and species. The sea of concrete buildings in Tokyo and the mass of people who dressed up in cartoon caricatures to run it or spectate. The red sand of the Australian Outback with only shadows of the Aborigines allowed in the picture. Antarctica, and its icebergs floating in hues of the hours of sunrises and sunsets. I had stockpiled all the pictures of the porters on Kilimanjaro and the victory stance when reaching the top.

Summiting that mountain seemed easier than the steps I was trying to take toward meeting my dad on this day. I was only hours into sorting what would take years to finally be compiled into the making of this book. But it was a start. Starting is the way to get to the finish.

My dad was in a regal, leather chair. His long legs were crossed. The chair was turned, facing the window. I could only see his hand resting on the arm. But I knew it was his with the distinguishable USC Doctorate ring. My dad teased that he had to get a doctorate to drop his middle name. For some reason even his own mom had no answer for, she had given him the middle name, Llewelyn. That got to go away when a proper Dr. was placed in front of his first name. And I think, with it, a lot of other things went away. He was no longer defined by anything in his past, but by the things he had been able to accomplish. I liked this best about him. And it was well deserving of admiration. He had quite a successful career. Was he finally calming into his accomplishments and less likely to grind others on his way up now that he had arrived? I hoped so.

I went and sat in the equally high sided chair to the right of him. He sensed someone next to him.

"I am waiting for my daughter. She is to arrive at ten a.m. to meet with me." His voice was his, just weaker than I had ever heard it before.

Airy. I pulled forward and peered around the side of the chair. He was on a small, portable oxygen tank. And yet, he was royal. Not a hair out of place. Dressed famously. And a smile spread across his white bearded face in recognition of me.

"Oh, there you are. Right on time, I see." He rolled his arm to uncover a watch that sparkled like a Lamborghini.

"Yes, Dad. Here I am."

He patted my hand and looked out the window. "Oh, look. The first butterfly I have seen this year." A yellow flutter with black and purple was dancing around the windowsill and drifted out of sight. That was the first time I had ever seen him recognize and value nature. It had always been about how grand the situation of standing in it had made him feel. Not an enjoyment for something as simple as the beauty of a butterfly fluttering. I didn't know he could notice. My coming all this way fluttered, and in some very simple, significant moment, my dad and I sat there and accepted each other.

"It has been a hard-physical fight." I believed him. We sat for a long time. I knew to enjoy this moment for the moment it was. A time to simply be a daughter and be with my dad. Something new, like that caterpillar that transformed into an altogether, new thing with beauty and wings and becomes a butterfly. That was this kind of a moment. I was able to take wing and fly with forgiveness. Experience grace and mercy for and from all of it. This was huge.

I had in the journals of my heart, many ills, questions, confusions, destructive habits, and such. I had lived in wonder as to why this man was so puzzlingly detached. My childhood and young adulthood left knots in my stomach. I finally got so busy with raising my own family and providing for them, I just let go of the drain of holding onto his ability to be so heartless and purposefully distanced. I knew I couldn't understand this man who continually and almost systematically hurt, cut down, squashed, and denied real needs. But, here, on this day, somehow, I could forgive him. It was its own Mt. Kilimanjaro.

Dear Dad, I thought to myself, *I raised my own two kids and helped five others get through college. I ran a solid race timing company. I hope I was a good wife though I fumbled the ball in the last minute of the final quarter. You know dad, I FOUND what it took to stand on a world podium in Track & Field. I ran a marathon on every continent. I did it. Me. Your daughter. Not to gain your approval anymore. I did it because I enjoyed trying. I did it because it brought enhancement to my own life. I did it because it taught me so much about myself and others. And I did it because it was interesting. I got to FIND ways to meet people, and cultures, and help spread hope in tangible ways. I am a butterfly. We can all be. We all are. I'm okay, Dad. I have FOUND something very important. I can forgive you. I can let you be you. That has wings.*

We finally changed the silence. I wonder what the universe was doing in his. It was throwing a relief party in mine.

I offered, "Your granddaughter, Carrie, got married."

"Oh yeah? I heard that. How is that going?" I knew he wasn't looking for an answer, so I did not bother to reply. I just let him talk about his new surroundings.

A lady strolled through the lobby. "Oh, there's so and so," my dad said. He leaned in. "She has blah, blah brand shoes on and a blah, blah brand purse." He took an inventory of me from head to toe. "I think they will still let you in at the top floor for lunch dressed as you are." I was perfectly fine and was dressed perfectly fine. I now knew not to take that as any reflection of who I was. I knew I was a butterfly even though he was calling me a caterpillar. *Thank you, good Heavenly Father, for showing me who I am. I choose to be defined by the original Creator, not my dad's need to push me under. And dear Dad, I won a World Champion title. Two of them. And I ran a marathon in some of the most remote and amazing places on earth. Those defined me better. I can love you, Dad. I understand so much more about you by understanding so much more about me.*

He looked at his watch again. "It is time for lunch." I watched this mighty man fight off frailty. He lifted his tall stature and carefully stood, putting the portable respirator over his shoulder. "How do you like this?" he tapped. "It's a blah, blah model. Best in the industry. It does allow me to walk about." He is handsome. He walks slow. Too slow. My heart aches. As we walk, he shares that he meets every morning with men in this complex and they debate world issues over coffee. That his wife grows her herbs in the indoor garden. That there is jazz night tonight. And movie night and a gym. I am warmed that my father is sincerely enjoying a scheduled life that includes community. He has friends. Acquaintances. And a wife he loves. The dining hall is on the top floor and towers above the hospital and reaches to views of trees far beyond the town.

"Well. It has sure been nice meeting with you today," my father concludes as they take the dessert dishes away.

"Yes, Dad. Me too. I really enjoyed being here with you." And I sincerely did. I knew that we were saying goodbye in the only way my dad knew how.

My dad offered to call a cab. I thanked him but told him I would enjoy the walk back. I crossed past the breakfast diner, the coffee roaster shop, the hospital. I walked across the entire town with my head down. I was trying to be deep into letting the goodbye be a goodbye. I wandered around a few parks before going back to my motel room. I plopped on the bed and decided I better go running to digest things better. I kicked off my dress shoes and put on my still damp running shorts and shirt that had been hand washed and hanging on the shower. When I sat on the edge of the bed reaching to lace up a shoe, I saw it.

My laptop screen was flashing with a big warning message. You have been hacked with RANSOMWARE.

What the frazzle was that?! I pounded on keys and every file containing pictures and documents were encrypted and frozen. Nothing would open.

Another screen popped up. Your files will be destroyed in …there was a clock ticking down in the frame like one does for a time bomb. It was at 10 hours and 33 minutes and a fast moving bunch of seconds were going by. There was a simple "Click HERE" button. $5000 was the ransom demand.

Could this be for real? This was like some scene right out of a movie. I had no idea there was such a thing as holding your computer hostage for money. I went to the hotel lobby and used their computer to research what this was. My hack was a very sophisticated malware that used crypto virology to encrypt files that would not be released unless funds were sent electronically to an unknown source. It seemed it was coming from a Russian or Eastern European country.

I went back to my tacky room and stared at the time bomb style clock on the screen. I scooted back as far as I could get away from the laptop. My back hit the backboard of the bed. I drew my legs in and wrapped my arms tightly around them. I let my chin slump in rest on my knees. My whole life felt like it had been hacked.

When I left the motel to head to the airport, I dropped the laptop in the trash. It was one of those cans that have the lid on it. The ones you must step on to open. It felt too much like the one my daughter dropped grandma's life into. Bang. It slammed open. SLUNK. The laptop went in. BANG. It closed as my foot came off the pedal.

I was not going to be held hostage. Not anymore.

40

Summitting the Insurmountable
Continent 4 Repeat: Asia — The Everest Marathon

The seven continent marathon goal was finished. But was it? The fact that my Tokyo Marathon in Japan had no recorded time made me feel the score was incomplete. There was a lingering lack of finality. I had surmounted so many things. It felt like there should be something BIG to hang all these years on. A final act. One so lofty it towered as high as the obstacles I had overcome. I Googled Asian Continent marathons and scrolled and scrolled. And then I saw it. Tucked away, as if as obscure and hard to get to as it would be, a website locater was promoting the Everest Marathon.

"There's an Everest Marathon?!"

I sucked in such an instant surge of delight and surprise, I almost forgot to take the next breath. I couldn't be more enticed. I have been mesmerized by the Himalayas since sixth grade. In a desire to thumb through every volume of The World Book Encyclopedias from A to Z, I had cruised by the H's and learned that two tectonic plates of Asia and India slammed together before time and formed this incredulous mountain range called the Himalayas. Living and trekking among these were the Nepalese on one side and the Tibetans on the other. I gobbled up books and expedition stories, interested in the people who carried their loads on their backs, or the backs of their yaks. This area accounted for many of the earth's outdoor adventures.

In adulthood, my awe for what felt like going to Shangri La never subsided. The definition of Shangri-La: 1) A remote beautiful imaginary place where life approaches perfection 2.) A remote idyllic hideaway. The Himalayas lured because they were so tucked away. I yoked onto a few restaurants in the USA, one in Big Bear Lake and the other in Pasadena, California and one called the Everest Momo Shack in Jackson Hole, Wyoming. All were operated by Nepalese, many with the last name Sherpa. They had the fortune of getting the lotto for work visas. I hung on all their stories and descriptions as if they were talking about Shangri La. I ate at them often, as if by doing so I was traveling vicariously to their country.

The Himalayas are a mountainous region of ravines, steep chiseled steps, hanging bridges, and the highest snowcapped peaks in the world. Everest looms at the mother of them all. At 29,032 (and I heard still growing) feet

(8,848.9 meters), it is the highest mountain on earth. A basecamp to start climbing the mountain is arranged at 17,598 feet (5363.9 meters). This is where the Everest Marathon website said the race started. Right at the wall of the Khumbu Icefalls. The only way to get there, or the right way to get there, is on foot. Carrying your own daypack or full pack and having the porters carry the rest. Trekking there and back, I knew would make THIS marathon a signature event. THIS was a BIG undertaking.

The website said to trek to Everest Basecamp and back would take no less than 15 days. Evacuation insurance was required to be in the race, and a signed release of good health from a certified doctor. I poured over the daily itinerary beginning with flights landing and departing in Lukla, which is considered one of the world's most dangerous landing strips. From there the walking started and each day was filled with five to eight hours of required hiking. We would have to traverse through villages chiseled into the mountainsides, clinging to high elevation plains and canyons which were only accessible by foot travel. This was a place that all the upper villagers had the last name Sherpa. I was pulled to it like a magnet.

I filled out the race registration and pushed send on the computer. I found a travel agency that had pre-set itineraries, guides, porters, and a formula for how to get there…and just as important, how to get back. I was going. It was December 2019, and the trip was set for mid-May of 2020. Of course, I had no idea how tumultuous our planet would almost instantly become with a surprising, and quickly spreading COVID virus pandemic. The entire planet came to a trepid halt.

The Everest Marathon was cancelled in 2020, as were almost all athletic gatherings around the world, though fees and airline tickets were already purchased. It was an unpredictable year. Everything went into an "on hold" chaos. And so did all my calls to 800 numbers to try and preserve my flights and plans. I was put on hold for days on end. But I had learned to not give up and to be more patient when faced with ordeals. To be wise and strategic in resolutions. "Resolve", I coached myself. "Don't dissolve." It was hard to do.

The trick was to re-train for 2021. I think I invented the excuse to do so. It would require me to tailor my agenda to include mountains and mountain living. I rented a small cabin in the San Bernardino mountains and called it my own 'basecamp'. I had already had the high-altitude experience of Kilimanjaro. I knew what near 20,000 feet was going to ask of me. But that trip was only five days of stair stepping up a towering cinder cone. This would be a much lengthier kind of a trek, staying at higher elevations longer, going deep into the Himalayas, which would not be easily retractable. On Mt. Kilimanjaro in Africa, I was able to descend to safety in a day. That would not be the case in the Himalayas. Helicopter evacuations were the rescue way out.

I knew the Nepalese, though they would not ask nor beg, could use a few extra unexpected dollars. So, when trekking through their land, I vowed I would bring cash to convert into their currency in the form of $5s, $10s, and $20s equivalent to daily and weekly wages. My plan was to discreetly place unexpected money into the hands of yak or donkey herders, the elderly, young moms with young children, fathers needing to feed a family, and aspiring Nepalese that needed some supply to start a business. Just a simple way to gift hope. Suddenly, the Everest trip took on my kind of meaning with this sincere kind of giving in mind. I added some extra contracts and worked to be able to do so.

I had a problem to conquer. My stomach hurt. It had been hurting for a long time. I was dropping weight once again, though I was eating a volume far greater than most. Almost four full meals a day to fuel the training miles I was doing to be ready. But I was living in someone else's home and at sea level. And living someone else's life. Not one that carried my internal convictions. It was eating me up from the inside out. I had to change that. I couldn't be carrying a potential stomachache to a place that would require my own good health for me to be able to trek all the way to Everest Basecamp. I took the doctor's certification seriously and had a bunch of tests done to make sure kidney stones, an appendix bursting, or any unknown heart condition would pop up in such a remote situation.

My extreme choice of a marathon location became the greatest motivator to do what was the right and best for my body and vitality. It took some hard decisions to make some healthy changes, but I did them. And the training then became fun and really about my purposes and passion. It inspired me to get a place in the mountains. And to purchase a Labrador puppy from a breeder that her vibrant pups were known for being great hunting and outdoor dogs. I taught my pup to run trails with me. And I taught myself to run the mountains.

I was so determined to go, I booked a flight on Qatar Air to Kathmandu, Nepal for May 13 of 2021. Then I drove all the way to Laramie, Wyoming from California. I was getting pretty good at traversing all that stretch of open land America has best. It felt like such the right place and precise plan to begin the trip to the Himalayas from this, also, high and wild place. Plus, I needed to leave my Labrador dog with his kennel owner while I was gone.

That's when all perfect plans have a way of making us develop patience. The Delta variant, a strain of COVID, had materialized in India. Many Nepalese cross the border and work in that country to try and support themselves. The strain had been brought back into Nepal and the Nepalese government closed its borders. There is such a condensed population in the capital city of Kathmandu, where they literally live sandwiched together in a frenzy of scooters, cars, and affordable materials used for buildings. The fear of what a deadly strain might do to such a city was real. It had already had to survive past a devasting earthquake. Just days before I was to leave a message from Qatar said the flight to Nepal had been cancelled. The borders had been closed.

I had already arrived in Wyoming. I was packed and trained for what I hoped the Himalayas were going to be. Begrudgingly, as many of us had to do, I had to change plans. Over and over, and still throughout much of 2021. I flew to Alaska instead and drove a rented camper van with a friend across that vast state and tried to be a good guide to its wilderness. It felt like such a consolation. I tried hard to not be let down. Shangri-la was still out there. Just out of reach for now.

But something fun happened. I got to make that little cabin in the San Bernardino mountains a home. What I thought would be temporary turned out to be just the right space and place for me. The stars at night. The birds that chirped in the day. The deer, raccoons, coyotes, and even a rarely seen mountain lion. The tall cedars and all the trails and roads to run on. My dog, Champ Champion, and I folded in. He loved it as much as I did. I bought him a Kevlar, spiked collared coyote vest…in case of a run in.

The best part about the cabin was the doors opened to the outdoors. Oaks on the property provided shade, and a nice sound in the breeze. And up at the end of the street was the forest service land, a preserved swathe that reached all the way to the Mojave desert. As I moved my belongings into my new abode, I followed the late afternoon's rays up to the top of the rise behind the cabins. Golden beams were shedding a glow across the tops of the tall trees, and I could see them hitting the large, climbable boulders that are a unique part of this area's landscape.

And there it was… the setting sun. It was making its dip behind Mt. Baldy in the San Gabriel mountains. This perch gave me a view of the setting sun in almost 360 degrees. As the sun set way off behind that 10,000-foot mountain, it threw rays that colored the sky a dark spectrum of red and yellow and it made all the clouds behind me turn pink and orange. I would make a habit of running out there every evening I could to catch that setting sun. It was as if God led me to this perch to show me life would be okay. To be lofted and looking out…at the setting sun, walking a wooded path to get there. It was gloriously regenerating.

I was no longer racing against it and trying to out beat it. I FOUND… peace. Sunsets, were now, a best friend of sorts. A sign that I knew how to make a day be better or the best. I wasn't fighting with it. I was forging through it. And it took on such a healthier feeling. I started making it a hobby. To search for the best sunrise and sunset in a day.

The cabin gave me a solid base. Basecamp was the perfect name for it. The owners of the cabin and I became great friends. This had a warmth to it that the sunsets had in colors. There is a sense of stability in having a foundation while feeling untethered. And having friends that have your good will in mind was one of the most helpful healings. We held a commonality in experiencing great loss. I had befriended and coached their daughter in high school. I knew her like a daughter and fellow athlete. Unfathomable and a rabbit hole no parent, sibling, or left behind loved one ever should have to go into, this precious young lady ended her life. And we can only put one foot in front of another and try and learn to live beyond pain that never goes away. Her parents took up running in races. They knew not what else to do. On her behalf. Sharing a love their daughter had for the sport.

It was the sunsets. The sunsets that gave me a heavenly hug. And a reflective place to reason and grapple with all of life's losses, gifts, mysteries, and beauty.

I wasn't sure if life was going to get to be this kind of better. Yet, I made the changes to determine it would do so. Who would have known it would take almost three years to finally get to the Everest Marathon? We decided to launch an annual mountain community run in the meantime and quietly dedicated it to the cabin owner's daughter who had passed away in college and all the families out there that had to endure unfathomable loss. I continued to promote and passionately stage the themed running races though they were much more difficult with all the new protocols. And I waited for the day I could trek through the Himalayas and run the Everest marathon.

I placed my mom's upbringing, the losses of life, and most importantly, all I had learned at my basecamp cabin. I printed out beautiful pictures of all the places and people running these marathons in remote places has allowed me to experience. I plastered them on cabin walls as a daily reminder of the color and variety all these experiences were letting my life become. I FOUND what I was looking for—to live to be myself by relaxing in my own heart, and finally accepting that learning to be myself was the address I needed to aim toward all along. There was no set place to be, as much as there is a path to be on, letting myself bloom.

41

Trekking to the Everest Marathon

"It's not the mountains we conquer, but ourselves."
-Sir Edmund Hillary

The Nepali guide was ushering me as the last trekker onto the 18-passenger aircraft. The twin engines were roaring, and the airplane was spinning into take off position before I could hardly buckle in. We were headed to the village of Lukla where most expeditions start trekking toward Everest. It has the reputation of being one of the most dangerous airports on the planet because its short runway. It was built on an angle so the slope up would slow down the landing aircraft, and there would be extra umph on the downhill speed for a desired successful takeoff. When weather lifts, a conglomerate of trekkers and climbers sprint for the airport in the bustling capital city of Kathmandu, Nepal. The hope is the window will hold out long enough to allow a landing on that shortest of runways. It dead ends into the side of a mountain. So, why risk it? This cuts off 5 days of trekking.

I was scrambled, like eggs. All my meticulous overplanning and overpacking had just unraveled as fast as we were scuffling to catch this flight. In the lobby of our Kathmandu hotel, I discovered that each of us was only allowed 15 kilos total. That is about 35 pounds. The small aircraft could only carry so much to Lukla. Plus, the porters would be carrying up to four of our duffle bags. This made this a strict weight restriction. The weight of my full-size backpack when empty counted in that weight limit. So, an extra set of clothing, and all my shampoo and body comforts had to be tossed back into my suitcase that was being left at the hotel. All except my toothbrush, a hairbrush, and toothpaste remained going.

I weighed everything again. It still was not enough. My shower flip flops. Toss. My wool beanie. Toss. I was told I could buy one along the route. Still not enough. And finally, what I was holding onto… my daily allotment of healthy protein snacks. That was the scariest. I burn calories as fast as I feed them into my body. The guide was so anxious we were going to miss the bus, he tossed that bulky bag of snacks on the scale by itself. The red numbers displayed it was the exact amount that would bring my total to permissible. He tossed that into my suitcase and slammed it shut.

When he wasn't looking, I flipped it back open and stuffed as many protein bars into my rain jacket pockets as I could. I was wearing one full layer to cheat the limit. I blindly felt through the bag until I hit two small square packets I knew would be Honey Stinger Waffles. And I continued to frantically forage until I felt a squishy foil wrapper I knew would be Gu.

The sugar energy one I pulled out was chocolate flavored. My least favorite. But in fear of taking too much time, I accepted that would be my race day fuel food. All the experience I had learned from the marathons and bonking told me I would need these protein bars for the trek days and that waffle sugar and one Gu for the race.

The bus was pulling away as the guide and I grabbed for the outdoor handle and jumped into the open stairwell. We rode most the way to the airport just holding onto the walls of the bus entrance. The guide gave me a slight smile, heightened by the adrenaline I caused as we had almost missed the bus. I liked him instantly. He was competent and easy going; unruffled and accepting of every one of us just as who were going to be. It took a while to understand his name was Bhim. Not Ben.

When we finally were on a straight away, he and I clambered to empty seats. We, an assortment of gals and guys, started shaking hands and settling in. This would be Bhim's next trekking party. And that made life interesting. He shared that all our personalities made his 19 year career as a veteran expedition guide worthwhile. I am sure it was challenging at times, but none of the guides nor porters would ever show that any of this diversity burdened them.

The small airborne craft was being tossed about in wind drafts the mountains must produce. I turned to ask the fit gentlemen across the aisle something just in time to witness his stomach's reaction to the turbulence. No apologies. Air sickness has no prejudices and can grab ahold of the refined and finest. While his head was in a white barf bag, the rest of us filmed how close our wings were to the sides of lush rocky ravines and held our breath as a speck of a runway was coming into view.

Our skilled pilot plopped that airplane down on screeching brakes. The nose stopped only inches from the wall that had a full mountain behind it. Like a cartoon scene, I think I felt the rear of the craft lift and slammed down in such an instant stop from our flying speeds. WOW. Everyone started to giggle and talk nervously in those quiet tones one does when they narrowly escaped death.

We disembarked into a world like no other. Whistles were blowing from officials in army green uniforms. But I think they were blowing the whistles because they were paid to be official. No malice was in their gestures. Just a hurry so the next plane could come in on that window of better visibility. "Step to here," they yelled in English.

We ended up in our first tea house and were warmly served drinks as our duffle bags were being assigned to porters. I think none of us knew what to expect. But all of us were excited and thrilled to actually and finally be here. Small talk began as we started to get to know each other. We would become our own special posse of people who trekked all the way to basecamp… together. Sixteen of us were Americans and added into our group was a South African father, his adult son, and an Australian who told us on this day one that he had never run an organized race before. We were dubbed the A TEAM, as we were mostly Americans. We felt the pride in that top graded letter and shouldered up to be A+ in fun and attitude.

Only a handful of us were over the age of fifty. Most were postgraduates and successfully traversing the early career road, or were self-made entrepreneurs, being personal trainers or product producers. All seemed super comfortable and confident that they were in for good times because they knew how to have a good time. I couldn't have been more instantly pleased to be with them. Hopefully, they were with being with me. I did something very necessary. I refrained from talking too much and asked questions about them and listened. My experiences had sculpted me into a new balance of introvert, and I often mixed that with my style of investigatory interaction. I was genuinely interested to get to know something that made each of them the unique person that they each were. The Nepalese took notice.

I utilized the free time after tea to go to the village's ATM. It would be only one of two on the entire trek. I wanted to make sure I converted the money I brought so I could give it away. It was a major part of my trekking. I wanted my presence in Nepal to be used by giving away a simple impact. I hoped my actions would be like dropping leaflets from heaven, sharing that life can have mini miracles in a day. Might they be blessed by some random woman giving away dollar bills along the way.

This heart of giving I brought to Nepal was not one that was extorted or conned or taken advantage of. It was a giving that butterflied down and landed on someone unexpectedly, in a fun way to make that day have a twinkle to it. I apportioned a small amount each day on my hike to and from Everest Basecamp and stuck it in my side pockets. I crumpled up $5, $10s, and $20s in their currency and made myself ready for who I would FIND to randomly give it to along the paths I crossed.

The trail out of Lukla left steeply downward, not up. And the undulating foot path to Everest Basecamp began with its indiscriminate pattern of ups and downs. But movement passed so full of new culture most of us hardly noticed the effort to walk it. It was so worth the ups and downs because each bend had a view, or a passing stream of yaks or donkeys, and little villages of people and houses.

The haul animals had colorful woven straps wrapped around their heads, and bells hanging from their necks. They carried a sound that would signify in my head a melody to always be associated with the Himalayas. The clang of bells to the rhythm of their swaying loads. We walked through the cobbled path of the little town of Lukla. As it passed away, we trekked most the day along ridges with river raging ravines and lush green vegetation.

We started to cross the first hanging bridges and dined in lunch spots that were quaint, manicured food stops made with indoor and outdoor seating. I was taken aback by the care and cleanliness of each abode. Flowerpots, rock walled courtyards, open for business flags flying. I can only imagine the shutdown COVID caused in these remote areas that were trying to newly become trekkers havens and a so-called tourist route.

But the Nepalese know how to farm their land and seem to do both. Lunch spots came with all the guides indulging on us, serving hot tea, coffee, and a hot type of lemonade. The food was basic and fresh and always centered on the potatoes they could grow even up at villages over 15,000 feet. They seemed to go outside and get things from their gardens to feed us. And they showered their best hospitality and best produce on us. We ate what someone carried on their backs or on a yak or they grew or raised.

I passed a family washing their baby in a tub. I brushed past clothes hanging to dry in the wind. The wind always played a soft sound with the prayer flags hanging tethered between trees and poles. Blue, white, yellow, green, and red. Tibetan Buddhism has meaning to each color. Blue means space. It is believed that anger can be transformed to wisdom when meditating on this color. White means air. It is practiced that focusing on white can cut down the delusion of ignorance and turn into wisdom of reality. Yellow means earth, green means water, red means fire. All five colors together signify balance.

Finding Fit

There are prayer mantras written on the flags. They are hung on high places so that when the winds blow, the prayers are carried to spread over the land. The prayer flags held significant beauty in this Himalayan terrain, flapping with something that raised a culture on values with character and carried their culture in the air. It was another sound I took in and marked as special to this remote region.

I let my own prayers be whispered in the wind. I thanked the God of heavens, the wind, and the earth for my being here. Healthy and with a vitality that thrived on getting to experience this. I said a thankful prayer for who I had finally, in all these years, learned to accept and be. For being alive. For learning. For living. For pushing past the fear of the unknown and courageously crossing parched parts of my life to FIND the mountain top experiences. For being spunky enough to keep climbing. For not giving up. For all that this book FINDING FIT has journeyed you through in my life. I'm grippingly thankful.

For my mom. My dad. My upbringing. For my marriage. My mistakes. My start overs. For the ashes of Janiece gifted to me by the cabin owners, inside a little card that held so much for me to carry here for them. From a family's heart. It was tucked carefully in the liner of my pack. The small picture her mom had pasted on the card was of Janiece readying to clear a high jump height. Standing erect and on her tippy toes, the picture captured her look of determination. Her spirit would weather this quest to get to Everest Basecamp and run this highest altitude marathon… with me.

I talked to God in the playful winds of the Himalayas. Yes, there were questions. Lots of whys? And there were the why nots. And that monster of a mountain called regrets. But I thanked the heavens for the races I started and the needs the proceeds were getting to help. All this, being me…was trekking with me. My life. My life experiences. In them, I felt the strength they all added up, giving me confidence and experience to be heading toward tackling the world's highest and one of the hardest marathons on the planet. I knew I could do this. And would be thrilled to meet the people who learned to live this high.

My getting to Everest Basecamp held so much. The word attached to it became SURMOUNT. This held more far-ranging meaning than the word summit. My marathon effort at the Everest Marathon was a SURMOUNT of all I had come through and overcome. It held an acceptance that was so genuine I started to smile and never stopped. The setbacks in my life may have felt as big as this monstrous mountain, but how else would I have learned to tackle them well and surmount them often without them?

There's a little girl with pretty cheeks holding a live chicken. There were boys and men carrying inhumanly heavy loads of plywood, store stock supplies, and crops in baskets. I even saw a Honda generator in among a heavy load. They did so with a strap that adhered the weight to their heads. Leaning over they moved among the trails between villages, hardly able to give the world eye contact. I felt for their loads and realized the western world carries some invisibly heavy loads that we should recognize as we pass each other. Not ignore the valor it takes to carry them.

I stuffed my $10s and $20s into the porters' hanging hands and a cocked head with only one eyeball able to look at me stared at me in disbelief. I leaned down to their vision and motioned a hand signal from my heart to theirs and walked on. Their hand slid the bill very carefully into a pocket. They would find the next object, a rock, or a wall, and carefully position their burden on it and the weight from them. As the burden fell off their body, they sat back and waved to me in humble and unexpected gratitude. I just handed them a week's worth of wages they would get paid for carrying that load. Most have no choice and do so for the only income they can secure. Most use it to clothe, school, and feed families.

There were large prayer wheels, brightly painted in the center of the squares of precision chiseled rocks that lined our path as we passed them. We kept all mantra carved rocks and prayer wheels to our right and passed them on our left. We spun all the lines of prayer wheels, a cylindrical container on a metal pivot, respectfully, using our right hand. Inside these prayer wheels is up to 32,000 printed mantras. Spinning them sends those mantras through the village and beyond. And, meditating on spinning them is a Buddhist practice that assists with good and bad karma. It felt very attune to do so. There was a huge respect for their culture. Hinduism and Buddhism are the prominent religions of Nepal. Both influences were uniquely visible.

Sudip was our hiking guide. He was athletic and energetic yet walked us at a pace that would be enjoyed by all and successful in the ascent and ability to acclimate. It took me a long time to get his named ingrained in my brain. I kept saying soup-dip. Sun-dip. It is sue-dip. Sudip.

Sudip wore sunglasses that reflected the Himalayas back at me in stunning colors. His smile was equally reflective. We felt his thrill to be with us. I asked him what religion he was, and it took a while for him to answer. I saw him stiffen, and then relax and let it be said with boldness and no refrain. He looked around to make sure I would be the only one to hear his answer. "I'm Christian."

"Wow," I replied. "So am I." He stared at me in such a look of relief.

It was meant to be. Somehow, in all the two-year delays, I happened to end up in the A group, and he happened to be assigned to it. I was from a country that was founded on a GOD they stamped on our coins—In GOD we trust. And in God, my mom taught me to trust. We were glad to be able to share that commonality.

He rambled on about his village, his wife and two small girls. At the next stop, there they all were. The porters. They had gotten the porter job, being assigned from Sudip's village area. Each porter had to carry 3 or 4 of our red duffle bags tied together and on their backs. They all had the last name RAI. I had just been told that villagers carried the name of their village as their last name. It was kind of like, in the state of Wyoming, the driver's license plate has a number in front of the personal number. It corresponds to what town the owner of the vehicle is from.

Most of these porters were teens. They had ample personalities to match their unpronounceable first names. I filmed them. I loved them in heart, almost instantly. Right there, on the trail into the second day of trekking, I felt like I adopted an entire village.

Halfway up the steep descent to the village of Namche, I spied an entrepreneurial gal with a lemonade stand. She had drinks and snacks for the trekkers to buy. I wiggled out my money and told her to give all those porters something they wanted. The porters were tickled. They gobbled a shared can of Pringles potato chips and drank some form of a soda drink that had caffeine in it. I could see it added delight to help get those loads up to Namche. The trail leading up was a maze of almost never-ending switchbacks.

I never saw the Nepalese buy themselves snacks. I think it took too much of their wages to afford brand wrapped treats most of us think of as a daily norm in western diets. I never saw them complain that they could not. Nor complain of their loads. They rested. Ate nothing between meals. Positioned that white strap on their foreheads. Then hoisted their load that seemed to weigh as much as them and headed onward and upward. I had felt so often I was the only one on earth who carried a heavy load. I was humbled.

There was a sense of relief and appreciation that they had been picked to do a job. And they each seemed so determined to be the best at it. We had just crossed the highest hanging bridge. They never faltered on the swaying structure that saw ravines almost 2000 feet below the footing on the metal rungs. We did, without their loads. It was like riding a roller coaster. We pitched, and tossed, our hands having to grip the wire siding.

The prayer flags fluttered rapidly over these open ravines. I think our hearts palpitated at the same rate and were saying prayers just as breakneck as the flapping squares.

I decided each night I would buy one of our guides a can of Pringles and a bottle of Coke. Those and Snicker Bars were the only snacks that seemed to be carried into the Himalayas and put into the display counters at the tea houses for the tourists. I decided that I would try and produce an Everest Energy Bar to sell in the USA and have the proceeds make it here to help these people through their monsoon season. I had fun giving the rare treats to the guides, and they had fun taking turns getting them. The guides again showered us with doting attention at the dinner meals. Tea, coffee, and juice drinks. And they waited until afterward to be fed themselves.

The porters stayed in some form of communal lodging, or tents, or maybe slept under the stars. We rarely saw them outside of passing us adeptly on the trail. The guides stayed with us, but never ate until we were all served. Serving was a huge part of their guiding us. It was delightful to watch the true camaraderie amongst them as they finally did all sit down to dine. I loved watching their natural rhythm of stirring their Dal Bhat into their rice and eating it with their hands while enjoying conversation that always seemed filled with laughter.

Each day we walked. We filled it with talking or going stretches enjoying the silence. Each day arose with the sun and wound down with after dinner teas and small talk. Lights were out around 9pm because solar power ceased, and generators were trying to power only the essentials. It was a natural rhythm my overly pressured and high speed body soaked up and wound down into happily accepting… the pace.

I found this so reparative. So recuperative. Rejuvenating. Regenerating. To be experiencing days in the rhythm of nature. Sunrises. Sunsets. Self-powered transportation. Self-reliance. I got enough sleep. There was no worry in the day without the business and harried hurry. Our phones turned into cameras, and we hardly thought to glance at anything else on them without any Wi-Fi connectivity.

A surprising thing was happening. We were not tired. Maybe fatigued by the challenge of climbing up in altitude yet energized. A sort of wholesomeness was here, and it was contagious. We were getting stronger and staying healthy without so many things. We barely had opportunity for hot water. But it was available if you strategized to shower at unconventional times and gave it time to reheat. Sometimes, cleaning consisted of wet wipes. But to be honest, dirt doesn't hurt. It's mold and bacteria and spoiled things that can cause illness. Dirt without that is, well, dirt. We enjoyed being allowed to be so…dirty.

We slept on wood frames with hard mattresses and were issued a colorfully thick blanket and a pillow. I learned that many guides, and most of the porters did not have these luxurious blankets. I opted for a single occupancy tour so I could revise in my moments of quietude. Each night I had a room to myself. Many of the lodges had two beds so I got to use the second bunk to spread out all my goods and inventory the pace I was using them, trying to conserve lotions and toothpaste and my foot tape to last the trek. But I didn't need that extra blanket with my own down sleeping bag. I started leaving it in the hallway by the duffle bags the porters carried for us.

Each night, the blanket was gone. Each morning, it was returned, carefully folded and where I had put it.

The lodge sleeping rooms were not heated. The tearooms watchfully were. At 5pm the stove was stoked. All meals and mid-day teas were served from each lodge's one large room, so everyone gathered into it. I learned to like them. Everybody was comfortably arranged in a daily form of the game, Ring Around the Rosy. Wherever there was room, that is where you sat. That is where the new conversation of that hour began. You almost always got to sit next to someone new.

People didn't rush from the dining table to go off to soccer practice or watch a show on Netflix. They played card games and read, talked and soaked in the warmth made warmer because the tearoom was filled with bodies and camaraderie. This was the home environment I never got to have growing up. I smiled at being able to FIND it in other places. I was comfortable. Comforted.

We stepped past Nepalese chiseling rocks to make blocks for future buildings and entered each establishment as if entering that family's own home. The grandmother and grandson might be in the back kitchen doing the cooking. Others were hauling water in large barrels to the washrooms. Some were washing the linens. Usually, one person worked the counter and issued the room keys. Their English was necessary and good. They knew speaking to the tourists was important to the family business. And they knew the comfort and acceptance a tourist felt in their lodge was vital.

On the third day of the trek, I landed on the last seat in the corner occupied by the A Team at our teahouse. I cozied in to make sure we all fit along the long table. I had been sharing postcards I brought that had the pictures of the other continent marathons and a corner picture of myself among all the Belmont boys and the one girl. In the few moments before tea was served, I shared the story of getting to raise them. I shared they were from the streets of Los Angeles, but originally from Mexico. One was indigenous Indian. That I had helped them all get into colleges.

Before I hardly put the period on those few sentences, the strong, quiet guy with lean fitness, wearing a boxing gym sweatshirt with the hoodie most often pulled over his head, had a reaction. He reached his tattooed arm across the table and slammed his fist atop my postcard.

"GOD DAMN. GOD BLESS YOU." His fist slam made the entire table listen, though I think he had no intention of doing that. He legitimately wanted me to feel his gratitude.

"THANK YOU for being that LADY to them. Had I not had a LADY take me in, I would have never gotten off the streets and became the one who trained people how to competitively fight instead of street fight."

He leaned fully back on the cushioned seat and led into an explanation of his childhood situation. He was left as that foster kid bounced around and labeled. We didn't shy away from his sharing. We leaned in to listen and really met who this guy was. This one lady came to break the foster care situation for him and was willing to raise him like a son.

He said it again, with almost a sincere tear in his eye. "GOD DAMN YOU for doing that for them."

By opening such a raw element of who he was, this guy become a hero to relate to. It was the magic that happens when the world spins at a natural pace and we share who we really are. When you get to know something about someone that makes you connect in a richer way. Funny, how, many times it is the hard things that people go through that make them so human and real. In the Himalayas, we got to know each other. In a day's race of life in the Western world, we would have simply brushed past one another.

There is a magic that happens when you share the real and raw…you. Knowing and discovering things about each other made us able to form an unspoken bond. Even with porters and the guides. It was the real, raw, hard things in life that mixed with the fun, awesome, other things that made each person a full spectrum. There's a reward in opening up and sharing what we have been through. This was a great place and situation to offer up a part of who we are, to the right people in the right timing. Like the blocks of rock being chiseled outside, we might not have become the better FIT unless we had marks from being hit with some sharp blows. Pounding can build something functional that becomes part of the foundation that makes us sturdy. This was remarkable to realize.

Namche Bazar lived up to its name. It really was Shang-Ri-la, a village nestled in a nook on a steep hillside at the convergence of two routes and two mountainous ravines. On a clear day, after hiking just above the village a first looming view of Everest could be seen. I was told about the town from a charity race organizer. When she heard I was training and going to Everest Basecamp, she told me I had to do something for her when I reached Namche.

The nanny to her two children was a Nepalese from Namche Bazar. Her nanny's sister was Pemba Doma Sherpa, the first Nepali female to summit Everest. In May of 2007, she was the first Asian woman to summit Mt. Lhotse. Unfortunately, she died in a fall on the descent. I was asked to take pictures of the monument I would find just as we entered the village. And there it was. A bronze bust of the honored woman, perched on a marble base under a well maintained and colorful pagoda canopy.

Marching up the steps past the monument was a cascading waterway and a volleyball game at an altitude I was told was only 11, 286 feet. We came into the bottom of the village staring up at a set of towering stairs. Lined along the way were the nicely kept businesses. Two bakeries. The second in only two ATMs on the entire route. A coffee shop. A restaurant with a handwritten sign that the documentary Sherpa was being played at 2pm every day and came with popcorn. A hair salon.

That caught my attention. I stuck my head in and made an appointment! I also rallied up interest to return to the movie for the popcorn. Our lodge was the highest one on the hill. It afforded a great view, but it was a real commitment to go all the way back down the rock chiseled stairs to the hair salon or to resupply my "Have a Heart Fund." Or to justify watching the movie with popcorn. But we all did it. The schoolkids of Namche did it with ease. Those carrying loads to villages further up had no choice.

The hair appointment was worth it. Just to meet the two young sisters who owned and operated it. They had a fancy salon they showed me pictures of in the main city of Kathmandu. The Nepalese could not afford to pay much for the haircuts, so these women made better money offering us trekkers a nice shampoo, a shoulder and foot massage, and a hair style. They knew they were offering this about when we were thinking it would sure be nice to have one. They did a good job. And they were impressive entrepreneurs.

I also bought a WIFI password from something called Everest Link that claimed I would find WIFI to hook up to all the way at Basecamp. Albeit weak WIFI. But it was worthy of getting some posts out that allowed my running audience to be an almost daily part of the trek. Charging phones became the game. Each tea house had a limited number of connections and a limited amount of electricity. I was grateful I brought two phones to use as filming devices, and a fast charger.

Best of all, I was able to receive one incoming video. It was a sonogram of my first, soon-to-be grandchild. My daughter was pregnant. The porters loved watching it. Over, and over again. I think they had not had the opportunity to see life moving from within. The word got out. There was an American woman trekking who had a video of a tiny peanut moving around in the belly. I ended up showing it to countless villagers.

When I got enough courage to descend the stairs to go shopping around this village of Namche, I was greeted with sincerity. This woman, my age, had made a yak wool jacket for my future grandchild. She motioned how special it was to become a beloved grandmother. The Nepalese seemed to honor the blessing of children. It was a genuine gift. It was colorful, hand woven and sewn. It smelled of the yak wool used to make it. It was a prized, and very unexpected gift that returned to me tenfold any $10 or $20 bill I gave out.

It made me smile even wider and grander. I really could not stop smiling. I was in a land that loved. It was reciprocal. This same talented lady wove a bell for my sister and her ranch horses when she found out she had horses. Her son gifted me with a painting of the Himalayas. I trudged up the village steps, totally out of breath, but cherishing that I had met its villagers.

I really liked the lodge we were staying in. It was right on the path out of town, and closest to the Everest Marathon finish line. Though it was a tough climb to keep getting back to, it sported the best view and overlooked the rooftops. The monastery chants could be heard coming from a building tucked higher up on the hillside.

When it was time to keep trekking toward Basecamp, I walked into the lodge's kitchen and handed twenty dollars to the grandma and another to the grandson who worked tirelessly in serving us hot meals during out stay in Namche. We were able to leave some clean clothes and items for our return at their lodge. That was helpful. I was able to neatly tuck away my unique gifts that were given me. I kept the yak wool hat that said "Everest" on it I had bought. I knew I would need that.

There were 160 entrants trekking to Everest Basecamp for the start of the marathon, but we were so well dispersed. All being at different lodges, it never seemed like there were that many heading in the same direction. Our guides took us up out of Namche on a side route. They let us know this would not be part of the running course and we were very thankful. It was steep. Almost a goat trail except made by yaks. Beloved yaks. I had huge respect for this animal that fit the slopes of the Himalayas so well and was tamable to turn into hauling animals. They ranged and were raised on these high slopes.

Khumjung is a Yak village. A Sherpa village where the names of the villagers all end in Sherpa. It lies in a high mountain valley that passes through a terrain known for its blooming Rhododendron flowers on the tree branches. I could feel the sturdiness and fortitude of the villagers as we entered the small path through their town. Buddhism had inscribed the rocks and had mantras on a pagoda. There was a drinking trough for the yaks, a coffee shop opened by a young villager who hauled a barista percolator all the way up from Kathmandu, and strong buildings made by those hand chiseled rocks. There were neatly painted wood windowsills, paint cans used to pot flowers lined up on the rock walls, and a handful of women were bent in the fields harvesting potatoes.

A beautiful lady was standing in front of her store of colorful yak wool scarves. I had to stop. I fondled her handwoven light blue, white, and brown scarf and gave her twice what she asked for it, which was very little. We snapped a fun photo and a short video blurb for the YouTube Channel. My hair had been washed and flat ironed, and she stood on a rock step, so we were on the same height. Somehow, in that small interchange there was a link of love. We both were businesswomen making our means to help raise our children into fine human beings. We shared this without words.

I looked around and my A team had disappeared. I saw Bhim trotting back to corral me to the lodge we were staying in. It was far up the path. After tea, I begged him for the opportunity to go back. I came here hoping to meet the sherpas in person. I had been hanging out for years rubbing elbows with any Nepalese I could find in the United States. I loved the hard-working family and personalities of those that owned and operated the Momo Everest Shack in Jackson Hole, Wyoming. I wanted to know these. Little did I know at the time, they were originally from this village.

I purposely tried to run a little at every village. The altitude made my eyeballs open wide and my chest want to burst. It was taxing to even walk at these higher heights, let alone run. I would have to start in little sips, running just a few yards out of sight of anyone to get my lungs and chest ready to pump that hard. I would then run the lengths of the villages and out to explore further up or down the Himalayan valleys. At a waddle.

The boys in Khumjung were gathered playing a game of marbles. They watched my first lap and decided it would be fun to join me. With glee, they raced ahead. I motioned that the course had to take the paths up and around the inscribed rocks. They liked that. They, to their delight, sprinted as fast as their healthy legs could carry them. And, of course, beat the huffing blonde lady who was older than their moms. They were a younger version of the same jocular teens the porters were. I saw purity in them having childhood time and space to develop…naturally.

The woman with the store across from where I bought my wool scarf was now open. She was so pleased by my entertaining the boys. Two of them were hers. She motioned me in but not to buy anything. She wanted to share her home. We didn't need to know the same spoken language. In a few words of English, she shared that she had a daughter in college in Kathmandu, that her husband was a Sherpa climbing guide who just successfully summited and had safely made it back down to Basecamp. She got out her phone and shared pictures and video. I turned to the two boys and told them how proud I was of their pappa. One smiled freely. The other seemed seriously cautious of this foreigner his mother was bringing into their home.

I turned back to the mom, and she had tears in her eyes. She wiped them and said, "He is finally safe." This was no small feat. An average of 16 Sherpas die each year. It is a lucrative business and helps them provide for their families. But the risk is very real, and they are courageous to do the work.

This family included a thirteen-year-old daughter. She had stunning eyes and an elegance to her that came from the mother. When asked her name and age she spoke in perfect English sentences practiced diligently at school. This was quite a family. The mom had the teenager offer me milk and tea and had her boys fetch the cookie wafers.

The warm kitchen was organized and clean, a testament to the pride she took in the care of her home and children. She took me into her teahouse. It was spacious with nice wood benches and curtains. There were handsome photos of her husband and family portraits of all her lovely children and herself. Two newly purchased toilets sat in the corner. She explained that they were working to complete a lodge, but it was a slow process as they had to earn the money for each stage. Now that they had toilets, lodge rooms would be the next step.

The money her husband made guiding helped pay for her daughter in college and feed the family first. What was left then went toward their future business. The mom added, "And I run this small shop." She had wool scarfs and sweaters and jewelry she and the children had made. I bought things to bring back to people in the States, and then I offered up some extra money for the children and her to make the summer season a better one.

When it was time to depart the guides always said, "Jum, jum…" Or was it "Yam, Yam?" Something of that sort. Which means, "Let's go. Let's go." As we passed by the shop I had visited, the owner ran out and wrapped a white scarf around my neck and tucked the ends of it into my waist. She smiled straight at me and squeezed my hands. It really had been a special meeting of the hearts.

"This is to send you on a safe journey to Everest."

We climbed onward toward the villages with the second syllable 'boche' in their names. Pangboche, Dingboche, and Lobuche. I'm not sure why there is a 'u' in this last one instead of an 'o'. The way to Everest Basecamp was a weaving, winding path, up and down valleys, across hanging bridges. Always standing off to the side of the trail to let porters and packing yaks pass, I would slip some money into the hand of the herder. It always got a look of surprise.

The villages were spaced about a day's hike apart. I never kept track of the mileage, nor the time of day. The Himalayas seemed to surpass the pressures we place on time. Up this high, the buzz and appearance and disappearance of helicopters was another memorial sound that I now associate with the Himalayas. Chop, chop, chop meant something of grave consequences was being rescued or higher paying tourists were getting to look around. Or a doctor was on the way.

Pangboche was a climb to get to. At its crest was a monastery. The Everest Marathon committee wanted to establish a sort of give-back to the natural state of the Himalayas. Here, each of us competitors were given a plastic sign with our name engraved in it. We each planted a tree sapling on a steep hillside to help restore vegetation. A token? Maybe. But it helped to have the mindset to try.

I happened to see a handmade sign pinned to the window of a building that had the word BAKERY painted across its tin roof. It read, "Movie showing of *Meru* at 2 p.m.…with baked goods or popcorn!" I rarely sit long enough to watch any movie, but the thought of getting to do so here in the Himalayas seemed fun. *Meru* is a 2015 documentary produced by Jimmy Chin and his wife. It won the Sundance film festival that year. It is the true story of Jimmy Chin, Conrad Anker, and Renan Ozturk trying to succeed in being the first to climb the Shark's Fin on Meru despite setbacks, failures on the first attempt, extreme weather, and near-death moments. This film, *Meru*, clamped a stamp of excellence on Jimmy Chin's ability to climb, and more so, his talent to film. He was still a young ski and climbing bum when I lived in Jackson. He started adeptly filming some of the most extreme stunts, and his film talent began to get noticed.

I jabbered a continued campaign to go back and watch as we hiked the rest of the way to our lodge. That would mean a long climb back up that torn apart portion of the trail. I did it. And to my delight, a portion of the A team filed in to watch also. We were watching a film powered from a solar generator up this high. I think we were approaching 15,000 feet. I didn't want to know the elevation. I wanted to listen to my body. It was telling me we were high. And it was developing a very serious sinus infection. I was bleeding from my nose. And a fluid of infection was draining out at a bothersome rate.

Each day thereafter, my voice had a rasp to it. And my cough was deep in the bronchioles. We were still in COVID restrictive times, and it was a potential nuisance to contract it somewhere. I wondered if I had it but had no way of knowing. A few others had started coughing before me.

Running with congestion was going to be hellish. I had never had so much infection drain out of my nose before. I had the doctor trekking with us keep an eye on me. There is a condition that develops in a dry climate that is also this high in elevation. In the Himalayas it is nicknamed the Khumba Cough, a dry hack that lasts weeks after descending. Breathing dry air irritates the lining of the lungs. We, though healthy runners, were starting to sound like a room of habitual cigarette smokers. It was worth contracting the condition though. The views were startlingly stunning. Jagged, snow-capped mountains loomed in all directions. If the villagers could grow potatoes at this highest farming village on earth, I would endure, without complaint, my new case of hacking.

While at Dingboche, one of our party opted to use the emergency insurance and get helicoptered out. The hacking concerned her and so did the terrain. She had never been hiking this much before and making it even this far was a life triumph. I also discovered that two of our A team had never made it past the hotel at Kathmandu. The wife had developed a lung infection from the pollutants in the air in Kathmandu or had arrived with some condition. After coming all this way, they ended up spending their days in the hospital.

We all were required to run a portion of the marathon course around Dingboche. To make the exact 26.2-mile distance from Basecamp to Namche and be a full marathon, a segment of the trail had to do an out and back. Of course, it was uphill and added another thousand plus elevation gain to the hard enough route. Plus, it was an out and back. It would reveal whoever was in front of you and who was behind at the halfway point in the race.

The fit personal trainer and I were the first ones back to our lodge on this training run. Of course, we were also the ones losing all our muscle. He joked about how awesome his abs looked and what he would do for the chance to eat three chicken patties in a row. We had those kinds of bodies that consumed rather than stored fat. I felt a tad dizzy, and admittedly intimidated by what even higher would be like if I was losing strength and weight.

After Dingboche, we arrived at the last village before the push to Everest Basecamp—Gorakshep. It's not a year-round village, but more a last stopping point before entering the base area known as the Khumba Icefalls, a moving glacier with lots of moraine. This is where helicopters were actively bringing climbers out from the end of the climbing season and porters were seen carrying the huge ladders, canisters of gas, tents, and materials that made the plain surface of the ice turn into a temporary tent city. All the materials from the climbing season were being packed out…on their backs. Snow had fallen and dusted the village valley with a look that matched the towering peaks. We were approaching the highest mountain on earth, and you could feel it.

We, the marathoners, were a welcomed added extension onto the climbing season. Our porters had to carry up enough tents and food for the 160 competitors. And were thankful for the chance and extra money we brought. This is when I saw the young teens rolling up slips of paper. They had just found out that not all of them would get to go to Everest Basecamp. Half of them would need to carry our gear back to Namche. They were drawing lots. Like my Belmont boys had to when we vacationed in Wyoming and only had two seats available for 5 of them, these boys would have to handle the lot they drew.

A porter came running in all out of breath. The mood changed instantly, and my guide Sudip disappeared into the dark night outside. A porter had his appendix burst while up at the Everest Basecamp and they were rushing to carry him down by headlamp in a snow flurry. He would not get a chance to be helicoptered out until the sun rose. I couldn't sleep either and waited with all the concerned guides for the fallen comrade to be brought down. The doctor shared how draining it was trying to keep him alive all night. And at 4:30am, in the rays of beautiful yellows and orangish red, a helicopter came and whisked the porter to hopeful safety. They never shared his fate.

The next day we climbed to the pinnacle of Kala Patthar—18, 519 feet or 5,534 meters. We did so on purpose. It was much higher than basecamp and was planned as to acclimatize all of us at a higher altitude before tackling basecamp. It was also the place to view Everest because you cannot see Everest from Basecamp. We all went. Guides and marathoners. It was a celebratory party. The accomplishment of the marathon soon to come, and that we all had made it this far.

I used the skills my mom taught to capture the eyes of all in our A team and snapped pictures for the guides. Luckily, someone snapped a shot of me that I will treasure. With prayer flags whispering their wishes from this highest of points, I sat on the ledge with them slapping their mantras in the background. A glacier-filled lake was far below, and the tip of the photo is the very top of Everest, looming so visibly above the clouds and over my head. Snap.

That picture is caught for posterity and will forever be etched in my soul. I had reached a height I knew I was capable of. One God knew all along. I was fulfilling a dream I finally got to make happen. There was an immensity in all of this. Dry tears of joy filled with simple, self-proven satisfaction welled up within me. I had no words to attach to this pinnacle moment. Wind swirled and carried my own prayers to the ends of the earth. I had been searching to FIND that I was right where I always needed to be. Right within myself. Right there, standing where I was. In any circumstance or situation. You are never lost if you know you are found.

I patted my backpack and let the journey of those who have battled unfathomable loss, or battled giving up on life, or thought they were not eligible, or had circumstances lower than the lowest of lows, or those who were just plain struggling… I let those be with me as I stared at the highest mountain on the planet. I asked the winds to carry everyone's struggles with my own—the continent marathons, the raising of my kids, my mentoring the Belmont boys, and all my journey of Finding FIT.

There they dispersed on the breeze. Mysterious and whispering as the depths of each of us are. In an invisible way, all the struggles fluttered and took flight, lessening their power. I felt a freeing, like a prison gate being unlocked and swung right open from that pinnacle.

I headed back down. I had a marathon to run.

42

Running the Everest Marathon

We departed for the Everest Basecamp, referred to as EBC, super early in the morning. It was snowing, letting our guide's footprints mark the way. We skirted the Khumbu glacier on a ridge that left sky, clouds, and mountains rolling into one crescendo of magnificence. An avalanche let loose across the valley reminding us of the magnitude of where we were. Again, the heavily loaded porters were passing us. Ladders, barrels, tent poles, even another Honda generator. The weather was moody and beautiful. And we finally arrived at a rock I had seen in photos. Someone spraypainted EVEREST BASECAMP on it and the elevation. We each took our turn to have such an iconic photo.

I loved basecamp. The orange tents dotted the glacier in any place the porters could find flat enough to pitch them. Square shaped tents covered holes with a barrel buried and constituted makeshift porta-potties. Large mess tents had tables and the fold out camp chairs, and the largest tent was bustling around the clock. It was the cook tent.

I was assigned an orange tent that someone had meticulously designed a rock step entry way for it. The guides teased it was for me, "The Queen of the mountains." It started to storm as if it would not be Basecamp without experiencing the mighty hand of unpredictability that nature could bring. Some of the A team called it the SNOW-pocalypse. It fell all night, blanketing each tent with over 12 inches of encasement. It now looked like Eskimo igloos instead of orange tents. But I loved that I was having to wear the clothing I had brought for just these circumstances. I was only missing the gaiters that I checked back into the suitcase at the Kathmandu hotel lobby. I had to be very careful the new snow did not slip into the tops of my boots and wet my only wool socks.

The next morning the sun shone superbly. It was so bright that all the worrisome snow melted away. So did the talk of how we were going to run not being able to see the indentations between boulders. We were asked to adorn our race shirts and took pre-race pictures. The guides assured us race morning would happen too quickly and all our cameras and extra gear must be given to the few porters who would have to carry it back to Namche. They encouraged us to take all our photos now.

I coughed up more mucus than I thought humanly possible. My nose bleed was so constant it appeared in all the pre-race pictures. Even a trek to the makeshift porta-potties winded our lungs. Running seemed a scary thought, but it is amazing what we can do, even beyond what we think. In order to acclimate properly, we spent two nights in basecamp. It gave us a lot of time to be mulling among our thoughts. I quietly hiked away from camp and did a self-video. It felt complete, and I felt confident. Yet, in the seconds walking back to the tents I doubted if I knew what the outcome would really be in trying to run this marathon.

To top it off, altitude makes you pee. Often. And so does altitude sickness medication. It was a real need to pay close attention to proper hydration. And it was a real problem to have to pee every hour on the hour. But I got to see something I may have missed. Again, like that lost moment in the middle of Nevada I may not have looked up. Every hour during the nights in Basecamp I had to suit up, put the boots on, unzip the cozy tent, and trample out to the remote commode area. And while I was there, I looked up.

What I saw was so startling. I trekked away from the potty area and found a boulder to lay back and gaze. Meteorite showers were happening. Shooting stars. And a twinkling I thought was only visible in the Outback and the middle of Nevada. But here it was. The universe was on display.

We forget so often, when we have our heads down bent over trying to battle life, that the stars and open expanse are out there. We forget there is a universe. But here at basecamp, it was void of light pollution. I spent a portion of each night gawking so I wouldn't forget. And, as the guides promised, the marathon morning start time came almost too fast. It was a mark, set, go, and we were tumbling over ice, pebbled rocks, and taking any route we could pick through, racing toward that rock that was painted Everest Basecamp. All 160 of us.

The runners with the last names SHERPA on their bibs had the Nepalese advantage of stamina and altitude adjustment. They were already out of sight. They would win the marathon hours ahead of the Westerners' times. A young porter took off with them with his full load. Determination was serious. He had something to show the world—that he could outbound the westerners even with that load on. I was motivated by his guts, and the guts of all the Nepalese. They didn't complain and wallow about their loads. They shouldered and carried them, and they accepted when their lot in life made them carry a load back to Namche and not get to see Basecamp for the first time. Wow. Were these thoughts taking my breath away, or was it the altitude?

I had read that some marathoners got lost on the course right out of basecamp. I had thought, "How ignorant was that?" Until I did it. A bundle of us were crossing the moraine with our heads down. I heard a muffled cry and looked to the right to see all the other marathoners going over a ridge. We were on a path that headed across the glacier in the wrong direction. With accelerated adrenaline, I screamed and steered all the foreigners I was running with to the point the marathoners had disappeared. We had to climb hand over foot up a loose rock embankment and over many boulders to get back on the right trail. In that time, we were now the back of the pack instead of the front, and we were doubled over and winded. What a costly mistake.

It took a mile to catch up and start overtaking some of the marathoners. And only when we hit that out and back point at Dingboche would I know that only one of our A team was still ahead of me. After I had passed most the pack again, I ran such a long stretch of that first half marathon by myself. One hundred and sixty people in the expanse of the Himalayas spread out quickly.

My stomach was righteously upset. It pained and rolled in protest at what I was asking my body to do. I fished for that dreaded chocolate flavored GU but knew my body would need some energy fuel. It stuck to the glop already in my teeth from gunky saliva and turned my smile brown. The entire race.

I typically take a ton of pictures and video moments, but only once on this entire marathon route did I fish out my phone. And only once did I record anything on that entire 26.2 miles. That was odd and irregular for me. I think it took that ounce of energy that I feared was the "straw that would break my Camel's back" to fiddle with the phone. I suffered out my only footage, talking about how isolated I was running in the middle of the Himalayas. My chocolate glued teeth looked like I was missing teeth. But the small snatch of footage did capture how beautiful and untouched these Himalayan outdoors were. And it proved I was here, in the moment.

The weather was fickle. It had a potential of being hypothermic when the clouds covered, and to shame you into thinking you were powerful when the sun came out. It beat you down and burned lips and ears. My clothing layers were peeled on and off. I think that constant need to unclothe and reclothe kept me from being willing to capture any more moments on film. Every excess action felt like it might sap needed survival energy. I didn't know what to expect and there was a dreaded tablespoon of fear in it, like having to take that swallow of cough medicine as a child. I was surprised, and so was my running audience, that I had no footage of the course, or the finish. I was just hunkered down to make it to the finish. And the experience would have to be in words and not film.

I wanted to finish in a respectable time. I wasn't even sure what that was. I was to find out that this Everest Marathon effort took about the same time a full ironman, with an added two-mile swim and a 112-mile bike would take! The A Team of Americans came in between 8 ½ hours up to 14 plus hours. The Sherpas ran it like a flatland marathon. I saw the fastest time was set in 2006 by Deepak Rai (same last name, from the same villages as my guide and porters) with a time of 3 hours 28 minutes and 27 seconds. I am not sure if this record has been broken, but this is proof. The Nepali are champions at this altitude. Their finish times speak for them.

I did have one smart move. I tossed my runner's pack at the half marathon checkpoint. This was at the start of our out and back uphill climb. The Nepali stationed there grabbed it and exclaimed that it was too heavy. It had all the water I thought I needed for the entire route stuffed in it. It was nice to lose the weight for a while, but I also did a not-so-smart thing. I left my pack with my water in it.

There was no water on this loop and fourteen miles into the terrain I felt the need for it. That is not a good thing. I high fived a fit ultra-runner from our group and the Australian in our group, who was running his first ever organized race. They were ahead of me. On the way down, I got a chance to nod and greet and high five a lot of people. It was a hard portion of the race. We were all doing respectably. We were doing it.

Somewhere before that torn up stretch of trail and the monastery checkpoint, one of the other ultra-runner gals in our group caught up to me. She was pacing at the exact cadence of another foreign runner. They couldn't speak each other's language, but they had linked in the race and ran like a duet. The two danced past me as we grabbed hot orange juice and a bite of naan. They were talking about the scrumptious hot meal the Nepali villager women had made at Dingboche. I was too busy reloading my pack of water back on my body, I had forgotten to nourish at that checkpoint. Plus, my stomach was still upset. It only let me take a few morsels of anything. I was deteriorating. I was feeling my age. I was one month from sixty years old.

Nearing the last stretches of the marathon surprised me the most. This was a killer of a challenge. The descent from the monastery went down so steeply I had to slow the pace to manage the jarring. I knew Namche was overhead, not below and that this decent would have to abruptly come as steeply back up. In fact, if you did not make it to the outside of this monastery by 4pm, you would be forced to return down to the village and find your own accommodations for the night. You would be permitted to continue in the morning, climbing all the way back up. Even though there were only ten kilometers left in the mileage of the race, it was grueling. School age teens bounced by me with backpacks on. I handed them the Snickers Bar the last aid station had given me. I could hardly stomach this climb up, let alone a candy bar. I resorted to walking and pressing my hands into my thighs with a will power needed for each lunge upward. It took forever and time ticked by. I felt I should have been at the finish by now.

Why do we do it? Because it shows us so much of what life requires. I just kept going. A British lady with grey hair went fist pumping by me. When I asked her age, she told me she was over sixty. She was the only other one who passed me in those last segments of that long climb up. She egged me to race her. I had nothing left, so I let her go. This was an event where simply finishing was a triumph. That was the race.

I staggered into the finish and the arena area, taking it all in. The villagers of Namche took the race seriously. They held out a finish tape for every finisher, even throughout the night. They made a huge food tent and finisher certificates with our finishing time proudly handwritten onto them. It took me nine hours, eleven minutes, and ten seconds. The certificate spelled out each pass we traversed and was signed by eight officials. The entire country of Nepal esteemed this race and the runners who ran the distance. It was a hero's welcome. And a hero feeling.

The village ladies begged me to go in the tent and sample their food. I couldn't. I decided it would be best for me to keep staggering back to the lodge and try and find a hot shower and dry clothes before my sweat cooled. I was already starting to shiver from pure fatigue.

Namche now had a problem. One hundred and sixty foreigners all needed housing on this marathon finish evening. Everyone would have to share rooms and double up. And many, including most of the A team, would have to sleep in basements and hallways. I could hardly manage the steps down to our lodge. But now, the lodge that was atop the town was a blessing. The finish had been at the top, and I only had to clamor down to the closest building.

By the time I entered the tearoom, the sweat had sealed a salt ring around my under arms. I could taste salt on my face. The man behind the counter grinned and explained his apologies for having to accommodate all of us in the basement. I didn't care as long as I got a hot shower. When I returned from those glorious minutes in the shower, the owner's son asked me to come into the kitchen area.

He pointed to the grandma and grandson. "Thank you for honoring them so much by recognizing their hard work to serve meals. They told me you gifted them some money. But more than the money, you encouraged my mother, and my son. We want you to stay in our upper guest room in our own home. It's the honeymoon suite."

He handed me a key and motioned to the nice wood stairs. The room had a window with a view. It had a private bathroom. And I couldn't have been more grateful. I was finished. I had finished. I had just run the Everest Marathon at almost sixty years of age. My muscles were turning sore and cramping. I crawled into the soft bed of this gifted room and fell into a deep sleep.

To be a part of all the congratulations, after power napping, I hobbled down from my attic and went to the tea house and awaited each triumphant arrival. It was a silly time of extreme exhaustion with the most rewarding sense of accomplishment. Even the guides did something equally courageous. They did the distance also with the added responsibility of making sure we all made it.

We spent the next two days nimbly descending and enjoying the time together. It had passed all too quickly. But now we had to get back to Kathmandu where the organizing committee had a hero's party planned at the palace for us.

An aircraft carrying twenty-two passengers had crashed while flying to another village in the Himalayas. It had two Germans, four Indians, and sixteen Nepalis, the two pilots, and a stewardess aboard. None survived what was supposed to be only a twenty-minute flight. I think this occurred while we were running the marathon. This left Lukla with less aircraft flying and 160 of us trying to get back at all the same time. Our guides found a compromised solution. They decided to fly a lot of us just over the mountain to a town that the road reached, and then we could take a bus back.

I found the porters all seated on the rooftop of the teahouse in Lukla. They were showered and dressed in attire I think they had left at this town so they would have it when they got back. They seemed as proud of themselves as they should have been. They did it. They carried those monumental loads all the way to get us to Everest Basecamp and back. I couldn't thank them enough. We all seemed sad that it was over. We were comrades.

I went inside and asked what it would take to serve all the porters lunch just like we got served. Money. I gave them what they thought was asking a lot. It wasn't. And we invited the young teens and experienced adults of the Rai village to have lunch with us. We also pulled together, as is tradition with the expeditions, money from all of us to provide a meaningful tip to each guide and the porters. This would be all they had to survive on during the long monsoon rainy season. The next morning, we hurried to wait for the aircraft with the pilot who was willing to use his day and all his gas to take us over the mountain.

The porters and my guide, Sudip, stood watchfully on the roof of the teahouse. They had a two-day, grueling hike back to their village. But they were not going to start for home until they made sure we were given a proper good-bye. We could still see them heartily waving through the windows of the buzzing prop plane. It was backing its tail to the mountain, revving its engines, and we lost sight of the hands as the craft picked up speed on this downhill runway to glide off into space on the earth's shortest runway. Again, there were those nervous jokes. I overheard someone say, "It has sure been nice knowing you all." Swaaaah. It became almost soundless. We were in the air bouncing with those mountain air turbulences. We made it through the take off.

The cool thing is we were not saying good-bye. It had been a forever hello. I had used a computer in Namche and secured a visitor visa appointment for Sudip to come to the USA. We knew by gifting him, his entire village and surrounding area would get to come with him in the experience. I was struck when I saw the soonest visa interview available was an opening in June of 2023. More than a year of waiting just for the chance to ask for a visa to visit the USA. I thought this incorrect, so I even took a taxi to the American Embassy in Kathmandu. In those few days, the appointments filled up and were now into August of 2023. This was June of 2022.

So, in the meantime, I asked what would help get them to be with their families, get them through schooling, and such. He said he was saving his earnings for a small refrigerator and lunch pails for his daughters. Someday, he hoped to raise enough money for a motorcycle so he could be the one that could come to Kathmandu and get supplies and act as a courier. He was halfway there in personal savings. Saving in a way one does with a piggy bank fund in much the same way I earned my way to run the remote marathons. I wired the funds from my self-made Have a Heart Fund, and my own Fun Fund to match what Sudip would have to earn to buy the used motorcycle.

Videos he has sent are priceless. Sudip getting a ride from another villager to get to Kathmandu. The motorcycle being washed. The motorcycle license to drive it being successfully accomplished. His little gifts of dresses and shoes for his wife and children, and a citrus orange each, plus the purchase of the refrigerator. Getting the motorcycle back was no easy task. The monsoon season had already started. Roads were being washed away and there were rivers which had to be crossed.

I have his footage of a group of 15 Nepali with wooden poles carrying each other's motorcycles across the torrent of the rivers. I can hear Sudip's voice in the background with a low whispered plea, a sincere prayer. "Oh, my God. Don't drop it."

He made it home many days later than expected, and his film footage shows the delight of daddy's return. My incalculably rich reward has been this bit of hope that my races have offered. But what became of the refrigerator?

"Oh," Sudip said without question. "We hired a guy."

His video provides a parting shot of Kathmandu. In among the scooters and vehicle mayhem is a refrigerator. It is strapped to someone weaving his way among the traffic and chaos. All that is visible are the calves of a man in flip flop shoes, bent over. He is determined to get his load carried to a village. For the price of $5 per day?

Carrying our loads courageously and getting them to a place of usefulness might be one of the greatest things any of us can do.

We can FIND FIT-ness, on the inside and out. We can shoulder our loads. We can adjust our surroundings and atmosphere by adjusting our attitude and fortitude. We can patiently wait for life to return, as sometimes is required. But we can also make life happen. We FIT perfectly into the puzzle of who we are… perfectly. There are no missing pieces. My FINDING wasn't far from home. It was in the heart.

Whether a confusing childhood, a devasting divorce, war breaking out on your home soil, losing a beloved child, having to work in the belly of a ship for 9 month stretches, or carrying loads up Kilimanjaro or high in the Himalayas, we can all do the tough parts of life. We can run marathons on every continent and score World Championship titles even in small ways in our own hometowns. In our hearts. We can handle the strike outs because there are home runs to be hit if we are open to the possibility. Can we use something as simple as FITNESS to propel ourselves toward being the healthiest "ourselves" we can be? You bet we can!

It is a journey. Trek through it! Grab ahold. RUN out and make your life active and a give back. As you do so, two great things will happen. You will FIND FIT. That you become in better shape physically. But equally important, you will FIND you FIT as a human being by being the best you. Put that puzzle piece in its final place, and the picture is a beautiful one.

I am grateful to have been given the name Caren with a C and the word care in it. To have had to keep telling every person I met that it was spelled differently until…I finally realized the point. We are all spelled differently. And that is the majestic meaning of it all. To FIND that we are perfectly FINE in just who the universe has let us so uniquely be. There is something deeply within each of us that is very special. Experience this.

Press on and FIND your dreams and ambitions. Especially, if you are at rock bottom. FIND the things that remake and make life become healthy again. There are many Everests out there. And climbing them IS the experience called life. Tibetan Buddhism lets the prayer flags fade instead of taking them down. They let nature naturally disintegrate them and hang new ones right next to the tattered ones as a way of displaying birth and death and newness over decay. What a great symbol of getting past things in life that fade us. Let them decay but hang new and bright colors right beside them. That was what this trek to Everest did for me. I started to smile and knew I had hung new, brightly colored flags on my heart next to the faded, tattered ones.

43

Patagonia: Bridges, the 7 Continents Medal, and a Windswept Marathon

The wind was fierce. It buffeted, then slashed, and whipped in all directions. It churned up the glacial, teal-colored lakes to a white capped froth I thought only possible in the ocean. It wasn't mad. It was determinedly sporting, boxing at me as if challenging me to a sparring match. I toed right up to it and took a punch. Right in its invisible face. I was in Patagonia, the Southernmost tip of South America, a place that can get this windy.

This happened to be marathon day for the Patagonia Running Festival, and I was at the starting line of the Half Marathon. Hunkered between the buses that brought us deep into Torres del Paine National Park, the wind was manageable. But once beyond any buffer, it literally knocked many of the participants right off their feet. I leaned in and accepted the chill that came with such a propulsion of fresh air whittling around this tip of the earth. I was proud of myself. I could face the wind.

Most of those stomping to stay warm at the starting line were jabbering in Spanish, but with such a rapid Chilean accent I could not understand them. Everyone was using high pitched voices to be heard above the howl of the wind. Their speech whisked away in a sound of garble. Someone shouted something a tad louder and we were off and running…up a very steep hill.

An abrupt start, trying to film the moment, starting on a hill, and having that intensity of wind…took my breath away. I went into that panic breathing I have not had to experience for many years. But I knew what to do. I relaxed. I backed off for a few seconds, took those expanded sucks in that would fill my lungs and let them out. And then, I continued running. My soul celebrated. I had mastered adrenaline. It had not mastered me. This was such a life win for me. The whole entire moment. Finishing a marathon on all seven continents. Getting here. And being so comfortable with the challenge because I was finally comfortable with myself.

I knew I was smirking. *Take that, you wind, you hill, you start that wanted to catch me off guard and by surprise. I can face all of you. And I can handle all of you.* I now had the life experience to adeptly do so. A quiet confidence had formulated in me over all these years. I ran on filming the fun that comes in pitting oneself against such odds. Others that were there were doing the same. We pulled each other along in encouragement, and shouted accolades in all kinds of languages as we passed one another. Peppered among the Chileans were an assortment of foreigners from all over. It's funny, I didn't think of myself as a foreigner. I felt like a joiner. Running all these vast, remote marathons in such various places had made us all be about one thing. Despite the diversity of people, those of us running had the same goal. To finish.

This half marathon was hard. Enduring. Yet, so beautifully triumphant. The race organizers set up the finish at a spa resort called the Rio Serrano. We ran through the national park on solid gravel roads, past pristine lakes with majestic mountains in all directions. They had built a makeshift lean to for the finish line that barely stood erect against such winds. Under it, I finished a wish since childhood. I wanted to experience the opposite ends of the earth, and the thought of Patagonia ignited an explosion of lust for the earth's unspoiled places and its furthermost reaches. Like Alaska is to Northern America, Patagonia is to South America. Is it possible to smile in the wind? My cheeks felt like they were flapping.

It was the culmination of what it takes to live life when you're willing to scale those hard routes. As my running friend put it, "Life is not a rehearsal, Caren. It IS one live performance." You only get to do it once!" Running is an addition to life. It gets us out there. Doing. Being. It's an if-we-only-get-to-do-it-once kind of thing then we have lived. Somehow, the character tools we need to make life happen, to interact and embrace people and situations, can grow greatly out of these kinds of experiences.

My mind was playing through all the things I had to tackle to get here. I had squelched the fear that comes with trying to navigate so many unknown foreign airports. I plowed through immigration check points still jittery from the pandemic and told myself I could handle the consequences. After two days of connecting misconnected flights, I landed a day earlier than the rest of the marathoners in a tiny town in southernmost point of South America. I needed a cab to the town to find a hotel.

The boy with begging eyes loaded my luggage. In his hand painted yellow car, he tapped the bumper of the car in front of us so he could get under the gate arm without paying the parking fees for the airport. What used to feel daunting and vulnerable, being solo, I now did with vigor. I felt as crystal clear as the clean drinking water far in these reaches of Patagonia…for maybe, the first time in my life. Can a person feel pristine? Like a beautiful butterfly spreading its wings? Like the one my dad finally noticed on the windowsill.

I realized I was carrying very little excess baggage. Emotionally. And physically. A weight on me had vaporized. I had conquered a marathon on every continent, and with that came the reward of learning, growing, changing, and finally becoming my best FIT. I FIT comfortably in being my own self and it felt good. I knew who I was, and what I liked, and wanted, and was capable of. I knew how to pack, prepare, and navigate life, even its setbacks. A smile I never knew before came with me from the Himalayas to Patagonia. A smile I intend to carry with me the rest of my life.

After being pampered with massages and excursions, the race organizers announced the winners at a lavish meal. I had traveled to Patagonia because Marathon Tours had prepared a travel package. They were also the ones that host the Seven Continents Club. And…I was now on the list of the few on this earth to have completed a full marathon on all seven continents. Included in tonight's ceremonies was the awarding of the most recent Seven Continent Marathon finishers.

I won my female age category of the Patagonia Half Marathon and was handed a hand-woven wall decoration made by the locals. Following that came an oval gold medal engraved "Seven Continent FINISHER." It was draped over my head and dangled right at my heart. Both awards could not have been more treasured. And, like all the marathon medals, they are made of material that holds so little monetary worth, yet they scaled the expanse of the universe in their value in personal growth, life interest, and the experiences earning the rewards these events had conjured up. I looked down at that medal and felt the enormity of it.

After the Patagonia Running Festival, I went trekking. Four young Chileans guided a group of us along what was dubbed the W circuit. Hundreds of miles of hiking trails have been established in Patagonia. Some are linked with refugios, little lodges that offered tents and basic bunks. And excitedly, hot meals. AND, if you hiked fast enough and were the first to arrive, there were hot showers.

We crossed Grey's Lake in a catamaran and sailed past Grey's Glacier. If it was possible, the wind was even more fierce than the day before. Life vests were mandatory on deck, not in fear that the boat would sink, but more for if you were blown overboard. I took selfie snapshots of all of us with wildly windy hairdos. We played on the deck like school children at recess and got to know each other in a fun way. I liked the youth and vigor of the Chilean guides. They were a ditto of myself as the camp counselor/activity director at their age. They were loving their livelihood choice as equally as I did. Somehow, we fist pumped each other from the get-go… knowing that we all valued the experience the outdoors offered for anyone.

A crewmember shared that Doug Tompkins had died of hypothermia at the age of 72, after capsizing in a kayak when such winds kicked up like the one we were handling. They can come out of nowhere. I could see the gravity of the situation if I was thrown into a lake that had house sized ice chunks from the glacier floating in it. He mentioned this man's name like I should recognize it, so I looked it up when I could purchase WIFI.

Doug and Kris Tompkins moved to Patagonia after very successful careers in owning and working for clothing companies like The North Face, Esprit, and Patagonia. Doug, feeling disgruntled with corporate America, took his amassed fortune and he and his new wife, Kris, started buying up land in Patagonia to preserve for the world in the form of National Parks. Over 2.2 million acres have already been set aside for the world to enjoy from the Tompkins Conservatory. It is the first time in history, and hopefully not the last, that a private person has purchased land solely for making national parks. The mission of wanting all to enjoy a pristine outdoor experience in Patagonia has set a tone that rubs off on those that feel privileged to guide in it, and those that feel awed to hike in it.

"The bridges," the guides declared. "We must backtrack before we begin trekking the W circuit and see the bridges."

Before the bridges were built, past hikers would have had to clamber down and back up the dangerous sides of ravines. But now, the tottering set of bridges swayed and swung over the canyons. The guides were so proud of the bridges. They said they opened up access to trek all the way around in what is now being called the O Circuit.

"This would not have been possible if a forest service group and a conservatory from the USA didn't help us engineer, secure funds, and build them," they excitedly told us.

There were bridges throughout the trek that made the hiking much easier had they not been there. I loved stomping across them because I felt what they meant. And, what they symbolized for me. It wasn't about just getting to our own heights in life. It was about building bridges so all that needed to cross those hard ravines could do so in a less treacherous way and get to better places quicker. It was about FINDING ways to ease the hardships for not just ourselves, but, yes, for others also. Appreciating the journey all of us are on, and sharing our experiences so that we support each other along the way. It's not always a smooth process. We all totter and sway, but when we have strong bridges anchored in our past with our present, when we bridge our differences, and reach out and help each other, we FIND a way to cross even the hardest of places.

Finding Fit

44

Heart Shaped Rocks

I shared with the bouncy Chilean guide, Marjone, that I was carrying a special card with a picture and a dash of ashes for a dear family whose daughter took her life in college. The guide stopped.

"Bullying," she said. "I believe bullying murders lives. Envy and meanness are a crime ignored on earth. Was she bullied?" She walked on, then stopped again. She had been taking three striving women at a blistering pace, but I think it was to gift us space. She wanted to get ahead of the others and let us be out in Patagonia …free of other trekkers. Once she blazed us this far ahead, she slowed to a relaxed pace that was meant to give us time relating to one another, something as beautiful as the scenery.

"Let's let who this girl was walk with us today!" she declared. Then she turned and pointed, "LOOK! There's the highest peak. It is so rare to see. Maybe 10 days out of a year." She was ignited by the shear majesty of the mountain. I liked her and her zeal. She walked with a strength unspoken— one that says life should be lived with gratitude and gusto, and treated as the gem that it is. A strength that comes from going through a lot. "Only 5 people have ever climbed it. And one of them was a Chilean woman," she prided.

She started a story. "My dad had a brain tumor when I was 2 years old. He was given 6 months to live. He told the doctors he would live to see me get out of high school. He had three more tumors but lived 17 years. I am convinced the spirit of who he was lives on in me. One time I was very lost in the Peruvian Andes mountains. I was very sick from the water and a storm was overtaking me. I had a high pass to cross to get below to a town, but in the wind and snow of the storm I lost my way. There were valleys and passes in all directions. I prayed to my dad to help me. Protect me. Help me find my way.

"When I opened my eyes from crying out, there was a heart shape rock on the ground. I said, 'Thank you, Dad… I know you are with me in heart.' I got out my camera which had a zoom lens and looked up the mountain to the only area that had a beam of light from a break in the clouds. In the zoom of my lens, I saw rocks marking the pass and the trails. The clouds enclosed, and I only got that view for a split second, but I knew that was the pass. I would have been heading in the wrong direction. Since then, I look for heart shaped rocks. And since then, I do believe that a person's life lives on in us, even if it is in memories, or for us to call upon for strength and guidance. Heart shaped rocks are rare. Try to find one."

I looked down at her feet … where we had stopped. It was a dirt path, that had only a few rocks on the trail. One was about the size of the palm of a hand. It was polished grey…and perfectly…heart shaped. Her story opened the four of us trekking to share random things about each other, much like I have done in this book FINDING FIT. We felt the awe that life is such a mystery of living …and dying… and full of experiences, memories, and people. We picked up the rock and dedicated this day to the beautiful spirit of the young gal who had to walk life with us…in spirit only. And all other parts of lives that were hard. It was interesting, the more one shared of what they have lived through, the more drawn we were getting to know them better. We chatted in a way that was as magically uplifting as the mountains were. Four gals who otherwise would have never met were able to share tidbits of life that made life…life.

Finding Fit

Our guide stopped us for lunch on the shores of a lake that didn't have a ripple on it. We were experiencing a serene, sunny day in Patagonia. The saying goes, you can experience all four seasons…in one day down here. Or, one a day, as we were getting to witness. Just yesterday, we had trekked the entire day in blizzard conditions. And we awoke to today's calm sun with no wind. I liked it. It was like moving props for scenes in a rapid moving play.

In our short break, I traversed a half mile stretch of that pebbled beach… looking for more heart shape rocks. Marjone yelled after me, "Bet you don't find one. They are rare."

I didn't. Nor did I on the entire rest of the trek…though I was looking. We traveled 30 more miles stepping over a ton of tiny rocks, and I never found another heart shaped one.

When we arrived back to the last refugio, after having a perfect window of weather to trek to the three towers (torres), Marjone ran up to me ecstatically. "I have something for you. I have little money being a guide, but I have vitality and this grand landscape." She had her hands behind her back. "Pick one."

I did. I saw her shift her object into the hand I picked. When she unfolded her fingers, nestled in her palm was a tiny, shiny black rock... shaped like a heart.

She smiled. "Take this heart as a piece of mine. Thank you for staying kind and living your own courageous life." I palmed the treasured tiny rock that cost nothing, as do the most valuable gifts of life, and I felt the love that comes from sharing something so meaningful.

I realized that the heart IS the heart of it...all. It should be the biggest muscle we train and shape. And be less rare to FIND.

The Youthful Chilean trekking guides.

If *FINDING FIT* can offer anything, it's that FINDING the will to survive is a hard-earned honor. Having the tenacity to get up after being knocked down, even when you're knocked down over, and over again, is where real valor comes in. If we can stand up to life and use experiences and wisdom to reach out and help others in the process, then we will climb the most ultimate peaks. Run the marathon called life. And FIND how you FIT.

May my journey help you summit yours.

May you climb your mountains with confidence.

May you build bridges with people, places, and yourself to make the climb easier.

May you share your heart openly with everyone you meet.

May you FIND you FIT, perfectly!

Caren Ware

45

A Healthy Life List. What's Yours?

What I FOUND paves a HEALTHIER road in my life:

Things in my career that are habitual that I believe reduce burnout and have led to my longevity:

- Try to sleep 7-8 hours a day.
- Try even harder to eat healthy.
- Win with respect.
- Lose with humility.
- FIND FIT things to do.
- Try new things.
- Maintain a healthy relationship with your body. It's the only one you get.
- Go outside often.
- Run a lot.
- Explore more.
- Reach out and help people.
- Make love an action. Caring a daily activity. Kindness your mantra.
- Celebrate YOU! Who you are and are going to get to be!
- Honor and Respect the Creator.
- Have Fortitude.

Here are my own life notes I made to myself:

What I FOUND to be unhealthy	What I replaced them with that IS HEALTHY!
Fixing others	Sincerely helping others
People Pleasing	Pleasing to be around
Co-Dependency	Freely independent
External Validation	Internal and Eternal validation
Live on High Alert	Living a heightened life
Fear of Abandonment	Secure in God's love
Deprioritizes Own Needs	Looks out for self. Practices self-love
Needs to Prove Themselves	Excels to excel
Tolerates Abusive Behavior	Won't allow maltreatment of any kind.
Attracts Narcissistic partners	Rallies wholesome relationships
Difficulty in setting Boundaries	Has lines already drawn. God's rules. Safe pastures.

What should your healthy list be?

___

___

___

___

___

46

Conclusion. My Challenge to You.

May my journey be of help to yours. May you see it takes courage, fortitude, and a willingness. We CAN re-route destructive paths and get on with life on winning routes. Name the trails you should not be on and re-route them to go the opposite direction. Pick peaks and head toward them. It is about moving in the right direction.

Let's SEE who we RUN into next!
Get after it.
GET FIT. Feeling like you FIT. And enjoy FITTING in together.
Make being actively outdoors a big part of who you are.
And, let's see what we GET to FIND when we RUN into ourselves…daily.

– CAREN WARE

ABOUT THE AUTHOR

Caren Ware makes running and active outdoor living her profession. It all started with an elementary school jog-a-thon and reaching the summit of Mt. Whitney at the age of twelve.

She is a...

* USA Track & Field Level II coach.
* 2x Masters Track & Field World Champion
* Holds 17 USA Track & Field Master's National Championship titles in the Heptathlon, Pentathlon, hurdles, steeplechase, long jump, triple jump, and high jump.
* Has a BS Degree in Education and Camp & Recreation Administration from Biola University
* Has a Master's Degree in Public Administration from Cal State San Bernardino
* Worked as a Coordinator, Supervisor, Superintendent, and Acting Director of Parks & Recreation programs & a Camp Activities Director.

* Owns and operates Itz ABOUT TIME, a professional RFID Chip Race Timing Company
* Stages her own themed running events: Caren Ware Events, the Something for Every Body & Everybody Races.
* Launched Ware in the World Adventure Travel, so you can experience Running travel adventures that care about cultures.
* Creating the Everest Energy Bar, a healthy protein snack food. Proceeds to help villages in Nepal during the Monsoon Season, providing schooling, clothing, food, hope, health, and opportunities.
* Raised 2 children of her own & helped 5 inner city youth get through college.
* She loves cultures and people, and has taken in countless Japanese, Tahitian, and Romanian exchange students.
* Caren assists villagers and their families who guide up Mt. Kilimanjaro in Africa, and the Nepalese Everest Basecamp guides, porters, and Sherpas in the Himalayas of Nepal. She is working at turning this into Ware in the World Foundation.

Caren Ware has a heart shaped heart and a zeal for life and adventure. As a gifted storyteller and writer, she is a sought-after author and inspirational speaker for running clubs, races, corporate and private events.

Be sure to follow Caren at:

FB: @carenware
IG: @caren.ware.events
YouTube: caren.ware.events
Email: carenfasttrack@aol.com

Caren Ware is available for speaking engagements, active corporate events, & healthy team building.

Watch for these books by Caren Ware

SNARED
Trapped by your own Ignorance
What can happen to Kind, Kind of People
(Coming soon)

Up 'n Running & Racing Through Life
All the people, adventure, cultures,
and life learning (the sequels to FINDING FIT).
(Coming soon)

LIVING WHILE MAKING A LIVING
Why wait until the end. Do it now. How?
(Coming Soon)

Carenwareevents.com
Staging Best themed running races

Itzabouttime.com
Premiere RFID Chip timing and fundraising jog-a-thons

Ware in the World Adventure Travel
WareInTheWorld_Adventures.com
Combining Great running experiences in remote places with caring about the culture. Join in adventure travel with a running excuse.

Caren Ware has made running & outdoor adventures,
not only a life passion, but a career.

She is esteemed as the leading expert in healthy, active events.

"You will show me the path of life;
in Your presence is fullness of joy;
at Your right hand are pleasures forevermore."

– Psalm 16:11